ARAB MASCULINITIES

PUBLIC CULTURES OF THE MIDDLE EAST AND NORTH AFRICA

Paul A. Silverstein, Susan Slyomovics, and Ted Swedenburg, editors

ARAB MASCULINITIES

Anthropological Reconceptions in Precarious Times

—m—

KONSTANTINA ISIDOROS
AND
MARCIA C. INHORN,
EDITORS

INDIANA UNIVERSITY PRESS

This book is a publication of

Indiana University Press
Office of Scholarly Publishing
Herman B Wells Library 350
1320 East 10th Street
Bloomington, Indiana 47405 USA

iupress.org

Manufactured in the United States of America

First printing 2022

Library of Congress Cataloging-in-Publication Data
Names: Isidoros, Konstantina, editor. | Inhorn, Marcia C., editor.
Title: Arab masculinities : anthropological reconceptions in precarious times / Konstantina Isidoros and Marcia C. Inhorn, editors.
Description: Bloomington, Indiana : Indiana University Press, [2022] | Series: Public cultures of the Middle East and North Africa | Includes bibliographical references and index.
Identifiers: LCCN 2021022626 (print) | LCCN 2021022627 (ebook) | ISBN 9780253058928 (hardback ; alk. paper) | ISBN 9780253058911 (paperback ; alk. paper) | ISBN 9780253058904 (ebook)
Subjects: LCSH: Men—Middle East—Social conditions—21st century. | Masculinity—Middle East. | Arab Spring, 2010—Social aspects. | Middle East—Social conditions—21st century. | Middle East—Economic conditions—21st century.
Classification: LCC HQ1090.7.M628 A73 2022 (print) | LCC HQ1090.7.M628 (ebook) | DDC 305.310956—dc23
LC record available at https://lccn.loc.gov/2021022626
LC ebook record available at https://lccn.loc.gov/2021022627

CONTENTS

ARAB MASCULINITIES

INTRODUCTION

—w—

MIDDLE EAST ANTHROPOLOGY AND THE GENDER DIVIDE

Reconceiving Arab Masculinity in Precarious Times

MARCIA C. INHORN AND KONSTANTINA ISIDOROS

THE MIDDLE EAST IS A vast and complex region, stretching from Morocco in the west to Afghanistan in the east. The region is host to three major Abrahamic traditions (Judaism, Christianity, and Islam) and four major languages (Arabic, Hebrew, Persian, and Turkish). In addition, multiple ethnic minority populations, with their own languages and cultural specifities, are found across the Middle East and North Africa (MENA), in some cases forming large nations without states (e.g., Berbers, Kurds). In the Arab world alone, there are eighteen Arab-majority countries.[1] Along with four additional nations where Arabic is also spoken, they make up the twenty-two nations of the Arab League.[2]

No one scholarly discipline has been able to adequately capture the complexity of the Middle East, including its social, cultural, linguistic, ethnic, racial, religious, political, and economic diversity. But the discipline of anthropology has certainly tried. Of the five major social sciences—anthropology, economics, political science, psychology, and sociology—anthropology has been the most devoted to regional and area studies. The disciplinary hallmark of anthropology is ethnography, an immersive form of field research in which the anthropologist learns the local language, lives with the community for an extended period of time, engages in both participant observation and in-depth interviewing, and attempts to represent the lives of interlocutors through writing that is thick with ethnographic description. Ethnography is sine qua non for anthropology. It is the process of research that defines our discipline. It is also the product of our efforts. Anthropology produces ethnographies, or full-length books describing the results of our field research.

MIDDLE EAST

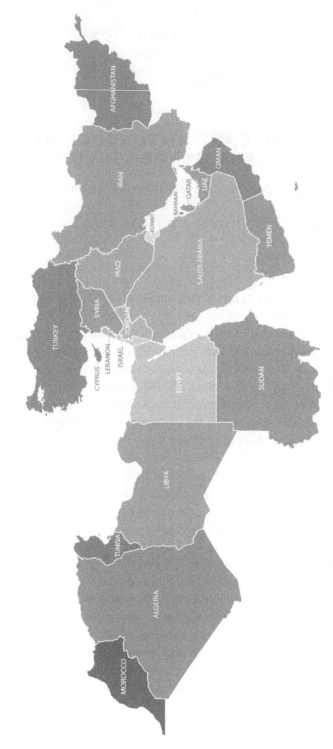

Figure 0.1: Map of the Middle East.

Hundreds of ethnographies now focus on the MENA region, constituting a remarkable anthropological corpus. As of 2020, there were 570 solo-authored ethnographies in English,[3] as well as a number of major ethnographic compendiums on the anthropology of the Middle East.[4] These volumes cover every Arab country, as well as Turkey, Iran, and Afghanistan. But very few of these ethnographies shed light on the lives of the men who live there. Middle East anthropology, as we shall see, suffers from a serious gender divide, promoting a view of Middle Eastern masculinity that requires reconception.

MIDDLE EAST ANTHROPOLOGY AND THE GENDER DIVIDE

In her seminal article on Middle East anthropology in the late twentieth century, anthropologist Lila Abu-Lughod (1989) pointed to particular zones of theory, or areas of scholarship that had dominated the Middle Eastern ethnographic tradition. At that time, Abu-Lughod was able to identify three major theoretical trends. First was segmentary lineage theory, or the way in which Middle Eastern tribes were purportedly organized. Second was Islam, which she argued had become a theoretical metonym for the region as a whole. Third was harem theory, or the assumption of a vast gender divide, in which Middle Eastern women were relegated to the private sphere.

This latter issue—of a so-called public/private gender divide between Middle Eastern men and women (Nelson 1974)—was the byproduct of two powerful forces. Middle East anthropology up until the 1980s was dominated by male ethnographers, who were almost exclusively interested in nomadic life, tribalism, and political leadership.[5] Most of these anthropologists were Europeans and Americans, and through their work in the MENA region, some became anthropology's most important luminaries (e.g., Talal Asad, Frederik Barth, Robert Fernea, Clifford Geertz, Ernest Gellner, Paul Rabinow).

In general, these early male anthropologists were interested in men's power, authority, domination, and violence—terms that often appeared in the titles of their books.[6] The men in their studies were variously described as "warriors," "heroes," "lords," "masters," "saints," "shaykhs," "khans," "shahs," and "notables," perpetuating a very masculinist ethnographic tradition in which the attitudes, values, and actions of the most powerful men were revealed. This interest in what might be called the "tribal hero warriors" of the Middle East continued throughout the 1980s and 1990s and into the new millennium (Dresch 1990; Peters 1990; Tapper 1979, 1996), with a particular focus on (1) men's leadership of insurrections and resistance movements (Davis 1987; Edwards 1996, 2001, 2017; Fischer 1980; Hart 1981, 2001; Peters 1990); (2) men's public war oratory and poetic contestations (Caton 1990, 2005; Gilsenan 1996; Meeker 1979; Reynolds 1995; Shryock 1997); and (3) men's religious leadership and authority (Eickelman 1976, 1985; Gaffney 1994; Geertz 1968; Gilsenan 1973, 1982; Hammoudi 1993, 1997; Hirschkind 2006; Messick 1992; Munson 1984, 1993).

Manhood itself—or how men experienced their day-to-day lives as men (Gutmann 1997)—was never the inherent interest of these male anthropologists, nor were gender relations between men and women. Because they gained little access to women's worlds—arguing that such access was simply impossible—these male anthropologists rendered ethnographies of Middle Eastern social life in which women rarely made an appearance, whether as mothers, wives, sisters, daughters, friends, or lovers. In other words, this early male-dominated Middle East anthropology upheld the notion of a great gender divide, one that Abu-Lughod (1989) described as anthropology's harem theory.

A second wave of Middle East anthropology set out to correct the ethnographic imbalance but unwittingly magnified the perception of a Middle Eastern gender divide. In the late 1970s, second-wave feminism emerged, and with it the entrance of hundreds of women scholars into the academy. By the early 1980s, the Association of Middle East Women's Studies (AMEWS) was formed by a group of feminist scholars (Inhorn 2014a), including prominent anthropologists who were concerned with the effects of patriarchy, or male power and authority, over Middle Eastern women's lives (Joseph 1993, 1994; see also Kandiyoti 1988). During this early period, feminist anthropologists began to trace the outlines of the feminist movement within the MENA region itself (Hale 1996; see also Badran 1996; Hatem 1993; Moghadam 1994), a scholarly theme that would continue for decades.

This new genre of woman-centered Middle East ethnography eventually prevailed in terms of the sheer number of volumes published, comprising one-quarter of the entire ethnographic corpus by the year 2020. Middle East women's ethnography covered many topics, including (1) women's poetry, storytelling, and oral traditions (e.g., Abu-Lughod 1986, 1993; Arebi 1994; Early 1993; Grima 1992; Hoffman 2008; Kapchan 1996); (2) women's reproductive practices and motherhood aspirations (Ali 2002; Boddy 1989; Delaney 1991; Fadlalla 2007; Inhorn 1994, 1996, 2003; Kanaaneh 2003); (3) women's increasing access to literacy and education (Adely 2012; Barsoum 2004); and (4) women's entrance into informal and formal labor markets (Cairoli 2011; Chakravarti 2016; White 1994). However, as in the original zones of theory outlined by Abu-Lughod, the dominant focus of this literature was on women and Islam, including (1) women's practices of veiling and seclusion (El Guindi 1999; MacLeod 1992; Rugh 1986; Sedghi 2007; Zuhur 1992); (2) the effects of

Islamic personal status laws on women's marriages and family life (Haeri 1989; Hoodfar 1996; Moors 1995; Tapper 2006); (3) the growth of Muslim women's piety movements (Deeb 2006; Hafez 2011; Mahmood 2006; Torab 2008); and (4) how these faith-based movements contrasted with more secular forms of feminist activism (Al-Ali 2000; Brodsky 2003; Peteet 1992; White 2003).

In all this work by women anthropologists, men were hardly present. Women's fathers, husbands, brothers, sons, friends, and lovers were shadow figures looming largely in the background of these ethnographic studies. Husbands and wives were almost never portrayed together as couples, given that marital ethnography was entirely undeveloped in the field of anthropology as a whole (Inhorn 2014b). Thus, the burgeoning anthropological literature on Middle Eastern women's lives gave little sense of wider gender relations, or how men and women might interact meaningfully and compassionately as fathers and daughters, husbands and wives, brothers and sisters, mothers and sons, and friends and neighbors. Instead, much of the anthropological literature on Middle Eastern women's lives operated from an implicit feminist assumption that all Middle Eastern women are subject to patriarchy and oppression.

To summarize, then, the purported gender corrective undertaken by women anthropologists of the Middle East had much the same effect as the earlier male-dominated ethnography. Women ethnographers worked only with women subjects, thereby perpetuating their own separate spheres research. Furthermore, because many women anthropologists were inspired by second-wave feminism, they searched for signs of patriarchy and oppression in Middle Eastern women's lives (Inhorn 1996).[7] Whereas male ethnographers were relentless in searching for signs of men's power and domination in the public sphere, female ethnographers were adamant in documenting signs of this male domination in the private sphere. Together, they reinforced the concept of a stark gender divide between Middle Eastern men and women, with men often represented as brutal oppressors.

NEO-ORIENTALISM AND MIDDLE EASTERN HEGEMONIC MASCULINITY

In these ways, the discipline of anthropology has unwittingly contributed to dominant stereotypes of Middle Eastern men as dangerous Others, a view that harkens back to the time of the Crusades. In his brilliant analysis entitled *Orientalism*, literary theorist Edward Said (1978) examined Western perceptions of the Orient, or the Middle Eastern lands where women were thought to live in harems—veiled, shut away, and controlled by polygamous men. According to Said, Western Orientalist scholarship portrayed Middle Eastern men as direct threats to women, as well as to Occidental security and Christian morality more generally. A millennium on, neo-Orientalist caricatures of Middle Eastern men carry forward—today in the powerful terrorist trope that portrays Middle Eastern men (invariably thought of as Muslim) as perpetrators of religious fundamentalism, jihad, barbarous violence, hatred of religious minorities, and misogyny toward women (Inhorn and Wentzell 2011).

Such neo-Orientalizing views of Middle Eastern men and the "trouble" they cause have been incisively questioned by political scientist Paul Amar (2011, 2013), who critiques omnipresent discourses for "misrecognizing, racializing, moralistically-depoliticizing, and class-displacing emergent social forces in the Middle East" (Amar 2011, 36). Such neo-Orientalizing discourses—recast today as toxic masculinity in the Middle East—render illegible more progressive, twenty-first-century men's social realities, including the changing contours of gender and sexuality in the region, and men's participation in social movements for justice and human dignity, of the kind that led millions of young Arab men onto the streets in the much-hoped-for Arab Spring.

Amar points particularly to hegemonic masculinity theory and the ways in which it has been systematically used to popularize discourses of toxic masculinity and Middle Eastern men in crisis. Hegemonic masculinity theory, which has dominated intellectual thought for more than three decades, was forwarded in 1985 by Australian sociologist and gender scholar Raewyn Connell and her colleagues (Carrigan, Connell, and Lee 1985; Connell 1993, 1995). Drawing explicitly from feminist theory and Marxist sociology, Connell sought to reconcile the lived reality of inequality among men with the fact of men's group dominance over women. Connell drew on Antonio Gramsci's (1971) concept of hegemony, a social mechanism through which various groups develop the "will to conform" with a leading group's way of being, thereby facilitating class-based domination. She argued that by using hegemony to understand masculinity, scholars could reveal the various hierarchies within masculinities and the dialectical relationships between social structures and masculine practice.

Connell defined hegemonic masculinity as the strategy for being a man that legitimizes patriarchy in current, local practices of gender. In this formulation, masculinity is shaped by cultural ideals of manliness (e.g., attributes such as wealth, power, and virility). Specifically, Connell argued that most men are not fully able to practice hegemonic masculinity because it requires access to particular social resources. Hegemonic masculinity thus creates inequality among men, making some men hegemonic or dominant over others, whereas subordinate men can only aspire to elements of hegemonic masculinity as the ideal type. Crucially, the theory of hegemonic masculinity is about relationships—among men, between men and women, and between men and their ideas of other men. Connell (1995, 37) argued, "We must also recognize the *relations* between different kinds of masculinity: relations of alliance, dominance and subordination. These relationships are constructed through practices that exclude and include, that intimidate, exploit, and so on. There is a gender politics within masculinity."

Because of this focus on masculine relationality, hegemonic masculinity theory, once applied by other gender scholars, has tended to cast masculinity into two static types—hegemonic versus subordinated (a.k.a. marginalized, subaltern). Hegemonic masculinity, furthermore, is often conflated in scholarly discourse with dominant notions of manhood that are toxic in practice (e.g., promiscuity, overdrinking, use of force, oppression of women). Thus, portrayals of hegemonic masculinity end up powerfully reinforcing pernicious stereotypes. When hegemonic masculinity is viewed in such negative terms, it may lead to a toxic trait list of manhood—which may or may not reflect men's (and women's) actual social realities and gender relations in practice (Inhorn 2012).

Anthropological representations of Middle Eastern men—whether by male anthropologists enchanted with the hegemonic tribal hero warrior or women anthropologists critical of men as hegemonic patriarchs—have unwittingly served to reinforce these views of toxic masculinity in the MENA region. Marcia C. Inhorn (2012) identifies what she calls the four notorious P's—patriarchy, patrilineality, patrilocality, and polygyny—which are often represented in ethnographic accounts as characteristic of Middle Eastern family life but which may end up vilifying and caricaturing Middle Eastern men in what she describes as "hegemonic masculinity, Middle Eastern style."

The first feature of this caricature presumes that hegemonic Middle Eastern men are family patriarchs who exert their power and authority over women, junior males, and children in their families through coercion and even force. Second, hegemonic men's marriages are never thought to be characterized by love because they are presumed to be arranged by families for the purposes of patrilineal tribal alliance, lineage continuity, and men's power. Third, women who marry into hegemonic men's patrilocal extended households are thought to be in an extremely vulnerable position. If they challenge their husband's hegemonic male authority, they are at risk of violence and repudiation, an Islamic form of divorce in which a man need only utter his intentions without recourse to formal legal proceedings. Fourth, hegemonic men's primary emotional commitments are said to remain with their own patrilineal female relatives (i.e., mothers and sisters) rather than with their in-marrying wives, which purportedly increases hegemonic men's likelihood of polygyny, or the taking of multiple spouses.

Furthermore, and as noted in Inhorn's critical analysis (2012), hegemonic masculinity in the MENA region is considered by default to be heterosexual, because homosexuality represents the ultimate form of male subordination. In short, Middle Eastern men who perform hegemonic masculinity are necessarily heterosexist and sexist—gaining respect and authority over women and "lesser" men through domination, fear, and threats of violence.

THE NEW MASCULINITY STUDIES IN
MIDDLE EAST ANTHROPOLOGY

But do these extremely negative portrayals of hegemonic Middle Eastern men's toxic masculinity bear any resemblance to the reality of modern men's lives across the region? When portrayals of Middle Eastern men as dangerous terrorists and brutal oppressors of women circulate freely around the globe, it becomes incumbent on anthropologists to engage with these discourses and attempt to deconstruct them.

In twenty-first-century anthropology, a move is afoot to reconceptualize masculinity and, in so doing, advance gender studies. Anthropologists of Latin America were among the first to investigate the meanings of manhood, in part to explore gay men's lives in the new era of HIV/AIDS (Carrillo 2001, 2018; Parker 1991, 1998) but also to unseat prosaic and taken-for-granted assumptions of Latino men's irremediable machismo (Brandes 2002; Gutmann 1996). The work of anthropologist Matthew Gutmann was crucial in this regard. He interrogated the meanings of macho in his ethnographic research on young men's lives in Mexico City (Gutmann 1996). In his now famous *Annual Review of Anthropology* article "Trafficking in Men: The Anthropology of Masculinity," he defined four ways in which masculinity could be conceptualized: (1) as "anything that men think and do," (2) as "anything men think and do to be men," (3) as "some men [being] inherently or by ascription considered more manly than other men," and (4) as "anything that women are not" (Gutmann 1997, 386).

Gutmann went on to edit a seminal volume on *Changing Men and Masculinities in Latin America* (Gutmann 2003), which was followed in short order by three other edited collections from around the world: *Asian Masculinities* (Louie and Low 2003), *African Masculinities* (Ouzgane and Morrell 2005), and *Men and Masculinities in Southeast Asia* (Ford and Lyons 2012). Middle East anthropology was not immune to this new wave of masculinity studies. Indeed, three edited volumes touching on Middle Eastern masculinities actually predated some of these other works even though they received less attention, perhaps because the editors were mostly women.

In 1994, Andrea Cornwall and Nancy Lindisfarne published a globally encompassing ethnographic compendium called *Dislocating Masculinity: Comparative Ethnographies*. Two chapters focused on Middle Eastern men: one on the "honour and shame" complex and the stresses of male (im)potency during wedding-night defloration ceremonies (Lindisfarne 1994), and the other by Turkish feminist scholar Deniz Kandiyoti (1994), who questioned the taken-for-granted assumption of male privilege in homosocial settings where some men may face significant forms of masculine vulnerability and discrimination.

Men's vulnerability was also a major theme in Mai Ghoussoub and Emma Sinclair-Webb's (2000) collection on *Imagined Masculinities: Male Identity and Culture in the Modern Middle East*. Both a literary and ethnographic compendium, this book offered a major section on military masculinities, or the ways in which Middle Eastern youth are "made into men" through conscription in the army, sometimes in dangerous roles such as commandoes (Sinclair-Webb 2000). In one ethnographic account focusing on Israel's Zionist masculine ideology, mandatory military service was deemed "a second bar mitzvah" for young Israeli men (Kaplan 2000). However, for Palestinian youth living under Israeli rule in the occupied West Bank, beatings and detentions were framed as rites of passage, becoming "central in construction of an adult, gendered (male) self with critical consequences for political consciousness and agency" (Peteet 2000, 103). The Palestinian-Israeli conflict was also a central theme of a third edited volume, Lahoucine Ouzgane's (2006) *Islamic Masculinities*, which showed how Palestinian men living in Israel attempted to navigate their Otherness—their "stranger masculinities"—in a postcolonial setting (Monterescu 2006).

Military masculinity in the Middle East has continued to absorb a newer generation of anthropologists. Six ethnographies focus on Algerian ex-combatants (Bucaille and Rundell 2019), Israeli soldiers (Ben-Ari 2001; Grassiani 2013), Turkish soldiers and veterans (Açiksöz 2019; White 2012), and Palestinian Bedouin soldiers serving in the Israeli military, often as scouts and guides (Kanaaneh 2008). The most recent of these volumes, by anthropologist Salih Can Açiksöz, focuses not on combat per se but on the aftermath of war. Calling his book *Sacrificial Limbs*, Açiksöz (2019) highlights the experiences of masculinity and disability among wounded warriors, most of whom are Turkish veterans of the country's war against the Kurds.

To some degree, these new ethnographies of Middle Eastern soldiers represent a continuation of the earlier Middle East anthropological focus on tribal hero warriors. Although men who have fought in wars deserve to be seen and heard—perhaps especially when their masculinity is tested by disability—it is extremely important to recognize that most Middle Eastern men are not combatants. Portrayals of ordinary civilian men in the Middle East—for example, recent accounts of Palestinian stone masons (Ross 2019) and Egyptian migrant workers in the Gulf States (Schielke 2020)—are also necessary, in part to move the new masculinity studies in anthropology beyond the recurrent trope of men's toxic violence.

In this regard, four recent ethnographies on the lives of ordinary Middle Eastern men bear mentioning and are significant for several reasons. First, they are all written by women anthropologists who conducted research directly with men, thereby disproving the long held but untested assumption that cross-gender research is impossible in the MENA region. Second, these ethnographies focus on gender relations, or the ways in which Middle Eastern men and women actually interact in daily life, shaping each other's senses of masculinity and femininity. Third, they focus on new themes, including men's fertility and use of new reproductive technologies; men's work and participation in community life; men's capacities to nurture their families in the domestic sphere, partly by getting food on the table each day; and men's support for their families through careers in the Middle Eastern music industry.

The first of these books to be published was Inhorn's (2012) *The New Arab Man: Emergent Masculinities, Technologies, and Islam in the Middle East.* In her study, Inhorn foregrounds the reproductive life histories of Lebanese, Palestinian, and Syrian men who are struggling to become fathers, sometimes because of their own male infertility problems but also because of their wives' reproductive troubles. Through marital ethnography conducted with husbands and wives, Inhorn demonstrates how Arab men are embracing new medical technologies and reproductive practices, decoupling manhood from fertility and virility in the process. Analyzing these changes as emergent and transformative, *The New Arab Man* not only questions patriarchy within marriage and family life but also foregrounds the changing emotional worlds of Arab men as they describe their love stories, their family commitments, their friendship circles, and the ways they have struggled within their nations in a postwar setting.

The New Arab Man forwards the trope of *emergent masculinities* to capture all that is new and transformative in Arab men's lives in the twenty-first century. Inspired by Marxist scholar Raymond Williams's (1978) concept of emergence, Inhorn argues that the term emergent masculinities—intentionally plural—can be used to embrace historical change and new patterns of masculine practice. Emergent masculinities encapsulate individual change over the male life course, change across generations, and historical change involving men in transformative social processes (e.g., male labor migration, new forms of political protest, the harnessing of social media). In addition, emergent masculinities highlight new forms of male agency, including men's desires to enter into romantically committed relationships before marriage, live in nuclear family residences with their wives and children, use the latest technologies (from mobile phones to reproductive technologies), and be involved in political and gender equality activism.

The local social and emotional worlds of Arab men are also highlighted in anthropologist Farha Ghannam's (2013) book *Live and Die Like a Man: Gender Dynamics in Urban Egypt*. Based on more than twenty years of ethnographic research in a low-income neighborhood in northern Cairo, Ghannam shifts the attention away from gender oppression and patriarchy to explore how men are collectively "produced" as gendered subjects, including through interactions with the women in their lives. Forwarding the conceptual analytic of *masculine trajectories*, Ghannam traces how masculinity is continuously maintained and reaffirmed by both men and women under changing socioeconomic and political conditions.

In the economic aftermath of Egypt's failed 2011 revolution, Ghannam shows how adult men struggle daily to provide for their families, often engaging in physically taxing, backbreaking forms of labor to do so. Focusing on the stories of ordinary, working-class Egyptian men, *Live and Die Like a Man* considers the extraordinary efforts that many men make to care for their families, as well as how the masculine caretaker role has been complicated by the challenges generated by Cairo's rapid urbanization, neoliberal policies, and political and economic instability. Ghannam's sensitive study underlines the affective dimensions of men's lives, exposing the vulnerabilities, dependencies, and inner conflicts faced by poor and working-class Egyptian men, particularly as they struggle to put food on the table.

In a similar vein, anthropologist Nefissa Naguib (2015) questions the so-called public-private gender divide in her book *Nurturing Masculinities: Men, Food, and Family in Contemporary Egypt*. Based on long-term fieldwork in Egypt among men of a variety of social classes, Naguib explores men's practices of food provision, nurturance, and care in the domestic realm. Egyptian men's practices of food provision are one measure of their lives as active and caring family members. Attention to individual men's aspirations as providers and ideas about masculine fulfillment capture the variety of ways in which Muslim men conduct themselves in a caring, nurturing mode as sons, husbands, fathers, friends, and community members.

Developing the concept of *nurturing masculinities*, Naguib (2015) argues that humanizing ethnographic portrayals of ordinary Arab men render legible the social realities of gender relations, including how the lives of Arab men and women often intersect on a much different, more humane level in relation to care, respect, love, nurturance, and intimacy in domestic life. Furthermore, beyond the domestic sphere, *Nurturing Masculinities* focuses on the tumultuous days of the Egyptian revolution, revealing how male protestors managed to feed and care for one another while occupying and defending Tahrir Square.

Finally, the newest ethnography, also from Cairo, Egypt, focuses on the life history of one man, Sayyid Henkish, who is a musician from a long family line of wedding performers. Anthropologist Karin van Nieuwkerk (2019) uses Henkish's autobiography to explore changing notions of masculinity over the male life course. Sayyid Henkish's story is one of an *ibn al-balad*—or an "authentic" Egyptian male of the lower-middle class who articulates his manliness as being associated with nobility, integrity, and toughness. However, like many Egyptian men of the *baladi,* or working classes, Henkish faces profound difficulties in providing for his family in the face of the socioeconomic and political changes taking place in contemporary Egypt.

Van Nieuwkerk situates Sayyid Henkish's account within the professional context of the Middle Eastern music and entertainment industry—an industry in which the performers, both male and female, face distinct moral ambiguities for being part of a religiously debated profession. However, van Nieuwkerk shows that the moral challenges faced by Egyptian men like Henkish are not limited to the world of entertainment. Through one man's autobiography, van Nieuwkerk is able to offer many insights about masculinity and moral uncertainty in today's Egypt, where profound post-2011 economic and political disruptions are transforming and unsettling received notions of manhood.

Since the publication of these four books—all of which focus on heterosexual married men and their families—a new focus on queer men in the MENA region has also emerged, perhaps inspired by anthropologist John Borneman's (2007) auto-ethnography of his own gay desires and encounters in the Syrian city of Aleppo prior to the civil war. A decade on, a generation of younger scholars has begun to study queer life in the Middle East, mostly in the major cities of Beirut, Lebanon (Merabet 2015; Moussawi 2020); Ramallah, Palestine (Atshan 2020); Istanbul, Turkey (Özbay 2017); and Tehran, Iran (Kjaran 2019). These books chart the ways in which Middle Eastern gay men are navigating urban and sometimes transnational spaces in order to express same-sex desires and enjoy relationships with other men. Yet all these ethnographies also focus on queer men's struggles in their own societies against inequalities and discrimination, homophobia, religious condemnation, threats of violence and detention, and human rights violations. Indeed, as argued by Ghassan Moussawi

(2020) in his book *Disruptive Situations*, which focuses on gay men, lesbians, and transgender people, the daily survival strategies of LGBTQ people in Beirut are not only "queer" but are made even queerer by living in the midst of a "queer situation." *Disruptive Situations* in Lebanon examines profound economic precarity, sectarian strife, the arrival of millions of refugees in the country, and the ongoing threat of regional war.

PRECARIOUS TIMES FOR ARAB MEN

Indeed, it is fair to say that no other region of the world has suffered so much war and population disruption than the Middle East, including the majority of Arab nations within it. By 2011, the year of the Arab uprisings, fifteen of twenty-two Arab League nations—comprising 85 percent of the region's population—had already suffered from complex emergencies due to protracted conflicts (Mowafi 2011). By 2011, Arab countries already had the largest percentage of forced migrants in the world, the majority of whom had fled from ongoing conflict, persecution, and political instability by crossing international borders as refugees or by becoming internally displaced persons (IDPs) within their own countries.

In the decade following the 2011 Arab uprisings, hopes of a revolutionary Arab Spring were dashed by the collapse of states, increasing authoritarianism, escalations of sectarian tensions, new wars added to ongoing conflicts, high rates of civilian casualties, refugee and humanitarian crises, and unrelenting economic despair. According to the United Nations High Commissioner for Refugees, by 2020, Arabs and Afghans made up the majority of the more than 70 million forcibly displaced persons in the world (UNHCR News 2019). Of the world's 25 million refugees registered with the United Nations, the largest population consisted of Palestinians, 5.5 million of whom were living since 1948 under the mandate of the second largest UN refugee agency, the United Nations Relief and Works Agency (UNRWA). Syrians comprised the largest newly created refugee population, with nearly 6.7 million refugees and an equal number of IDPs in need of humanitarian assistance (UNHCR 2019, 6). The non-Arab country of Afghanistan placed second on the UNHCR's list of globally displaced persons, with 2.7 million Afghans registered with the United Nations, despite not having formal refugee status in the neighboring host countries of Iran and Pakistan. Adding up these numbers, Middle Eastern refugees made up more than half of the world's total refugee population.

What's more, the worst man-made humanitarian crisis in the Arab world was unfolding in Yemen, where Saudi Arabia led a nine-state coalition in a devastating war. By 2020, UNHCR (2019) estimated that 24 million Yemenis, or 80 percent of the total population, were in need of some form of humanitarian assistance. Two out of three Yemenis were unable to afford food, and half of the country was on the brink of starvation. One million cholera cases occurred in Yemen between 2018 and 2019, 25 percent among children, making this the largest cholera epidemic in the world.

Beyond the suffering of refugees and IDPs, the certainty of daily life has diminished for ordinary people in many Arab nations, especially in the aftermath of 2011. The post-2011 period has brought with it unprecedented levels of economic, political, and social upheaval. Arab men and women who have remained in politically precarious home countries often face disappearing labor opportunities, high unemployment rates, rampant corruption, oppressive military rule, and increasing (although often internalized) rage against governing forces.

How have Arab men responded to these political disruptions and economic uncertainties in the post-revolutionary period? A state-of-the-art survey—undertaken by a nongovernmental gender advocacy organization called Promundo, in conjunction with UN Women and a variety of international funding agencies—attempted to answer that question. Called the "International Men and Gender Equality Study in the Middle East and North Africa" (IMAGES MENA, or IMAGES for short; https://imagesmena.org), the study relied on local teams in four MENA countries (Egypt, Lebanon, Morocco, and Palestine) where quantitative and qualitative research was undertaken with nearly ten thousand Arab citizens, mostly men between the ages of eighteen and fifty-nine.

The IMAGES study was unprecedented as the first large-scale empirical investigation of the lives and struggles of Arab men since the uprisings of 2011. This comparative study was designed to assess Arab men's involvements as sons, husbands, and fathers at home and at work, as well as in public and private settings, in an effort to better understand how Arab men see their positions as men in the current economic and political climate, and to explore contemporary male attitudes toward gender equality. The results of this study were published under the title *Understanding Masculinities: International Men and Gender Equality Survey (IMAGES)—Middle East and North Africa* (El Feki, Heilman, and Barker 2017).

The IMAGES study highlighted the tremendous levels of stress in Arab men's lives, particularly in countries affected by conflict and displacement. Across all four countries surveyed, half of the male respondents said that they fear for their family's well-being and safety, as well as for their own.[8] In Palestine, for example, 65 percent of men reported at least one form of occupation-related violence or discrimination. In Lebanon, where Syrian refugees were also included in the study, Syrians were at least two to three times more likely than Lebanese men to report that they had experienced some form of physical violence or been arrested, imprisoned, or detained by police.

These effects of conflict—as well as the challenges of finding paid work and fulfilling the traditional masculine provider role in times of economic scarcity—were frequently cited in the study as the main reasons for, or aggravating factors in, men's depressive symptoms. For example, the majority of Palestinian men in the IMAGES study reported being frequently stressed or depressed because of unemployment and underemployment. Similarly, in Lebanon, both Lebanese and Syrian refugee men showed signs of stress and depressive symptoms related to their inability to find remunerative work. All told, one-fifth to one-half of Arab men in the four countries reported being ashamed to face their families because of their lack of work or regular income.

Despite the many challenges facing Arab men across the region, *Understanding Masculinities* concluded on a positive note. In its final analysis, the IMAGES study emphasized that a "sizeable minority" of Arab men in the four countries surveyed—from the most elite to the most marginalized—showed support for gender equality and women's empowerment. Arab men were described as cracking the armor of patriarchy and encouraging an equal playing field for men and women. Moreover, qualitative interviews undertaken with Arab men in all four countries yielded many "stories of tenderness, of deep caring and caregiving" (El Feki, Heilman, and Barker 2017, 20). As the IMAGES authors concluded, "While it is fashionable to talk about a 'crisis of masculinity,' in reality, men and women are at a crossroads as they try to find their way in a shifting world" (El Feki, Heilman, and Barker 2017, 263). The goal of the IMAGES report, then, was to "cut through the stereotypes and prejudices that too often obscure the complexity of dynamic gender identities and relations in the region" (El Feki, Heilman, and Barker 2017, 14).

The IMAGES study was historic as the first large-scale social survey to examine the views and lived experiences of Arab men on a comparative basis across the MENA region. Yet in typical fashion, the Western media reported the study results in highly negative terms. For example, the right-leaning British journal the *Economist* led with this nested series of headlines in its May 4, 2017, edition: "Down and out in Cairo and Beirut," "The sorry state of Arab men," "They are clinging to the patriarchy for comfort."[9]

Unfortunately, the *Economist*'s reporting is nothing new. As argued by media scholar Jack Shaheen (2008), ever since the 2001 terrorist attacks on the World Trade Center and Pentagon, Arab men have been deemed intrinsically

Guilty—the title of his book—in popular Western media representations. This portrayal of Arab men as dangerous Others has been fueled by unrelenting media attention on Islamist terrorist activities and attacks, especially violence inspired by what is known as the Islamic State of Iraq and Syria (ISIS). As a result, amid the worst Middle Eastern refugee crisis since World War II, many European countries justified their refusal to accept Arab refugee families by claiming that Islamic terrorists were entering Europe disguised as refugees. Similarly, in the United States, President Donald Trump's 2017 Executive Order 13780, entitled "Protecting the Nation from Foreign Terrorist Entry into the United States" but commonly known as the Muslim ban, clearly drew on the terrorist trope to keep Muslim men out of the country, despite the fact that not a single terrorist act had ever been committed by a refugee on US soil (Inhorn 2018).

As clear from these studies, statistics, and executive orders, Arab men have found themselves in increasing situations of precarity in the post-2011 period, with economic insecurity and violent political upheavals compromising men's daily lives, including their sense of security, moral order, future aspirations, political rights, and overall human dignity. According to social theorist Judith Butler (2009, ii), precarity is "that politically induced condition in which certain populations suffer from failing social and economic networks of support and become differentially exposed to injury, violence, and death. Such populations are at heightened risk of disease, poverty, starvation, displacement, and of exposure to violence without protection." Central to Butler's notion is the politically induced nature of precarity, which can result in "maximized vulnerability" of human beings through exposure to violence perpetrated by the state or other actors, or through inadequate state protections.

In short, Arab states are no longer able—if they ever were—to adequately protect their citizens. Where does this leave Arab men today? The chapters in this volume aim to provide answers to this question.

ORGANIZATION OF THE VOLUME

In the midst of such life-shaping precarity in many Arab countries, it is vital to understand how Arab masculinities are being experienced and reshaped. This is the goal of the present volume. Through thick ethnographic descriptions of Arab men's lives across the region, we intend to examine in concrete detail how men's current understandings of their *rujula*, or masculinity, are being affected in these precarious times.

Our aim as anthropologists is to innovatively challenge received wisdoms in the long-standing debates on Middle Eastern patriarchy and the gender divide, and to further explicate the political contexts in which gender relations are actually conducted. This collection of groundbreaking ethnographic studies reflects our mounting dissatisfaction with earlier anthropological and feminist works that treat Arab patriarchy as timeless and intractable and that reinforce untested assumptions of toxic, hegemonic Arab manhood. Instead, we attempt to contest crisis of masculinities discourses and the reentrenchment of Western political interventions to "save" Arab women from Arab men (Abu-Lughod 2013).

The foundational premise of this book is that there is an urgent need for a more profound anthropological understanding of Arab men and masculinities that breaks away from the political debates, media hysteria, and misinformed stereotypes of Arab men that are unequivocally intensifying, particularly in the United States and Europe. In challenging these representations, this book offers unique insights into the mostly private spaces of Arab men's lives—stories that rarely enter the public arena. Each author delivers stimulating and thought-provoking analysis from rarely accessed field sites to understand the everyday realities of Arab men, women, and children—in their lives together, as well as apart.

All the anthropologists contributing to this volume have undertaken ethnographic research projects within the same four countries as the IMAGES MENA study—namely, Egypt, Lebanon, Morocco, and Palestine. Although there is no formal connection between the IMAGES study and our anthropological investigations, these overlapping sites of research clearly reflect issues of research access and closure in the turbulent post-2011 period. (For example, scholarship within war-torn Syria or Yemen is now virtually impossible.) Furthermore, the anthropological studies carried out by researchers in this volume are of a fundamentally different nature than those of the IMAGES study. Whereas IMAGES researchers collected large-scale, aggregate, quantitative data, the anthropologists in this volume offer small-scale ethnographic portrayals of particular men's lives while at the same time innovating methodological, epistemological, and conceptual approaches to Arab masculinity more generally.

In this regard, it is important to note that the anthropological research presented here foregrounds the voices and stories of male interlocutors. Nonetheless, we take methodological care to skillfully interweave gender more broadly so that women also inform the analyses about Arab men's lives, hopes, and dreams. Indeed, this volume provides a rare opportunity to look closely at the ways in which both men and women are rethinking and unseating Arab patriarchy today.

Part I. Masculinity and Precarity: Class Conflict and Economic Indignity

Because of the overarching attention to conflict in the MENA region, structural and economic forces have received relatively less attention. Yet economic conditions either create possibilities or intensify struggles in the everyday life worlds of Arab men. In the three chapters in this section, the authors interrogate the meaning of masculinity when morality, piety, dignity, and justice are continually being undermined by economic and political powers beyond men's individual control. The first two chapters offer postrevolutionary reflections on Egyptian men's perceptions and experiences of the country's worsening economy and growing social class disparities. These two chapters argue against monolithic constructions of Egyptian masculinity. Instead, they capture the ways in which differently positioned Egyptian men, living in the same society, actively choose to respond to their local class ascriptions. In the third chapter on Morocco, men's very personal efforts to renegotiate and reconstitute the social and moral order amid intensifying class stratification suggest that social class and class-based identities are being reinterpreted in the present era, often along religious lines.

In chapter 1, Bård Helge Kårtveit explores the new othering taking place between middle-class and working-class men in the setting of Alexandria, Egypt. Among middle-class Alexandrian men, Kårtveit finds men placing conjugal connectivity (Inhorn 1996, 2012) at the center of their masculine aspirations, in their intentions to strive toward better communication with their fiancées or wives, and to achieve a greater sensitivity toward their needs. Kårtveit argues that middle-class Egyptian men are attempting to break away from certain patriarchal ideals, enabling them to establish, explore, and initiate "softer" forms of masculinity with middle-class group approval. In doing so, they define themselves in opposition to men of earlier generations but also in opposition to the uneducated working-class men, or *fellahin,* that constitute their masculine, predatory Other. Seen as lacking in culture and civility by middle-class men, these working-class men are regarded as sources of trouble and as perpetrators of sexual harassment in public spaces. Thus, Kårtveit's study is a powerful reflection on how worsening, postrevolutionary economic conditions in Egypt are exacerbating preexisting class tensions.

In chapter 2, Jamie Furniss examines the reactions of young working-class men in Cairo to popular media representations of themselves as violent "thugs." In a nuanced ethnographic portrayal of audience reactions to the 2016 summer hit series *Al-Ustura (The Legend),* Furniss examines which men liked and disliked the television show and why working-class men identified with the show's violent and vengeful folk hero. Furniss's ethnographic analysis captures how middle-class Egyptian men condemn what they see as the working-class predisposition toward violence. But the chapter focuses primarily on working-class men's reactions because these men perceive quite differently the moral of the story of *Al-Ustura*. In the process of outlining and describing these class-based masculine perceptions, Furniss shows how Egyptian working-class men resist their stigmatization and, in so doing, redefine meanings of masculinity and violence.

In chapter 3, Hsain Ilahiane captures the experiences of working-class Moroccan men who, unlike many of their counterparts, chose not to migrate to Europe. Making a living in the streets of Casablanca, they take their chances as informal laborers. But as these Moroccan men struggle to earn a daily living, they also lament the compromised ethical order of things, a time of injustice that they call *al-hogra*. This chapter examines contemporary meanings of al-hogra in Morocco and North Africa more generally, where feelings of al-hogra were the very spark that ignited the Arab Spring protests in Tunisia. Ilahiane's chapter focuses on the stories of individual Moroccan men, whose circumstances render them economically vulnerable and who rail against the perceived corruption and domination of society's ruling elites. Ilahiane finds that these working-class men—who toil to be good providers and to pursue a decent way of life—must face inherent contradictions between making a living and achieving their Islamic ideals of masculine piety. Ilahiane voices Moroccan men's stories of pain as they struggle to "earn a piece of bread." In search of dignity and fulfillment, Moroccan informal laborers imagine a day when al-hogra will no longer exist and men can provide a decent standard of life for their families without compromise.

Part II. Masculinity and Displacement: Moving, Settling, and Questions of Belonging

In many ways, the first three chapters of the volume are about internal transformations in social and moral ideas of manhood. The four chapters in this section turn to external worlds, particularly to the displacements of Arab men as both migrants and refugees. In this section, we see the complex interplay between "moving" and "settling," and how manhood is being made and contested in these oscillations. In chapters 4 and 5, movement emerges as a key domain through which Arab masculinity is shaped. Clearly, movement is essential to understanding the experiences of Arab men who have been forced to migrate because of economic circumstances. However, for Arab political refugees who have already fled their homes, displacement and resettlement may render them "stuck in place." In this next section on refugee displacement, we focus on the relative immobility of refugee men who have been encamped across national borders in other MENA countries. In some cases, such refugee displacement can last for generations, with little hope of return. How do Arab men respond to such circumstances? Chapters 6 and 7 attempt to answer this question, arguing that displaced Arab men find creative ways of "doing" gender and masculinity, including in their encounters with the nongovernmental organizations (NGOs) and UN agencies that often structure their refugee camp existences.

In chapter 4, Alice Elliot focuses on the ceaseless movement of Moroccan men who migrate to Europe for work. Here, migration simultaneously ensures, but also erodes, men's social, physical, and gendered existences, given that repeated movement can either underpin or undermine the making of manhood. Elliot's ethnographic study traces how migration becomes constitutive of what it means to be a Moroccan man, as well as how repeated movement can become corrosive of the very familial, social, and existential trajectories that migration is usually imagined (and assumed) to sustain. Classic analyses have tended to portray male migration as a definitive rite of passage from boyhood to manhood. But Elliot's work focuses instead on the difficult challenges—emotional, structural, and physical—required of Moroccan emigrant men in order for them to remain men despite the odds. Elliot coins the term *repeating manhood* to argue that masculinity can be built up or diminished over time through repeated movements. Thus, becoming a successful migrant man is never guaranteed. As the stories of Moroccan men in this chapter show, migrant manhood is always a precarious achievement.

Whereas Elliot's work focuses on migrants still on the move, chapter 5 takes us to Denmark, where Arab migrant men attempt to resettle with their families. As seen in this chapter by Anne Hovgaard Jørgensen, fatherhood among Arab migrant men becomes a sociomoral battleground in which Arab men must repeatedly attempt to overcome what Jørgensen calls *mistrusted masculinity*. Jørgensen's study focuses on interactions between Arab migrant fathers and the schools in which their children are educated by Danish professionals. In the Danish school system and in the welfare state more generally, Arab men often try their best to act on behalf of their children's best interests. Yet these efforts are frequently hindered by inherent distrust on the part of Danish teachers. Through nuanced ethnographic stories, Jørgensen focuses on fathers' reactions to these negative ascriptions and on the strategies men develop to forge new fatherhood identities for themselves. The chapter showcases Arab men's investments in their children's futures, including their hopes that their Arab offspring will eventually be integrated as part of the Danish "next generation."

In chapter 6, Gustavo Barbosa takes readers to the Shatila refugee camp in southern Beirut, Lebanon, where NGOs and development projects are active. His ethnographic study captures the dynamics of gender workshops sponsored by NGOs, as well as the responses of the young men (*shabāb*) who question the meaning of these various "gender performances." As Barbosa shows, the promotion and framing of gender by certain NGOs as solely relations of power and subordination fail to capture the experiences of young Palestinian men in Shatila. These shabāb have limited access to power and become framed as emasculated, due to the political-economic constraints placed on them. Barbosa challenges this by developing a very different frame, that of the *NGOization of gender.* He argues that once gender is reconceptualized beyond NGOs' limiting frames, shabābs' lives appear ethnographically much richer than those suggested by the stereotype of brutalizing and brutalized Arab men. Outside of these gender workshops, Barbosa's study shows how Palestinian shabāb excel in both care and competition of prized pigeons—whose flight outside the camp is a poignant reminder of young Palestinian men's relative captivity. For the Shatila shabāb, much more than "just gender" is at stake; the well-being and survival of their pigeons serves in some ways as a metaphor of Palestinian refugeehood.

In chapter 7, Konstantina Isidoros also finds definitions of gender to be similarly displaced in her study of Sahrawi refugees in North Africa. This chapter focuses on Sahrawi men's ancient practices of full facial veiling—a form of veiling quite different from those of most other Muslim and Arab societies. Furthermore, Sahrawi men are increasingly becoming admired by international legal campaigners and aid organizations as steadfast refugee-statesmen, human rights activists, and skilled diplomats. Isidoros explores a poignant political moment in 2016 when these warrior-nomads lowered their customary male veils—while still using a traditional camel and goat hair tent—to receive then UN secretary general Ban Ki Moon in their desert heartland. She argues that these customary practices of *masculinity on the threshold* have become woven into new ideas about what it means to be a "modern" Sahrawi man and statesman. Like Barbosa in chapter 6, Isidoros finds conventional gender constructs to be rendered almost useless when differentiating cultural norms around gender. Instead, masculinity is best understood as skirting thresholds—sitting on the edges of habitable domains, circumnavigating the boundaries of international law, or adjusting the folds of cloth around the face. Today for Sahrawi refugee men, masculinity is achieved by successfully managing, moving with, and sitting in these risky, life-changing thresholds.

Part III. Masculinity and Familial Futures: Sex,
Marriage, and Fatherhood under Threat

Men's deep concern over domestic responsibilities reemerges in the final section on masculinity and familial futures. These chapters follow Arab men in their roles as husbands and sexual partners to their wives and as fathers to their children. These chapters highlight the importance of marriage and family-making in the Arab world, with men achieving full adulthood through these accomplishments. However, marrying, having sex, and making a baby are not always easily achieved. These chapters focus on masculine embodiment by exploring the most intimate realms of sexuality and reproduction, where men's bodies may be imperiled. As we shall see in this section, Arab men may be forced to put their bodies on the line—facing imprisonment as political activists or undertaking risky medical treatments to restore their threatened sense of masculinity.

In chapter 8, Sabiha Allouche's Lebanese interlocutors reflect on their futures in a country that has faced twenty-five years of civil war and Israeli occupation, an ongoing Syrian refugee crisis, and decades of economic precarity. Drawing on narratives collected during fieldwork with men and women in Tripoli, Allouche captures the affective components, such as hope and desire, that accompany discourses of ideal masculinity. Allouche's key finding is that Lebanese women construct the ideal husband along highly nationalistic lines, often referring to the slogan "Lebanon is for the Lebanese." Allouche argues that such findings are paradoxical given the long history of interaction and kinship alliances between the Lebanese, Palestinians, and Syrians in the region. Yet Allouche shows that this new interest in the Lebanese man occurs at the same time as Lebanese men struggle to function in a stagnant economy with high unemployment and emigration rates. Moral discourses of Lebanese emasculation are increasing, along with this escalating precarity. Thus, far from being fixed, ideas about Lebanese masculinity are constantly shifting, particularly as Lebanese men and women struggle to come to terms with Others (i.e., Palestinian and Syrian refugees) in their midst.

In chapter 9, L. L. Wynn forwards the concept of *masculinity under siege* to examine married men's sense of embodied peril. In Cairo, Wynn discovered Egyptian men's widespread and often daily use of the narcotic pain reliever, tramadol, thought to give them energy and treat their erectile dysfunction. As an opioid, the neuropharmacology of tramadol would predict an erection-wilting, rather than an erection-producing, effect. Yet as Wynn found, this narcotic pain reliever is being used as a substitute for Viagra, and both drugs are claimed to restore Egyptian masculinity and sexual vigor. In her chapter, Wynn offers an important contextualization of this emerging opioid epidemic. Namely, socioeconomic hardships in Egypt today make men feel that they are constantly gripped by pain and physical depletion. Thus, Egyptian men ingest tramadol to help them absorb the shocks and blows of an ailing economy, as well as to uplift their exhausted and failing bodies in order to meet the challenges of domestic life, including men's conjugal responsibilities.

In chapter 10, Laura Ferrero starts by critiquing the research on gender in Palestine, which she argues has overemphasized fighting, resistance, and imprisonment as crucial attributes of Palestinian masculinity. As Ferrero shows, the Palestinian struggle can have a twofold effect on manhood. On the one hand, it affirms masculinity through political resistance, but on the other hand, it may lead to long periods of detention in which reproduction and aspirations for fatherhood are at stake. Because scholarship on Middle Eastern men has emphasized their masculine reproductive imperative (Inhorn 2012), Ferrero's ethnographic research shows how imprisoned Palestinian men work with their visiting wives to secretly smuggle sperm outside of the prison complex. As a result, between 2012 and 2017, more than fifty Palestinian in vitro fertilization (IVF) babies were born using smuggled sperm. These "miracle" births have often been greeted with public announcements and widespread celebration. Based largely on ethnographic interviews with prisoners' wives, Ferrero finds that this recent practice of sperm smuggling has enabled prisoners' wives to become mothers and has offered Palestinian political prisoners a life-affirming chance at fatherhood.

CONCLUSION

The chapters of this volume offer rare ethnographic insights into the shifting ideas and practices of Arab masculinity. These emergent masculinities (Inhorn 2012) are being shaped by particular historical temporalities and political conditions, which render Arab masculinities in a current state of flux. Even so, as shown in these chapters, Arab men are setting out to counteract, amend, and reset new principles for what it means to be a good man in difficult times, thereby achieving personal senses of achievement and life fulfillment. The studies in this volume illuminate how men develop alternative strategies of affective labor and how they attempt to care for themselves and their families within their local moral worlds. Indeed, these chapters offer fresh insights into what it means to be an Arab man—a father, a husband, a son, a lover—but also what kinds of difficult compromises Arab men must sometimes make in order to fulfill these masculine commitments.

The chapters in this volume capture Arab men's unhappy awareness of how the post-2011 nation-state and world order have failed them, thrusting them into new conditions of political and economic insecurity. Indeed, as of this writing, the MENA region finds itself in the midst of a new form of life-threatening precarity as the COVID-19 pandemic spreads across the region, causing infection, death, and mass burials. How Middle Eastern men's own health, employment, and family well-being will be affected by COVID-19 remains to be seen and studied. But it is likely that with COVID-19, Arab men will again become caught up in the responsibilities of manhood as they care for their sick relatives, bury the dead, and, in the midst of government-imposed quarantines, attempt to put food on the table.

Ultimately, Arab men's longing for security and relief from unremitting stress may be this volume's most important, overarching message. Arab men face the discomfort of being betwixt and between worlds—worlds that involve both movement and stasis, acceptance and distrust, hope and despair. Caught in a precarious world, Arab men in Egypt, Lebanon, Morocco, and Palestine long for a different future in which political stability, economic security, health, and well-being enable their best selves and ideal masculinities to emerge.

ACKNOWLEDGMENTS

The editors and contributing authors are immensely grateful to the Wenner-Gren Foundation for Anthropological Research. The foundation's generous support with a Workshop Award for a conference held in March 2017 and hosted by the Middle East Centre and Institute of Social and Cultural Anthropology at the University of Oxford led to the development of this edited volume and to a special issue in *Men and Masculinities* (Inhorn and Isidoros 2018). We thank our colleagues Soraya Tremayne of the University of Oxford and Nefissa Naguib of the University of Oslo for lending their support as conference chairs and co-conveners.

NOTES

1. These countries are Algeria, Bahrain, Egypt, Iraq, Jordan, Kuwait, Lebanon, Libya, Morocco, Oman, Palestine, Qatar, Saudi Arabia, Sudan, Syria, Tunisia, United Arab Emirates, and Yemen.

2. The four additional countries are Comoros, Djibouti, Mauritania, and Somalia.

3. This is the total number written over a seven-decade period, from the end of World War II to the beginning of the 2020s.

4. These include Soraya Altorki (2015); Daniel Bates and Amal Rassam (1983); Donna Bowen, Evelyn Early, and Becky Schulties (2014); Dale Eickelman (2001); Sherine Hafez and Susan Slyomovics (2013), Judith Scheele and Andrew Shryock (2019), and Lucia Volk (2015).

5. Seminal ethnographies included Richard Antoun (1979), Talal Asad (1970), Thomas Barfield (1981), Frederik Barth (1961), Daniel Bates (1973), Donald Cole (1975), Ian Cunnison (1966), John Davis (1987), Edward Evans-Pritchard

(1949), Robert Fernea (1970), Ernest Gellner (1969), David Hart (1981), William Irons (1975), Fuad Khuri (1980), William Lancaster (1981), Richard Tapper (1979, 1996), and Amal Vinogradov (1974).

6. Some examples include Asad's (1970) *The Kababish Arabs: Power, Authority and Consent in a Nomadic Tribe*; Eickelman's (1985) *Knowledge and Power in Morocco: The Education of a Twentieth Century Notable*; Fernea's (1970) *Shaykh and Effendi: Changing Patterns of Authority among the El Shabana of Southern Iraq*; Khuri's (1980) *Tribe and State in Bahrain: The Transformation of Social and Political Authority in an Arab State*; Michael Meeker's (1979) *Literature and Violence in North Arabia*; and Paul Rabinow's (1975) *Symbolic Domination: Cultural Form and Historical Change in Morocco*.

7. Inhorn's (1996) second book, *Infertility and Patriarchy: The Cultural Politics of Gender and Family Life in Egypt*, was devoted to this search. Although Egyptian women unable to have children "lived" patriarchy in their interactions with their in-laws and community members, their husbands were often extremely supportive, protecting their infertile wives and helping them to seek treatment. Inhorn coined the term *conjugal connectivity* to capture these marital commitments.

8. See Promundo's main website for the full range of country-specific reports, regional reports and executive summaries: https://promundoglobal.org (retrieved April 2018).

9. https://www.economist.com/news/middle-east-and-africa/21721651 -they-are-clinging-patriarchy-comfort-sorry-state-arab-men (retrieved April 2018).

BIBLIOGRAPHY

Abu-Lughod, Lila. 1986. *Veiled Sentiments: Honor and Poetry in a Bedouin Society.* Berkeley: University of California Press.

———. 1989. "Zones of Theory in the Anthropology of the Arab World." *Annual Review of Anthropology* 18:267–306.

———. 1993. *Writing Women's Worlds: Bedouin Stories.* Berkeley: University of California Press.

———. 2013. *Do Muslim Women Need Saving?* Cambridge, MA: Harvard University Press.

Açiksöz, Salih Can. 2019. *Sacrificial Limbs: Masculinity, Disability, and Political Violence in Turkey.* Berkeley: University of California Press.

Adely, Fida. 2012. *Gendered Paradoxes: Educating Jordanian Women in Nation, Faith, and Progress.* Chicago: University of Chicago Press.

Al-Ali, Nadje Sadiq. 2000. *Secularism, Gender and the State in the Middle East: The Egyptian Women's Movement.* Cambridge, MA: Cambridge University Press.

Ali, Kamran Asdar. 2002. *Planning the Family in Egypt: New Bodies, New Selves.* Austin: University of Texas Press.

Altorki, Soraya. 2015. *A Companion to the Anthropology of the Middle East.* Hoboken, NJ: Wiley.

Amar, Paul. 2011. "Middle East Masculinity Studies: Discourses of 'Men in Crisis,' Industries of Gender in Revolution." *Journal of Middle East Women's Studies* 7, no. 3: 36–70.

———. 2013. *The Security Archipelago: Human-Security States, Sexuality Politics, and the End of Neoliberalism.* Durham, NC: Duke University Press.

Antoun, Richard. 1979. *Low-Key Politics: Local-Level Leadership and Change in the Middle East.* Albany, NY: SUNY Press.

Arebi, Saddeka. 1994. *Women and Words in Saudi Arabia: The Politics of Literary Discourse.* New York: Columbia University Press.

Asad, Talal. 1970. *The Kababish Arabs: Power, Authority and Consent in a Nomadic Tribe.* New York: Praeger.

Atshan, Sa'ed. 2020. *Queer Palestine and the Empire of Critique.* Stanford, CA: Stanford University Press.

Badran, Margot. 1996. *Feminists, Islam and Nation: Gender and the Making of Modern Egypt.* Cairo: American University of Cairo Press.

Barfield, Thomas. 1981. *The Central Asian Arabs of Afghanistan: Pastoral Nomadism in Transition.* Austin: University of Texas Press.

Barsoum, Ghada F. 2004. *The Employment Crisis of Female Graduates in Egypt: An Ethnographic Account.* Cairo: American University of Cairo Press.

Barth, Frederik. 1961. *Nomads of South Persia: The Basseri Tribe of the Khamseh Confederacy.* Boston: Little, Brown.

Bates, Daniel G. 1973. *Nomads and Farmers: A Study of the Yoruk of Southeastern Turkey.* Ann Arbor: University of Michigan Press.

Bates, Daniel G., and Amal Rassam. 1983. *Peoples and Cultures of the Middle East.* Upper Saddle River, NJ: Prentice Hall.

Ben-Ari, Eval. 2001. *Mastering Soldiers: Conflict, Emotions, and the Enemy in an Israeli Military Unit.* New York: Berghahn Books.

Boddy, Janice. 1989. *Wombs and Alien Spirits: Women, Men, and the Zar Cult in Northern Sudan.* Madison: University of Wisconsin Press.

Borneman, John. 2007. *Syrian Episodes: Sons, Fathers, and an Anthropologist in Aleppo.* Princeton, NJ: Princeton University Press.

Bowen, Donna Lee, Evelyn A. Early, and Becky Schulties, eds. 2014. *Everyday Life in the Muslim Middle East.* 3rd ed. Bloomington: Indiana University Press.

Brandes, Stanley. 2002. *Staying Sober in Mexico City.* Austin: University of Texas Press.

Brodsky, Anne E. 2003. *With All Our Strength: The Revolutionary Association of the Women of Afghanistan.* New York: Routledge.

Bucaille, Lætitia, and Ethan Rundell. 2019. *Making Peace with Your Enemy: Algerian, French, and South African Ex-Combatants*. Philadelphia: University of Pennsylvania Press.

Butler, Judith. 2009. "Performativity, Precarity and Sexual Politics." *Revista de Antropología Iberoamericana* 4, no. 3: 321–336.

Cairoli, M. Laetitia. 2011. *Girls of the Factory: A Year with the Garment Workers of Morocco*. Gainesville: University Press of Florida.

Carrigan, Tim, Raewyn W. Connell, and John Lee. 1985. "Toward a New Sociology of Masculinity." *Theory and Society* 14, no. 5: 551–604.

Carrillo, Héctor. 2001. *The Night Is Young: Sexuality in Mexico in the Time of AIDS*. Chicago: University of Chicago Press.

———. 2018. *Pathways of Desire: The Sexual Migration of Mexican Gay Men*. Chicago: University of Chicago Press.

Caton, Steven C. 1990. *"Peaks of Yemen I Summon": Poetry as Cultural Practice in a North Yemeni Tribe*. Berkeley: University of California Press.

———. 2005. *Yemen Chronicle: An Anthropology of War and Mediation*. New York: Hill and Wang.

Chakravarti, Leila Zaki. 2016. *Made in Egypt: Gendered Identity and Aspiration on the Globalised Shop Floor*. New York: Berghahn Books.

Cole, Donald. 1975. *Nomads of the Nomads: The Al Murrah Bedouin of the Empty Quarter*. Arlington Heights, IL: Harlan Davidson.

Connell, Raewyn. W. 1993. "The Big Picture: Masculinities in Recent World History." *Theory and Society* 22:597–623.

———. 1995. *Masculinities*. Cambridge: Polity.

Cornwall, Andrea, and Nancy Lindisfarne, eds. 1994. *Dislocating Masculinity: Comparative Ethnographies*. London: Routledge.

Cunnison, Ian. 1966. *Baggara Arabs: Power and the Lineage in a Sudanese Nomad Tribe*. Oxford: Clarendon.

Davis, John. 1987. *Libyan Politics: Tribe and Revolution*. London: I. B. Tauris.

Deeb, Lara. 2006. *An Enchanted Modern: Gender and Public Piety in Shi'i Lebanon*. Princeton, NJ: Princeton University Press.

Delaney, Carol. 1991. *The Seed and the Soil: Gender and Cosmology in Turkish Village Society*. Berkeley: University of California Press.

Dresch, Paul. 1990. *Tribes, Government, and History in Yemen*. Oxford: Oxford University Press.

Early, Evelyn A. 1993. *Baladi Women of Cairo: Playing with an Egg and a Stone*. Boulder, CO: Lynne Rienner.

Edwards, David B. 1996. *Heroes of the Age: Moral Fault Lines on the Afghan Frontier*. Berkeley: University of California Press.

———. 2001. *Before Taliban: Genealogies of the Afghan Jihad*. Berkeley: University of California Press.

———. 2017. *Caravan of Martyrs: Sacrifice and Suicide Bombing in Afghanistan.*
Berkeley: University of California Press.

Eickelman, Dale. 1976. *Moroccan Islam: Tradition and Society in a Pilgrimage Center.*
Austin: University of Texas Press.

———. 1985. *Knowledge and Power in Morocco: The Education of a Twentieth-
Century Notable.* Princeton, NJ: Princeton University Press.

———. 2001. *The Middle East and Central Asia: An Anthropological Approach.* 4th
ed. New York: Pearson.

El Feki, Shereen, Brian Heilman, and Gary Barker, eds. 2017. *Understanding
Masculinities: Results from the International Men and Gender Equality
Survey (IMAGES)—Middle East and North Africa.* Cairo: UN Women and
Promundo-US.

El Guindi, Fadwa. 1999. *Veil: Modesty, Privacy and Resistance.* London: Berg.

Evans-Pritchard, Edward E. 1949. *The Sanusi of Cyrenaica.* Oxford: Oxford
University Press.

Fadlalla, Amal Hassan. 2007. *Embodying Honor: Fertility, Foreignness, and
Regeneration in Eastern Sudan.* Madison: University of Wisconsin Press.

Fernea, Robert A. 1970. *Shaykh and Effendi: Changing Patterns of Authority
among the El Shabana of Southern Iraq.* Cambridge, MA: Harvard University
Press.

Fischer, Michael M. J. 1980. *Iran: From Religious Dissent to Revolution.* Cambridge,
MA: Harvard University Press.

Ford, Michele, and Lenore Lyons, eds. 2012. *Men and Masculinities in Southeast
Asia.* Abingdon: Routledge.

Gaffney, Patrick D. 1994. *The Prophet's Pulpit: Islamic Preaching in Contemporary
Egypt.* Berkeley: University of California Press.

Geertz, Clifford. 1968. *Islam Observed: Religious Development in Morocco and
Indonesia.* Chicago: University of Chicago Press.

Gellner, Ernest. 1969. *Saints of the Atlas.* London: Weidenfeld and Nicholson.

Ghannam, Farha. 2013. *Live and Die Like a Man: Gender Dynamics in Urban Egypt.*
Stanford, CA: Stanford University Press.

Ghoussoub, Mai, and Emma Sinclair-Webb, eds. 2000. *Imagined Masculinities:
Male Identities and Culture in the Modern Middle East.* London: Saqi Books.

Gilsenan, Michael. 1973. *Saint and Sufi in Modern Egypt: An Essay in the Sociology of
Religion.* Oxford: Clarendon.

———. 1982. *Recognizing Islam: Religion and Society in the Modern Arab World.*
New York: Pantheon Books.

———. 1996. *Lords of the Lebanese Marches: Violence and Narrative in an Arab
Society.* Los Angeles: I. B. Tauris and University of California Press.

Gramsci, Antonio. 1971. *Selections from the Prison Notebooks of Antonio Gramsci.*
New York: International.

Grassiani, Erelle. 2013. *Soldiering Under Occupation: Processes of Numbing among Israeli Soldiers in the Al-Aqsa Intifada.* New York: Berghahn Books.

Grima, Benedicte. 1992. *The Performance of Emotion among Paxtun Women: "The Misfortunes Which Have Befallen Me."* Austin: University of Texas Press.

Gutmann, Matthew C. 1996. *The Meanings of Macho: Being a Man in Mexico City.* Berkeley: University of California Press.

———. 1997. "Trafficking in Men: The Anthropology of Masculinity." *Annual Review of Anthropology* 26:385–409.

———, ed. 2003. *Changing Men and Masculinities in Latin America.* Durham, NC: Duke University Press.

Haeri, Shahla. 1989. *Law of Desire: Temporary Marriage in Shi'i Iran.* Syracuse, NY: Syracuse University Press.

Hafez, Sherine. 2011. *An Islam of Her Own: Reconsidering Religion and Secularism in Women's Islamic Movements.* New York: NYU Press.

Hafez, Sherine, and Susan Slyomovics, eds. 2013. *Anthropology of the Middle East and North Africa: Into the New Millennium.* Bloomington: Indiana University Press.

Hale, Sondra. 1996. *Gender Politics in Sudan: Islamism, Socialism, and the State.* Boulder, CO: Westview.

Hammoudi, Abdellah. 1993. *The Victim and Its Masks: An Essay on Sacrifice and Masquerade in the Maghreb.* Chicago: University of Chicago Press.

———. 1997. *Master and Disciple: The Cultural Foundations of Moroccan Authoritarianism.* Chicago: University of Chicago Press.

Hatem, Mervat. 1993. "Toward the Development of Post-Islamist and Post-Nationalist Feminist Discourses in the Middle East." In *Arab Women: Old Boundaries, New Frontiers*, edited by Judith Tucker, 29–48. Bloomington: Indiana University Press.

Hart, David. 1981. *Dadda 'Atta and His Forty Grandsons: The Socio-Political Organization of the Ait 'Atta of Southern Morocco.* Boulder, CO: Westview.

———. 2001. *Qabila: Tribal Profiles, Tribe-State Relations in Morocco and the Afghanistan-Pakistan Frontier.* Amsterdam: Het Spinhuis.

Hirschkind, Charles. 2006. *The Ethical Soundscape: Cassette Sermons and Islamic Counterpublics.* New York: Columbia University Press.

Hoffman, Katherine. 2008. *We Share Walls: Language, Land and Gender in Berber Morocco.* New York: Wiley-Blackwell.

Hoodfar, Homa. 1996. *Between Marriage and the Market: Intimate Politics and Survival in Cairo.* Berkeley: University of California Press.

Inhorn, Marcia C. 1994. *Quest for Conception: Gender, Infertility, and Egyptian Medical Traditions.* Philadelphia: University of Pennsylvania Press.

———. 1996. *Infertility and Patriarchy: The Cultural Politics of Gender and Family Life in Egypt.* Philadelphia: University of Pennsylvania Press.

————. 2003. *Local Babies, Global Science: Gender, Religion, and In Vitro Fertilization in Egypt.* New York: Routledge.

————. 2012. *The New Arab Man: Emergent Masculinities, Technologies, and Islam in the Middle East.* Princeton, NJ: Princeton University Press.

————. 2014a. "Celebrating a Decade of Middle East Gender Studies: Reflections on the Tenth Anniversary of the *Journal of Middle East Women's Studies.*" *Journal of Middle East Women's Studies* 10, no. 3: 1–7.

————. 2014b. "Roads Less Traveled in Middle East Anthropology—and New Paths in Gender Ethnography." *Journal of Middle East Women's Studies* 10, no. 3: 62–86.

————. 2018. *America's Arab Refugees: Vulnerability and Health on the Margins.* Stanford, CA: Stanford University Press.

Inhorn, Marcia C., and Emily A. Wentzell. 2011. "Embodying Emergent Masculinities: Men Engaging with Reproductive and Sexual Health Technologies in the Middle East and Mexico." *American Ethnologist* 38, no. 4: 801–815.

Inhorn, Marcia C., and Konstantina Isidoros, eds. 2018. "Arab Masculinities, Anthropological Re-conceptions." Special issue, *Men and Masculinities* 21, no. 3: 319–449.

Irons, William. 1975. *The Yomut Turkmen: A Study of Social Organization among a Central Asian Turkic-Speaking Population.* Ann Arbor: University of Michigan Press.

Joseph, Suad. 1993. "Connectivity and Patriarchy among Urban Working-Class Arab Families in Lebanon." *Ethos* 21, no. 4: 452–484.

————. 1994. "Brother/Sister Relationships: Connectivity, Love and Power in the Reproduction of Arab Patriarchy." *American Ethnologist* 21, no. 1: 50–73.

Kanaaneh, Rhoda Ann. 2003. *Birthing the Nation: Strategies of Palestinian Women in Israel.* Berkeley: University of California Press.

————. 2008. *Surrounded: Palestinian Soldiers in the Israeli Military.* Stanford, CA: Stanford University Press.

Kandiyoti, Deniz. 1988. "Bargaining with Patriarchy." *Gender & Society* 2, no. 3: 274–290.

————. 1994. "The Paradoxes of Masculinity: Some Thoughts on Segregated Societies." In *Dislocating Masculinity: Comparative Ethnographies,* edited by Andrea Cornwall and Nancy Lindisfarne, 197–213. London: Routledge.

Kapchan, Deborah. 1996. *Gender on the Market: Moroccan Women and the Revoicing of Tradition.* Philadelphia: University of Pennsylvania Press.

Kaplan, Danny. 2000. "The Military as a Second Bar Mitzvah: Combat Service as Initiation to Zionist Masculinity." In *Imagined Masculinities: Male Identity and Culture in the Modern Middle East,* edited by Mai Ghoussoub and Emma Sinclair-Webb, 127–144. London: Saqi Books.

Khuri, Fuad. 1980. *Tribe and State in Bahrain: The Transformation of Social and Political Authority in an Arab State*. Chicago: University of Chicago Press.

Kjaran, Jón Ingvar. 2019. *Gay Life Stories: Same-Sex Desires in Post-Revolutionary Iran*. London: Palgrave Macmillan.

Lancaster, William. 1981. *The Rwala Bedouin Today*. Cambridge: Cambridge University Press.

Lindisfarne, Nancy. 1994. "Variant Masculinities, Variant Virginities: Rethinking 'Honour and Shame.'" In *Dislocating Masculinity: Comparative Ethnographies*, edited by Andrea Cornwall and Nancy Lindisfarne, 82–96. London: Routledge.

Louie, Kam, and Morris Low, eds. 2003. *Asian Masculinities: The Meaning and Practice of Manhood in China and Japan*. London: Routledge.

MacLeod, Arlene E. 1992. *Accommodating Protest: Working Women, the New Veiling, and Change in Cairo*. New York: Columbia University Press.

Mahmood, Saba. 2006. *Politics of Piety: The Islamic Revival and the Feminist Subject*. Princeton, NJ: Princeton University Press.

Meeker, Michael E. 1979. *Literature and Violence in North Arabia*. Cambridge: Cambridge University Press.

Merabet, Sofian. 2015. *Queer Beirut*. Austin: University of Texas Press.

Messick, Brinkley. 1992. *The Calligraphic State: Textual Domination and History in a Muslim Society*. Berkeley: University of California Press.

Moghadam, Valentine, ed. 1994. *Gender and National Identity: Women and Politics in Muslim Societies*. Helsinki: Zed Books.

Monterescu, Daniel. 2006. "Stranger Masculinities: Gender and Politics in a Palestinian-Israeli Third Space." In *Islamic Masculinities*, edited by Lahoucine Ouzgane, 123–142. New York: Zed Books.

Moors, Annelies. 1995. *Women, Property and Islam: Palestinian Experiences, 1920–1990*. Cambridge: Cambridge University Press.

Moussawi, Ghassan. 2020. *Disruptive Situations: Fractal Orientalism and Queer Strategies in Beirut*. Philadelphia: Temple University Press.

Mowafi, Hani. 2011. "Conflict, Displacement and Health in the Middle East." *Global Public Health* 6, no. 5: 472–487.

Munson, Jr., Henry. 1984. *The House of Si Abd Allah: The Oral History of a Moroccan Family*. New Haven, CT: Yale University Press.

———. 1993. *Religion and Power in Morocco*. New Haven, CT: Yale University Press.

Naguib, Nefissa. 2015. *Nurturing Masculinities: Men, Food, and Family in Contemporary Egypt*. Austin: University of Texas Press.

Nelson, Cynthia. 1974. "Public and Private Politics: Women in the Middle Eastern World." *American Ethnologist* 1, no. 3: 551–563.

Ouzgane, Lahoucine, ed. 2006. *Islamic Masculinities*. New York: Zed Books.

Ouzgane, Lahoucine, and Robert Morrell, eds. 2005. *African Masculinities: Men in Africa from the Late Nineteenth Century to the Present*. New York: Palgrave Macmillan.

Özbay, Cenk. 2017. *Queering Sexualities in Turkey: Gay Men, Male Prostitutes and the City*. London: I. B. Tauris.

Parker, Richard G. 1991. *Bodies, Pleasures, and Passions: Sexual Culture in Contemporary Brazil*. New York: Beacon.

———. 1998. *Beneath the Equator: Cultures of Desire, Male Homosexuality, and Emerging Gay Communities in Brazil*. New York: Routledge.

Peteet, Julie. 1992. *Gender in Crisis: Women and the Palestinian Resistance Movement*. New York: Columbia University Press.

———. 2000. "Male Gender and Rituals of Resistance in the Palestinian Intifada: A Cultural Politics of Violence." In *Imagined Masculinities: Male Identities and Culture in the Modern Middle East*, edited by Mai Ghoussoub and Emma Sinclair-Webb, 103–126. London: Saqi Books.

Peters, Emrys L. 1990. *The Bedouin of Cyrenaica: Studies in Personal and Corporate Power*. Cambridge: Cambridge University Press.

Rabinow, Paul. 1975. *Symbolic Domination: Cultural Form and Historical Change in Morocco*. Chicago: University of Chicago Press.

Reynolds, Dwight F. 1995. *Heroic Poets, Poetic Heroes: The Ethnography of Performance in an Arabic Oral Epic Tradition*. Ithaca, NY: Cornell University Press.

Ross, Andrew. 2019. *Stone Men: The Palestinians who Built Israel*. London: Verso.

Rugh, Andrea B. 1986. *Reveal and Conceal: Dress in Contemporary Egypt*. Syracuse, NY: Syracuse University Press.

Said, Edward W. 1978. *Orientalism*. New York: Pantheon Books.

Scheele, Judith, and Andrew Shryock, eds. 2019. *The Scandal of Continuity in Middle East Anthropology: Form, Duration, Difference*. Bloomington: Indiana University Press.

Schielke, Samuli. 2020. *Migrant Dreams: Egyptian Workers in the Gulf States*. Cairo: American University of Cairo Press.

Sedghi, Hamideh. 2007. *Women and Politics in Iran: Veiling, Unveiling, and Reveiling*. Cambridge: Cambridge University Press.

Shaheen, Jack G. 2008. *Guilty: Hollywood's Verdict on Arabs after 9/11*. Northampton, MA: Olive Branch Press.

Shryock, Andrew. 1997. *Nationalism and the Genealogical Imagination: Oral History and Textual Authority in Tribal Jordan*. Berkeley: University of California Press.

Sinclair-Webb, Emma. 2000. "'Our Bulent Is Now a Commando': Military Service and Manhood in Turkey." In *Imagined Masculinities: Male Identities and Culture in the Modern Middle East*, edited by Mai Ghoussoub and Emma Sinclair-Webb, 65–92. London: Saqi.

Tapper, Nancy. 2006. *Bartered Brides: Politics, Gender and Marriage in an Afghan Tribal Society*. 2nd ed. Cambridge: Cambridge University Press.

Tapper, Richard. 1979. *Pasture and Politics: Economics, Conflict and Ritual Among the Shahsevan Nomads of Northwestern Iran*. New York: Academic.

———. 1996. *Frontier Nomads of Iran: A Political and Social History of the Shahsevan*. Cambridge: Cambridge University Press.

Torab, Azam. 2008. *Performing Islam: Gender and Ritual in Iran*. Leiden: Brill.

UNHCR (United Nations High Commissioner for Refugees). 2019. *Global Trends Report 2018*. May 19. Retrieved from https://www.unhcr.org/globaltrends2018/.

UNHCR News. 2019. "Iraq Refugee Crisis Explained." November 7. Retrieved from https://www.unrefugees.org/news/iraq-refugee-crisis-explained/.

Van Nieuwkerk, Karin. 2019. *Manhood is Not Easy: Egyptian Masculinities through the Life of Musician Sayyid Henkish*. Cairo: American University of Cairo Press.

Vinogradov, Amal R. 1974. *The Ait Ndhir of Morocco: A Study of the Social Transformation of a Berber Tribe*. Ann Arbor: University of Michigan Press.

Volk, Lucia, ed. 2015. *The Middle East in the World: An Introduction*. New York: Routledge.

White, Jenny B. 1994. *Money Makes Us Relatives: Women's Labor in Urban Turkey*. Austin: University of Texas Press.

———. 2003. *Islamist Mobilization in Turkey: A Study in Vernacular Politics*. Seattle: University of Washington Press.

———. 2012. *Muslim Nationalism and the New Turks*. Princeton, NJ: Princeton University Press.

Williams, Raymond. 1978. *Marxism and Literature*. Oxford: Oxford University Press.

Zuhur, Sherifa. 1992. *Revealing Reveiling: Islamist Gender Ideology in Contemporary Egypt*. Albany, NY: SUNY Press.

MARCIA C. INHORN is William K. Lanman Jr. Professor of Anthropology and International Affairs and Chair of the Council on Middle East Studies at Yale University. She is author of six books, including *America's Arab Refugees: Vulnerability and Health on the Margins*; of *Cosmopolitan Conceptions: IVF Sojourns in Global Dubai*; and of *The New Arab Man: Emergent Masculinities, Technologies, and Islam in the Middle East*.

KONSTANTINA ISIDOROS is Lecturer in Anthropology at St Catherine's College and Research Affiliate of the Institute of Social and Cultural Anthropology at the University of Oxford. She is author *of Nomads and Nation-Building in the Western Sahara: Gender, Politics and the Sahrawi*.

PART I

MASCULINITY AND PRECARITY: CLASS CONFLICT AND ECONOMIC INDIGNITY

ONE

—҉Ѡ—

EGYPTIAN MIDDLE-CLASS MASCULINITY AND ITS WORKING-CLASS OTHERS

BÅRD HELGE KÅRTVEIT

INTRODUCTION: REFLECTIONS ON MASCULINITY

Since the late 1980s, Raewyn Connell's (1987, 2000) concept of *hegemonic masculinity* has been a dominant point of reference in masculinity studies. The term refers to a set of practices that, in a given society, constitute "the currently most honored way of being a man" (Connell and Messerschmidt 2005, 832). Within a hierarchy of competing masculinities, hegemonic masculinity represents an ideal that "all other men must position themselves in relation to" (Connell and Messerschmidt 2005, 533) and that is distinguished from subordinate and complicit masculinities. The term *hegemonic masculinity* connects the dominance of some masculinities over others with men's patriarchal dominance over women, thus representing two mutually constitutive relations of domination. Studies of Western societies include the following among the core tenets of hegemonic masculinity: physical strength, courage, self-assertiveness, and the absence of what are perceived as stereotypical feminine traits, such as emotional openness and vulnerability (MacDonald 2014). In a Middle Eastern context, patriarchal authority and patrilineal loyalty are also critical dimensions.

In this chapter, I argue that the masculine ideals and practices embraced by some middle-class Egyptian men—and their subsequent construction of a working-class masculine Other—challenge some of the central premises of Connell's notion of hegemonic masculinity. One such premise is that some form of masculinity must necessarily attain hegemonic dominance, thus becoming "culturally exalted above all other" (Connell 1995, 77). The case of middle-class men in the city of Alexandria, Egypt, teaches us instead that men belonging to different social milieus within the same society can embrace different and even mutually exclusive forms of masculinity that are hierarchically unrelated. Further, this case challenges the notion that dominant masculinities necessarily serve to reinforce patriarchal power structures (Christensen and Jensen 2014). Under some circumstances, resourceful, assertive men can aspire to masculine ideals that may challenge, or at the very least seek to decenter, patriarchy as a defining aspect of male-female relations. I use *patriarchy* here to mean "the privileging of males and seniors and the mobilization of kinship structures, morality, and idioms to legitimate and institutionalize gendered and aged domination" (Joseph 1993, 453).

Other scholars have sought to challenge, improve, or move on from Connell's concept of hegemonic masculinity. For instance, Ann-Dorte Christensen and Sune Qvotrup Jensen (2014) have introduced the notion of intersectionality by exploring how other criteria of stratification, such as race and class, serve to complicate relations between masculinities. Other researchers have argued in favor of inclusive masculinity, suggesting that a new form of masculinity, characterized by social tolerance and inclusion, is emerging in societies where homophobia has begun to decrease, thus challenging concepts of "orthodox" masculinity (Anderson 2005; Anderson and McGuire 2010). Parting with Connell, Eric Anderson and Rhidian McGuire (2010, 250–251) argue that this new form of masculinity can coexist with an orthodox masculinity that may be numerically but not hegemonically dominant, allowing for a horizontal rather than a stratified relationship between the two. Researchers working within a European context have likewise introduced the concept of caring masculinities, characterized by an emphasis on caregiving, compassion, and nurturing as central values and by an explicit rejection of patriarchy (Elliott 2016).

Working from within a Middle Eastern context and adopting Raymond Williams's (1977) notion of emergence, Marcia C. Inhorn (2012) introduces the concept of emergent masculinities to describe changes in masculine norms and practices. Inhorn (2012, 15) argues for the emergence of a "new Arab man," describing a new generation of males who are departing from the patriarchal ideals and practices of earlier generations and expanding "the terms for what it means to be a man in the Middle East." *The New Arab Man* (Inhorn 2012) has become an important reference well beyond the Middle East (Thompson, Kitiarsa, and Smutkupt 2016) and has been joined by other works on Middle Eastern masculinities, including Farha Ghannam's (2013) *Live and Die Like a Man* and Nefissa Naguib's (2015) *Nurturing Masculinities*. All these works share some important characteristics. First, they add nuance, complexity, and dynamism to the portrayal of Muslim men in the Middle East. Second, they focus on men's relationships and responsibilities toward their families and the women in their lives and on the importance of these relationships in shaping masculine subjectivities. In this sense, these texts stand out from a broader international literature on masculinity, which has focused heavily on homosocial relations—that is, on men's evaluation of and relations with other men. Third, these works focus on Muslim men without necessarily stressing the importance of Islam as a component of their masculine identities. There are good reasons for this approach: Islam is the majority religion in the region, and Muslim men are the primary targets of the static representations these scholars seek to challenge.

A central theme among many of these recent works is an effort to capture new forms of masculinity that break with previously dominant ideals that might otherwise be referred to as old, orthodox, hegemonic, or traditional. I borrow from all these contributions to explore how urban middle-class masculinities in Alexandria are taking many new forms. But at the same time, these emergent masculinities are constructed in opposition to a working-class masculine Other.

Negative stereotypes of Arab men have a central place in the Western representation, but they are also prevalent in the Arab world. These internal stereotypes serve multiple functions. For example, they serve to justify and reinforce social divides based primarily on class, regional origins, ethnicity, and other criteria. Furthermore, by offering the construct of a masculine Other, a masculinity ascribed with negative traits—one to which urban middle-class men can define themselves in opposition—these stereotypes also provide direction for the formation of positive masculine aspirations.

The masculine Other is a construct of a masculinity that can be found in any society, and it describes a series of traits that are traditionally associated with masculinity.[1] Notwithstanding, those men who self-identify with other masculine ideals tend to negatively view this masculine Other. In this chapter, I look at masculinity among middle-class men in their early twenties to midforties in the city of Alexandria. I explore the kinds of ideals and practices to which they aspire while also focusing on the masculine constructs to which they define themselves in opposition.

While sitting at a coffee shop in Alexandria, Mohammed, a well-groomed young man in his midtwenties, points to a group of men who are ten years his senior and wearing much plainer clothes than himself: "You see these guys over here? You can bet they are all married, and most of them have small children. Still, they hang out here with their friends all night. Every day. This is how they behave."

In criticizing a form of socializing and a way of prioritizing that is common, accepted, and even celebrated among Egyptian men, Mohammed and many of his peers are signaling a new set of masculine aspirations for themselves. Here, masculinity becomes centered around men's conduct toward the women and children in their lives, as well as their ability and willingness to embrace new expectations in handling these relationships. For instance, as young middle-class men describe their aspirations—and sometimes shortcomings—in connecting with their partners at an emotional level, they assume no such aspiration or capacity among men of lower socioeconomic status. When Mohammed looks at a group of working-class men at the coffee shop, he assumes that they are neglecting the needs of their families in order to socialize with friends. This chapter is based on fieldwork conducted in Alexandria, Egypt's second-largest city, in the spring and summer of 2014 and later in 2015 for a research project focused on masculinity among Egyptian Copts and Muslims. For this project, I connected with young men in coffee shops, at sport clubs, outside mosques, and at churches. I spent the evenings with several groups of young men hanging out in inexpensive coffee shops. After I explained my research project to them, they generously assisted me by connecting me with other male friends and family members, most of whom allowed themselves to be interviewed. As such, the material presented here is based on unstructured interviews, informal conversations, and personal observations, primarily among men of middle-class backgrounds between the ages of twenty and forty-five years.[2] While doing fieldwork, I presented myself as a North European of Protestant background but also as a married man in my thirties and a father of two small children. In my experience, this positioned me clearly as a foreigner and an outsider, but one who could connect with some of these men on the basis of shared concerns and experiences. In many cases, at least initially, my own background informed how some of my informants presented themselves to me. With time, they grew more candid and assertive in expressing attitudes and describing actions with which they knew I would not personally identify.

MOHAMMED AND ISLAM

Among my first acquaintances in the city were Mohammed, who was mentioned earlier, and Islam. These two young Muslim men lived in Bahary, a neighborhood in the western part of Alexandria. They were both bachelors in their midtwenties and men of relative privilege who came from families with some wealth and valuable connections. While growing up, they had attended church-run private schools. They had since completed studies in engineering and landed steady jobs. Both were socially and financially prepared to get married. Their families had also started nagging them about settling down.

The two talked about the challenges of looking for and attracting a suitable girl. "You've got to be hard," stated Mohammed. "Arab women want their men to be hard."

Islam reacted to his friend's assertion: "Hard? Any *fellah* [peasant] can be a hard man! You got to be able to talk to her! That's the difficult part." This exchange was followed by ten minutes of banter about which of the two was smoother in talking with girls.

The two young men argued that the informal rules of marriage arrangements had changed since their own fathers were young. They belonged to a generation of men whose search for a spouse would not be directed entirely by their families. Today, they stressed, a bachelor is expected to get to know the girl and establish some kind of connection, all without depending on family to act as intermediaries. Although there are clear social limits on what kind of direct interaction can occur between unmarried men and women, social media represents a new arena where young men can—and increasingly are expected to—express themselves and connect emotionally with their chosen ones while demonstrating wit, sincere affection, and romantic instincts. Such expectations are also shaped by Egyptian popular culture through music, television series, and social media. For young men such as Mohammed and Islam, the world of courtship is a difficult terrain where mistakes are easy to make but are not always easily forgiven. In this regard, Valentine's Day (February 14) was described by many as a minefield and viewed with absolute dread.

However, the rules of married life and family life are changing as well. Once married, young men now are expected to spend more time with their wives and children than was common just a few years ago. This is particularly visible at one of the primary areas of male interaction: the coffee shop.

In Egypt, as in other parts of the region, the local *qahwe* or coffee shop is an important meeting place for men of all ages. Young men can spend several hours here drinking coffee, playing cards, and socializing with their friends (Kreil 2016; Schielke 2009, 2015). Alexandria is known for its bustling coffee shop scene, and those facing the Cornish and Mediterranean are especially popular. These coffee shops often have a basic interior with many tables and chairs. They sell tea and coffee at moderate prices, thus boosting their popularity as social hangouts. Traditionally, the coffee shop is a space in which to assert masculine authority, both directly through interaction with other men and indirectly, in that by spending time at the coffee shop, a man demonstrates that he is in control of his household and needs not be physically present at home at all times.

These ideals are challenged by young men who want to retain control over their own households but who also wish to make their wives happy and be a central part of their children's lives. Among young men on the brink of starting their own families, challenging these ideals requires a careful consideration of their own priorities as husbands, fathers, and friends. Mohammed and Islam both have older brothers who are married with children and who rarely meet friends at the coffee shops because they spend what little free time they have with their families. Mohammed and Islam compared this to the behaviors of their fathers, whom they mostly saw on Fridays while they were growing up. This contrast between the priorities of their fathers and their own expectations of marriage was a point emphasized by other young men in Alexandria, both Muslim and Christian. Some men considered these changes to be significant, and some could face sanctions from their own families if they failed to adjust.

OMAR

Omar is thirty-two years old and holds an administrative position at Alexandria University. He has been married for eight years and has two daughters, ages three and five. His family lives in an apartment complex next door to two of his brothers and their families, and their parents live one floor down. He loves his daughters, but he has been deeply unhappy in his marriage, and so has his wife. When I first met him in spring 2014, Omar handled this situation by staying in his office much longer than his job required and then spending several hours with friends at his favorite coffee shop before going home around midnight. He did this every evening except on Fridays, when he had the day off. Though he felt guilty about not seeing his daughters very often, he believed that this coping mechanism worked for him.[3] When I met him again six months later, his two brothers had held an intervention, admonishing Omar to come home after work and to spend more time with his family. They told him that his wife was lonely and that there was no excuse for his behavior. He tried to defend himself, saying that this was how their father had behaved. His oldest brother gave him a stern look and said, "Yes, but that was a different time. We can't behave like that. You can't behave like that." Since this intervention, he has spent more time at home. He cherishes the time with his daughters and now gets along better with his wife. Though Omar had to be coerced into making this adjustment, his brothers' interference points to broader changes in the norms and expectations associated with marriage and fatherhood. These changes represent a break from the traditional structure of the Egyptian family, where the domestic space is viewed as a female arena and where staying out of the house has been not only a male privilege but also a male virtue, one traditionally appreciated by female members of the household.

Cutting back on coffee shop time with male friends may seem like a trivial sacrifice for young men about to settle down, but it is not. For many men, the coffee shop is where they confide in close friends and share their most personal feelings. It is a place where they enact masculine attributes that are held in high regard, seek the social approval of other men, and sometimes reveal their more vulnerable sides. In writing about the importance of the coffee shop as a social arena for young men, Aymon Kreil (2016) describes it as a zone of social intimacy that both complements and competes with the family sphere. Nonetheless, by talking to both bachelors and married men in their twenties to midforties, I found that most were keen to embrace these new norms—including the drift away from the coffee shop and into the home—and that they connected these changes with their own desire to experience an emotional connection with the women in their lives. Those from relatively liberal social circles also reported having some experience socializing with girls from outside their own families. Mohammed and Islam had attended a Catholic school in Alexandria, where they had interacted with girls their own age.[4] They felt that this background was an asset that better equipped them to become attentive partners who could communicate with and express their own feelings toward their future wives.[5]

The ability to connect with a future wife was something these young men regarded as an important quality for being a man today. Mohammed and Islam both had older brothers and expressed sadness that they had not been able to spend as much time with them as they might have wished. At the same time, they admired their brothers for being caring and attentive fathers and husbands, thereby serving as role models to them.

IBRAHIM

The young men I interviewed held up being considerate and attentive to the needs of one's wife as a central aspiration. However, there are boundaries regarding the extent to which a man is expected to accommodate his partner. What follows is an account of Ibrahim, a young man who has been perceived by many as crossing these boundaries.

Ibrahim teaches Arabic and English at a foreign school in Alexandria. He is thirty-two years old, as is his wife of eight years. The two met while studying at Alexandria University. In a break with local tradition, their families allowed the two to marry even though Ibrahim was unable to provide a house at the time. For four years, they had to rent an apartment before they were able to purchase a place of their own in the eastern part of Alexandria. His wife is also a teacher, and she works at another private school in Alexandria. They have two children, ages three and five, who attend nursery school and kindergarten near their home. Both parents must work full-time to stay afloat financially. In 2013, however, his wife decided that she wanted to pursue a master's degree; this would allow her to demand a higher salary from the school where she worked. However, her employer could not facilitate her studies in any way, so she had to complete her degree at a private college that offered evening classes over a four-year period.

Though the couple could rely on some childcare assistance from their parents and siblings, this situation required Ibrahim to stop working in the evenings. Like many teachers, he supplemented his salary by working after school as a private tutor for the children of wealthy parents. While his wife attended classes in the evening, he stayed at home at least three nights a week and took care of their children. When I met Ibrahim for the first time, the couple had been living like this for a year, and it was a comfortable arrangement for Ibrahim. He was still tutoring students in the evening at least twice a week, during which time his sister-in-law would care for the children. The other three nights in the week, he would take care of his children while his wife attended school. He found it tiring but also rewarding to be alone with the children. He has been an involved father from the start, so he has a very close relationship with his children.

His only concern is the attitude of those around him, from family members to colleagues and old friends. His parents do not approve of this arrangement. They question his wife's commitment to their children, and they argue that it is her job to take care of them and that it is bad for the children not to be around their mother. They were concerned that this arrangement makes Ibrahim look weak and asked him not to tell people about it. However, Ibrahim did not follow their advice and was unwilling to keep silent on matters of importance to him. After the ousting of former president Mohammed Morsi in July 2013, Ibrahim remained a lone voice of support for the Muslim Brotherhood amid friends and family members who had a hard time accepting his position. An independent thinker, Ibrahim expressed support for the value-centered politics of the Brotherhood, their resistance to the military's dominance, and their commitment to end a culture of corruption. At the same time, Ibrahim condemned Morsi for his failure to build alliances with non-Islamists. In a deeply polarized Egypt, this was a difficult position to defend. Others pointed out the inconsistencies to him, but he refused to see any contradiction between his somewhat conservative politics and his personal commitment to supporting his wife's professional ambitions.

Whereas his colleagues were mostly unfamiliar with his political views, his colleagues and friends were aware of his familial arrangement, and they teased him for it. They joked that he was being slapped around and controlled by his wife because he was at home with the kids while she was at school. Ibrahim wanted to remain unaffected by these attitudes, but he was not. He thought that he was doing a good thing and that his priorities were right. He found, however, that the negative reactions and the constant battle to defend both himself and his wife were difficult to handle, as was the complete lack of approval from everyone around him. At the same time, his wife was happy and grateful for the chance to pursue her studies, and Ibrahim was willing to go a long way to make her happy.

When he told me about this, he knew that I was a European man who was married to a woman with a career of her own. He was cautiously looking for approval from someone who might understand his priorities. Usually confident, Ibrahim talked about this arrangement with a tone of self-deprecation, constantly excusing himself. He was seeking assurances that what he was doing was not completely unheard of. According to Ibrahim, many of his male friends were married to working women with university degrees. As members of two-income households, they took some responsibility and abided by fairly progressive norms as husbands and family men.

Still, none of these friends had shown any empathy over his decision to stay at home with his children in the evening so that his wife could pursue her studies. On this issue, Ibrahim felt the social burden of pushing the boundaries too far. Nonetheless, when I contacted him two years later in 2016, Ibrahim's wife had almost completed her master's degree, and Ibrahim was looking forward to a new reality in which he could take on more tutoring in the evening and his wife could demand better pay as a teacher.

THE WORKING-CLASS MASCULINE OTHER

Some young men, such as Mohammed and Islam, place "conjugal connectivity" (Inhorn 2012) at the center of their masculine aspirations, explicitly striving toward better communication with their fiancées or wives and greater sensitivity to their needs. Ibrahim's actions reveal an intrinsic commitment to these ideals. Through their actions and stated aspirations, these men define themselves in opposition to men of earlier generations (though none spoke poorly about their own fathers). At the same time, they define themselves in opposition to the uneducated, predatory rural and working-class man who constitutes their notion of the masculine Other.

These men are seen as representatives of a brute form of masculinity, which lacks culture and civility and which dominates the urban spaces of Alexandria, such as parks, seaside boardwalks, busy commercial districts, and low-budget coffee shops scattered throughout the city. Their body language, tendency to speak loudly and animatedly, and inclination to play-fight during friendly arguments are seen as intimidating and primitive among their male middle-class peers. These men are often referred to in a dismissive tone as *fellahin* (or *fellah* in the singular). The term is well known to those who work in the region and has a rich history with local variations in its usage. Traditionally, fellah refers to someone of rural background who works in agriculture.[6] As part of the struggle for Egyptian independence, the fellah was elevated as a nationalist symbol and a source of pride. At the same time, the rural fellah has a long history as a figure of ridicule and class-based contempt in Egypt. Among middle-class Alexandrians today, the term is commonly used derogatorily, denoting a person as uncultured, uneducated, ill-mannered, and uncivil. The term has a clear social class dimension but does not refer to a specific religious background.

According to some locals, the use of *fellahin* as a derogatory term is particularly strong in Alexandria and has grown more so in the last two decades. With time, a massive influx of rural villagers from the Delta region is thought to have resulted in overcrowding, unemployment, traffic congestion, and growing social tensions between already settled Alexandrians and the city's most recent arrivals. These tensions are partly reflected in the contemporary usage of *fellahin*.

The fellahin are generally referred to with a mixture of fear and contempt. When visiting one of the coffee shops along the boardwalk, Mohammed and Islam refer to patrons who stand out as particularly loud-voiced and aggressive as fellahin. Ahmed is a lawyer in his late twenties and belongs to the same circle of friends as Mohammed and Islam. While sitting at a coffee shop on the day before a public holiday in Egypt, Ahmed broke from his usual mild-mannered demeanor to rant about the fellahin. "They behave like animals, they have no culture, they smell terrible, and they cannot behave around women." He described how, as an Alexandrian, he faces public holidays with genuine dread. During holidays, the city is invaded by thousands of fellahin, mostly young men from the Delta and from villages around Alexandria. On such days, Ahmed leaves the city, if he can, or locks himself in his apartment. This sentiment is widely shared, especially among middle-class Alexandrians. These tensions are further heightened during the summer months, when rural visitors flock to the public beaches of Alexandria. Although the fellahin presence on public beaches is a source of widely expressed anger, ongoing privatization of beaches—making fewer beaches publicly accessible—is barely discussed.

The fellahin are not just peasants who live in rural communities outside of Alexandria. A fellah can also be a third-generation Alexandrian city dweller of rural origins who has not attained a basic level of civility and who remains deeply ignorant, uneducated, and poorly mannered, even after generations of living in the city. The term thus refers more to a set of ascribed characteristics than to a rural origin. The youths and men who dominate shared public spaces in Alexandria are widely ascribed with these characteristics. The image of the well-mannered, educated middle-class man stands in sharp contrast to the construct of the fellahin. This contrast is perhaps most evident when the topic of sexual harassment is raised.

WHAT THE MASCULINE OTHERS DO

In a 2014 interview with the author, Fadi, who teaches at a renowned private school in Alexandria, discussed sexual harassment in the city.

> Fadi: It's an epidemic! Young boys don't know how to behave around girls. They do not learn to respect women, and they terrorize girls who walk around in the city, even when they have male company. You can see it in their eyes. You can see in the way they dress, and the way they behave among each other. They have no culture! They have no civility!
>
> Bard: Do you talk to your students about these things? Do you talk to them about sexual harassment?
>
> Fadi: No. We don't have to. *Our* boys don't behave like this.[7]

Harassment is a significant problem throughout Egypt and particularly in Alexandria (*Cairo Post* 2015). While the scale of the problem might be publicly disputed, the last decade has seen greater public acknowledgment of harassment as a real and widespread problem in Egypt (Abdelmonem 2015). While condemning harassment, some young men concede that most men have engaged in it at some point, often without thinking of their actions (whether physical or verbal) as harassment. Some recently married men, who found themselves in charge of protecting their wives, described having an epiphany in which they suddenly discovered that the culture of harassment was much worse than they previously thought. Others framed this problem in a way that was both troubling and cause for cautious optimism; they confidently asserted that men of respectable backgrounds did not engage in harassment and that harassment was something primarily done by those regarded as fellahin.[8]

It is reasonable to argue that this kind of framing of harassment belittles the problem and defines it as the shameful actions of other men in a way that discourages any unpleasant introspection among middle-class men. To some extent, this view also downplays the gravity of harassment by explaining it partly as an expression of poor social skills and ignorance rather than an issue of misogyny, male entitlement, or intolerance toward women's presence in the public sphere.

At the same time, these men define sexual harassment as a type of conduct that is anathema to their own form of masculinity. By defining harassment as a type of action found among their masculine Others, these young men see such behavior not primarily as expressions of a moral deficiency but as evidence of one lacking in the social skills and qualities needed to be the right kind of man. However, this denouncement of sexual harassment is not always reflected in their own conduct. When I talked to female students at Alexandria University, they stressed that they were harassed by men from throughout Alexandria's social spectrum. Young men of more privileged backgrounds may be more discreet and subtle than their working-class counterparts, but female students emphasized that they were no less handsy and no less disrespectful in their conduct. Nonetheless, the notion among many upper-middle-class men that they themselves are above this kind of conduct partly reflects their own class-based self-conceptions and attitudes toward men of lower socioeconomic status.

Such attitudes do not emerge in a vacuum. They are passed down through families and within an educational system that instills middle-class males with a clear sense of their rightful place in society. For the most part, these young men come from families of some means, have been able to attend well-renowned private schools, obtain university degrees, and for the most part—often through family connections—landed jobs that enable them to provide for their own families. They are very aware of and preoccupied with their own position on the socioeconomic ladder. There are several layers to the Egyptian class system; however, most of these men point to the immense social gulf between those who have had access to private school education and those who have been confined to the Egyptian public school system as the main overarching social divide. At the same time, they tend to describe the system itself as a brutal but seminatural order, where they find themselves at the level where they belong mainly due to their own skills, character, and social virtues. When describing men of lower socioeconomic status, they do so with reference to ascribed social and moral qualities, or a lack thereof—as in their descriptions of the fellahin. As such, their own class identification becomes a near all-encompassing identity that further serves to legitimize a social order marked by stark social and economic inequalities.

Fadi, the private school teacher quoted earlier, proudly described his male students as "future community and business leaders who will contribute to the Egyptian society in a positive way." He contrasts them quite sharply with the "simple, uneducated masses" that, in his view, comprise most of Egypt's population.[9]

These young men combine a strong class consciousness and an elitist attitude toward men of lower socioeconomic status, with masculine aspirations of emotional connectivity with and attentiveness toward the women in their lives. This attitude should encourage an active commitment to combat harassment against women and at the very least discourage them from personally engaging in acts of harassment. At the same time, the gap between their stated ideals and actions can also be read as part of a pattern whereby middle-class men distance themselves from a stereotyped other, further justifying the vilification of working-class men while at the same time asserting their superiority over women through their own more subtle forms of harassment.

RETHINKING MASCULINITY

These young, middle-class Alexandrian men illustrate the importance of moving beyond a focus on hegemonic masculinity when looking at masculine ideals, practices, and self-perceptions. Christensen and Jensen (2014) stress the importance of an intersectional approach that considers race, class, and other criteria of demarcation to explore how men identify themselves and are perceived by others. In an Egyptian context, social class is a vital factor in shaping masculine identities. Mohammed and Islam are both very conscious of their own socioeconomic backgrounds. They are aware of their privilege and that of their friends. They proudly ascribe a distinct set of social qualities to themselves and to other men of their own age and background. They strongly believe that men of lower socioeconomic status do not possess the same qualities but rather exhibit a set of other, widely negative traits, such as aggression, a violent disposition, poor manners, a lack of education and respect for females, and an inability to behave around women. These traits are viewed as more or less immutable among the fellahin, serving not only to justify their subjugation with lowly social status but also as motive for active efforts to minimize one's interaction with them. To a large degree, this construct of rural and working-class men reflects the scale of class-based insulation among some middle-class men and their lack of knowledge about the lives of their masculine Others.

While partly based on class-based segregation, the tensions that exist between men of different backgrounds and generations in Alexandria resemble the dynamics between male rugby players of different generations, as described by Anderson and McGuire (2010). Writing about social interactions within an all-male rugby setting in England, Anderson and McGuire (2010) describe the tensions between men of different generations. For instance, young players were dismayed by the homophobic and misogynist attitudes displayed by their older coaches. These younger players described homophobia and misogyny as defining features of a traditional, orthodox masculinity that they found outdated and off-putting (Anderson and McGuire 2010).

Here, Anderson and McGuire (2010) build on an earlier argument by Anderson (2005) that orthodox masculinity loses its hegemonic dominance in societies where homophobic sentiments are weakened, making way for the emergence of inclusive masculinities that are characterized by greater tolerance toward homosexuals, greater respect for women, and a willingness to express personal emotions. When represented with confidence and self-assertion, inclusive masculinity can coexist alongside an orthodox masculinity that remains numerically dominant, but that is no longer held in high regard. Anderson's (2005) focus on homophobia as central to orthodox masculinity might make sense in Western societies where homophobia and harsh sanctions against homosexual activities have a long history. But the notion that homosexuality is a phenomenon to be feared, condemned, and socially sanctioned does not hold a central place in all societies. As such, there is little reason to assume that socially cultivated homophobia is universally central to the formation of a masculine identity or the attainment of hegemonic masculinity. In Egyptian society, and certainly in a city like Alexandria, homosexuality is widely recognized as a phenomenon that is generally frowned on, but it is not seen as representing a significant moral danger. Most of all, young men do not experience a need to actively and explicitly distance themselves from homosexuality. For the most part, they socialize in mostly homosocial settings, often involving extensive physical contact with each other, a contact that is rarely interpreted in sexual terms. In this context, the display of homophobic attitudes is not a central mark of manhood.[10]

Nonetheless, if we follow the broader premise of Anderson's (2005) theory—that the diminishment of one set of widely shared sentiments has the ability to undermine the hegemonic hold of orthodox masculinity—it is possible that the fading of other sets of widely held sentiments (e.g., the assertion of patriarchal authority) may allow other forms of masculinity to challenge orthodox hegemony. Specifically, it is important to ask this question: If the norms regarding patriarchal authority are in flux, can nonpatriarchal or less patriarchal forms of masculinity emerge and gain equal status with an orthodox masculinity that fiercely upholds patriarchal structures? The development of a more connective masculinity among young middle-class men in Alexandria certainly points in that direction. Proponents of more traditional norms must view some of the ideals and practices pursued by these young men as a violation of patriarchy itself.

Although the inclusive masculinity described by Anderson and McGuire (2010) challenges the repressive features of an orthodox masculinity, Karla Elliott (2016, 241) discusses the potential for a further movement toward caring masculinity that "rejects relationships based on domination, and that seeks relational equality, emotional connectivity, and interdependence." Elliot's theory is based on gender and masculinity studies conducted primarily within a European and North American context.

In Egypt, the notion of a caring masculinity that involves an explicit rejection of patriarchy and any form of masculine domination is detached from reality. Patriarchy and its associated norms are deeply entrenched in Egyptian family structures, schools, religious institutions, political and economic structures, and popular culture. Young middle-class men in Egypt do not reject patriarchy. They will not question the patriarchal authority of their own fathers, nor will they relinquish their own in relation to their wives and children. However, they may seek their own ways of asserting authority while simultaneously seeking deeper emotional connections with their wives and a deeper involvement in the day-to-day care of their children. In other words, they are reworking the premises on which patriarchy can be practiced and reconciled with ideals of conjugal connectivity and involved fatherhood.

Within certain urban, middle-class milieus in cities such as Alexandria, these forms of masculinity may emerge through the gradual development of ideals and practices that elevate qualities traditionally viewed as feminine, such as the ability to connect emotionally with spouses (or prospective spouses) and a commitment to spending time with family at the expense of other social commitments. Adopting such practices in a society where traditional patriarchal ideals are still strong requires confidence and clear evidence that these practices resonate among other men and women of one's own generation. The burden of nonapproval was visible in Ibrahim's struggles with his commitment to support his wife's ambitions. If new ideals and practices are to gain ground, they must be viewed favorably in contrast to another set of ideals.

As a new form of masculinity emerges, it is defined in contrast to its polar opposite, a form of thuggish, predatory masculinity characterized by aggressive self-assertion, male entitlement, and a violent disposition. Yet middle-class

Alexandrian men's notions of working-class gender relations may in fact be based on stereotypes. More than twenty years ago, Marcia Inhorn's (1994, 1996) research with working-class Alexandrian couples offered moving accounts of the mutual love, affection, and support that held them together in their joint struggles to have children of their own. The very concept of conjugal connectivity emerged from her encounters with fellahin men and women in Alexandria, who were openly affectionate and emotionally committed to each other (Inhorn 1996).

CONCLUSION

The case of urban middle-class men in Alexandria challenges the central premise of Connell's (1987) gender hierarchy—namely, that men in hegemonic and subordinate positions practice manhood differently, even if their stereotypes of the other suggest this. In line with Anderson's (2005) theory of inclusive masculinity, these young men, in articulating their own ideals of masculinity, are moving away from more traditional norms and opposing other forms of masculinity that are considered numerically dominant but are not culturally exalted by others. It is also important to scrutinize the notion that dominant forms of masculinity reinforce patriarchy in the Egyptian setting. While this might be the case at present, the emergence of new masculine ideals among certain segments of Egyptian society suggests that such notions are changing. Even if urban middle-class men hold masculine aspirations that emphasize conjugal connectivity and greater sensitivity to the needs and concerns of the women in their lives, this does not necessarily represent a challenge to patriarchy. It may, however, pose a challenge to certain patriarchal practices, to some extent allowing men to prioritize their relationships with their wives and children over social commitments.

NOTES

1. In a separate work focusing on Coptic men, the concept of masculine Others will be explored from a different angle, focusing on how masculine self-ascription and othering can be informed by minority vulnerability and sectarian boundaries.

2. My interactions with informants took place both in Arabic and in English because some of my informants, due to private school education and international cultural exposure, had an excellent command of English. This goes for unstructured interviews as well as casual conversations. When conducting

interviews in Arabic, I would make my own notes in English (Egyptians, both researchers and others, had strongly advised against using any recording devices). At the end of the interview, I would go through my notes with the interviewee to confirm details and to clarify specific statements when needed. This way, I felt confident about my own translation, and the interviewee was left assured that his or her own words and reflections were properly presented. Among my male interlocutors in Alexandria, there was limited interaction between those of Muslim and those of Coptic background. On further inquiry, I found that many of my interlocutors had few, if any, personal acquaintances belonging to the other group. As such, I found myself splitting my time between milieus of Muslim and Coptic men who were of similar socioeconomic stature and who sometimes frequented the same public spaces without interacting with each other.

3. This was a common coping strategy among family men who were unhappily married, with men simply staying at work or out with friends and spending as little time as possible at home.

4. The school is an all-boys school. However, it organizes social events and cultural activities in cooperation with an associated girls' school, affording male and female students opportunities for supervised interaction.

5. This was a social asset highlighted by young men who had attended other church-associated but non-Catholic schools as well.

6. Historically, *fellahin* refers to people of modest rural backgrounds from all over Egypt. These days in Alexandria, people of rural origins from Upper Egypt are more commonly referred to as *saidis* (and only derided as fellahin when exhibiting exceptionally poor manners).

7. Interview with Fadi, teacher at a well-renowned private school in Alexandria, November 3, 2014.

8. This attitude was widely shared by Alexandrian Copts as well. Middle-class Coptic men in Alexandria stressed that sexual harassment was committed primarily by the fellahin, who in their accounts were primarily Muslims. While adding a sectarian dimension to their self-presentation, these Coptic men highlighted the same masculine ideals as their Muslim middle-class peers and defined themselves in opposition to the same construct of a masculine Other, represented by the fellahin.

9. Interview with Fadi, teacher at a well-renowned private school in Alexandria, November 3, 2014.

10. The term *khawal*, as in *ya khawal*, is sometimes used as a lighthearted insult. Khawal can mean gay man, sissy, girly man, and many other things depending on the context. Originally from the late eighteenth century, the term referred to men who dressed as women and who performed as belly dancers at public gatherings.

BIBLIOGRAPHY

Abdelmonem, Angie. 2015. "Reconceptualizing Sexual Harassment in Egypt: A Longitudinal Assessment of El-Taharrush El-Ginsy in Arabic Online Forums and Anti-Sexual Harassment Activism." *Kohl: A Journal for Body and Gender Research* 1, no. 1: 23–41.

Anderson, Eric. 2005. "Orthodox and Inclusive Masculinity: Competing Masculinities among Heterosexual Men in a Feminized Terrain." *Sociological Perspectives* 48, no. 3: 337–355.

Anderson, Eric, and Rhidian McGuire. 2010. "Inclusive Masculinity Theory and the Gendered Politics of Men's Rugby." *Journal of Gender Studies* 19, no. 3: 249–261.

Cairo Post. 2015. "Alexandria Saw Highest Sexual Harassment Rate in a Year: Survey." June 14. https://web.archive.org/web/20160704001954/http:// thecairopost.youm7.com/news/155344/inside_egypt/alexandria-saw -highest-sexual-harassment-rate-in-a-year-survey.

Christensen, Ann-Dorte, and Sune Qvotrup Jensen. 2014. "Combining Hegemonic Masculinity and Intersectionality." *NORMA* 9, no. 1: 60–75.

Connell, Raewyn. W. 1987. *Gender and Power: Society, the Person and Sexual Politics.* Cambridge: Polity.

———. 1995. *Masculinities.* Berkeley: University of California Press.

———. 2000. *The Men and the Boys.* London: Blackwell.

Connell, Raewyn. W., and J. W. Messerschmidt. 2005. "Hegemonic Masculinity— Rethinking the Concept." *Gender and Society* 19, no. 6: 829–859.

Elliott, Karla. 2016. "Caring Masculinities: Theorizing an Emerging Concept." *Men and Masculinities* 19, no. 3: 240–259.

Ghannam, Farha. 2013. *Live and Die Like a Man: Gender Dynamics in Urban Egypt.* Stanford, CA: Stanford University Press.

Inhorn, Marcia C. 1994. *Quest for Conception: Gender, Infertility, and Egyptian Medical Traditions.* Philadelphia: University of Pennsylvania Press.

———. 1996. *Infertility and Patriarchy: The Cultural Politics of Gender and Family Life in Egypt.* Philadelphia: University of Pennsylvania Press.

———. 2012. *The New Arab Man: Emergent Masculinities, Technologies, and Islam in the Middle East.* Princeton, NJ: Princeton University Press.

Joseph, Suad. 1993. "Connectivity and Patriarchy among Urban Working-Class Arab Families in Lebanon." *Ethos* 21, no. 4: 452–484.

Kreil, Aymon. 2016. "Territories of Desire: A Geography of Competing Intimacies in Cairo." *Journal of Middle East Women's Studies* 12, no. 2: 166–180.

MacDonald, Cheryl A. 2014. "Masculinity and Sport Revisited: A Review of Literature on Hegemonic Masculinity and Men's Ice Hockey in Canada." *Canadian Graduate Journal of Sociology and Criminology* 3, no. 1: 95.

Naguib, Nefissa. 2015. *Nurturing Masculinities: Men, Food, and Family in Contemporary Egypt.* Austin: University of Texas Press.

Schielke, Joska Samuli. 2009. "Ambivalent Commitments: Troubles of Morality, Religiosity and Aspiration among Young Egyptians." *Journal of Religion in Africa* 39, no. 2: 158–185.

———. 2015. *Egypt in the Future Tense: Hope, Frustration, and Ambivalence before and after 2011.* Bloomington: Indiana University Press.

Thompson, Eric C., Pattana Kitiarsa, and Suriya Smutkupt. 2016. "From Sex Tourist to Son-in-Law: Emergent Masculinities and Transient Subjectivities of Farang Men in Thailand." *Current Anthropology* 57, no. 1: 53–71.

Williams, Raymond. 1977. *Marxism and Literature.* Oxford: Oxford University Press.

BÅRD HELGE KÅRTVEIT is Senior Researcher at NORCE Research in Oslo, Norway. He is author of *Dilemmas of Attachment: Identity and Belonging among Palestinian Christians.*

TWO

AL-USTURA (THE LEGEND)—FOLK HERO OR THUG?

Class and Contested Masculinity in Egypt

JAMIE FURNISS

INTRODUCTION

During the month of Ramadan in Egypt, a number of television series play after iftar nightly for a total of thirty episodes. One of these in 2016 was called *Al-Ustura*, or *The Legend*. In the first several episodes, viewers are introduced to two brothers, Nasser and Rifaʻi, who live in the metalworkers neighborhood of Sebtiyya, a working-class area duly depicted as filled with street cafés, men with moustaches and galabiyas (loose-fitting male garments, often considered traditional), tuk-tuks, and other stylized markers of class and locale. Nasser, the clean-shaven younger brother, is an earnest young law student who graduates at the top of his class and therefore seeks what is, in the great Nasserian tradition of the civil service, the most prestigious position for law graduates: that of public prosecutor in the general attorney's office. After brilliantly passing an oral examination, he reaches the final stage, an investigation of professionalism that considers one's suitability on the basis of reputation and possible criminal records of one's relatives. Since the 1970s, this investigation has been a feature of these appointments in Egypt. Because the rules consider evidence pertaining to relatives up to the fourth degree (an exceedingly wide swath of people), this criterion is often considered to provide the pretext through which non-insiders are removed from the recruitment process. Nasser is informed that despite his outstanding academic results, he is not suited to the profession because his brother is a petty criminal.

After having been professionally spurned, Nasser suffers further rejection from his law school girlfriend. As the daughter of a former minister, she is from an upper-class background. When he comes to her house to propose marriage, the father refuses to give his blessing, explaining, "Nasser, my son, don't be up-set with me for the words I am about to say to you. You have nothing, no work, or apartment, and even if you had an apartment and work, I believe that they would not fit Tamara." The mother goes on to tell him that "our two families don't fit together *khallis*. *Pardon* [said in French], I don't mean it, but your family are very simple people, very common [*sha'abi*] people. . . . And we, my love, are, as you can see . . . [gesturing to the lavish setting of their home]." A sign of her sophistication, she drops some French; for example: "*Pardon*, but *jamais* there could be a common language between us at all."

This process by which Nasser is professionally and personally locked into a class identity from which education fails to liberate him precipitates a shift in his persona. This shift is marked by physical transformations: he adopts his distinctive look (a shaved head and very short, vaguely Islamic beard) and begins smoking (initially cigarettes and then increasingly cigars). After his elder brother is killed as a result of neighborhood rivalries in the metalworking business, he takes over the family workshop, transforming it into a full-blown weapons factory. He becomes incredibly rich, filling a vault with pallets of crisp US$100 bills. Although drawn into higher stakes and more complex rivalries on the national level, with great courage, cleverness, and aplomb, Nasser continually betters his rivals. A major subplot involves making the law school girlfriend who spurned him his third wife (by this point, he has already married Shahd, a wholesome neighborhood girl, as well as his brother's widow). After having rejected him when he was an outstanding student with no money, Tamara's family embrace him sycophanti-cally now that he is rich, avoiding questions about the source of his wealth.

The series ends with a confrontation between Nasser and his principal rival, Badr, over the course of which Nasser kills all Badr's men through a clever ruse. But Badr uses his mobile phone to order the execution of Nasser's mother and female relatives by men he has posted outside their home. Nasser shoots Badr dead. He would now be free to consolidate his domination of the business free of rivals, but after having caused the death of his mother, he is overcome with grief and remorse. In the last two minutes of the last episode of the series, text is shown on the screen explaining that Nasser turned himself in to the police. The final scene is of a hooded prisoner's head being slipped through a noose. This brief attempt to include a final "crime doesn't pay" moral was shot in extremis after ac-cusations had already surfaced that the show promoted violence and what is often referred to in Egypt as *baltaga*—a social category this chapter explores in-depth.

Inspired by two methodological premises, the goal of this chapter is to use the debate around *Al-Ustura* to examine how differing categories and subjec-tivities of masculinity and class are produced and contested. The first of these premises is that the way people interpret and engage with mass media depends on their cultural, social, and historical circumstances, which anthropology can contribute to unpacking through the study of "reception" (see, e.g., Abu-Lughod 1997). The second is that narrative depictions of "tough guy" figures such as the Syro-Lebanese *qabaday* (Gilsenan 1996; Joubin 2013, 2016), the Egyptian *futuwwa* (Armbrust 2000, 2002; Jacob 2007, 2011), and the main character of *Al-Ustura*—and in particular their construal in either positive or negative terms—are sites for the study of differing, often contested interpretations of masculinity (cf. Ghoussoub and Sinclair-Webb 2000 for some outstanding early examples of this approach).

This chapter argues that the varying degrees of approval, identification, and condemnation generated by the show bring to light differing ideas about society and male conduct that reflect different class positions. The show was wildly popular with a low-class, young, male demographic, but other groups criticized it for promoting violence and lawlessness. This sharp divide in the show's reception reveals some of the terms in which working-class men are stigmatized and othered in Cairo, particularly through their construal as violent, as well as how the nature of violence and the problem it poses are understood from different perspectives.

The chapter begins by giving a sense of the show's popularity, describing the *Usturamania* that swept over Egypt in the summer of 2016, and in particular by trying to provide a thumbnail sociology of the young men with whom the show was so popular. It then presents the contrasting reception the show received with more middle-class demographics through an overview of its condemnation in media outlets, as well as on the part of individual viewers. Because the emic category of *baltaga* was central to this condemnation, it then discusses this notion, drawing on extensive literature around the term to argue that it is best understood here as being enrolled in a process of class-based subject formation. Finally, the chapter explores the reactions of fans to the accusation that the show was violent, showing how they sought to redefine violence away from autonomous, individual recourse to force and toward structural forms of injustice and exclusion. My interlocutors did so principally through reference to plot elements that reflected actual events in recent Egyptian history and their own experiences of bureaucracy and the state.

MY FIELDWORK AND MY INTERLOCUTORS

The fieldwork on which the chapter is based and my awareness of *Al-Ustura* was thrown up from the folds of a separate, ongoing piece of research on Cairo's waste economy. Since 2007, by now for a total of approximately twenty-four months, I have been conducting fieldwork in neighborhoods where hereditary waste collectors and recyclers live, with special emphasis on Manshiet Nasser; I also lived in Ezbet Al-Nakhl for five months in 2009. Around 2013, I began spending time in Ezbet Abu-Hashish, where many of the city's itinerant scrap collectors live. This neighborhood is just north of Ghamra Bridge, next to the train tracks that run north from Ramsis Station. In the month of Ramadan 2016, in the context of a longer period of about six months of fieldwork that began in March, I divided my time between Manshiet Nasser and Ezbet Abu Hashish, often spending time with friends in the evenings after they finished work. I spent many evenings with Ibrahim (Manshiet Nasser) and Hassan (Ezbet Abu Hashish), who are both between the ages of thirty and thirty-five and of low social class by almost any measure. Like many young men in those neighborhoods, they were huge fans of Al-Ustura, and we often watched and discussed the show together. These conversations occurred in Egyptian Arabic, the language of the series, which I was constrained to watch without subtitles. I learned my Arabic mostly in the crucible of a diglossic fieldwork setting, where speech and literacy sometimes seem like two different languages, so writing has never been my forte. Although in the past Ibrahim has asked me to correct his SMS messages in Arabic before sending them, this is less a reflection on my literary prowess in Arabic than on his limited access to formal education. For this project, I worked alongside a paid bilingual assistant to ensure accurate translations of texts.

Ibrahim is soft-spoken and wary. An elementary school dropout, he later received some basic education through a nongovernmental organization devoted to projects for youth in the Zabbaleen neighborhood, which is how we met. His only daughter was born with a heart defect and spent a lengthy period of time in neonatal intensive care; his only brother, with whom he was on very bad terms and never reconciled before his death, was killed by sniper fire in a protest on the edge of their neighborhood. He has worked odd jobs, including carpentry and sorting waste plastic for resale. In recent years, he has struggled to subsist as the owner-operator of a government-subsidized bakery; he was fined a substantial amount for allegedly defrauding the subsidy system, and the bakery was closed for several years until he could negotiate a repayment schedule that allowed him to reopen with money lent or gifted by friends, of which I was one.

Hassan is married with four children and works independently as an itinerant scrap buyer, making daily rounds through the city on a motorized tricycle. We met when I sold him some scrap metal from an apartment in Abdeen. At that time, his wife lived in Fayoum with their children, and he worked shifts (ten or fifteen days in Cairo, followed by a few days back in the village), renting a padlocked room in a shared flat occupied by young male scrap buyers like him. He is full of swashbuckling stories about more or less believable exploits such as defending himself in street fights, getting back his mobile phone when it was stolen, enforcing payment from reluctant debtors, or engaging in close brushes with police in his twenties. He considers himself extremely lucky not to have ended up in jail during the years before his wife moved to Cairo.

Hassan and many of his buddies have clear notions of what it takes and what it means to be a man. For example, in addition to the usual religious expressions, they decorate their vehicles with rhyming phrases like *Al-rugula mish b-il-suhula* (Manliness doesn't come easy) or *'isht 'asfur, dabahuni, 'isht asad, ihtaramuni* (Live like a bird, you'll be slaughtered; live like a lion, you'll be respected). The latter phrase was superimposed on pictures of the star of *The Legend*, Mohammed Ramadan, in another series in which he previously acted. Another example of this explicit deployment of the semantic field of masculinity is in the memes they share on Facebook or over WhatsApp. One common meme features the phrase "The Republic of Ezbet Abu Hashish, Where Men are Made" (*masna' al-rigala*; this expression is also used to refer to the military). A number of these memes feature photographs of the actor Mohammed Ramadan and bear slogans like "I never felt sorry for anybody, because nobody ever felt sorry for me," "You're a good man and a role model of manliness," and "No doubt about it, you're a friend who can be counted on," often in phrases that rhyme in Arabic.

USTURAMANIA

In their respective neighborhoods, Ibrahim and Hassan were typical of their gender and age group in their liking of *Al-Ustura*. Many young men in Manshiet Nasser and Ezbet Abu Hashish followed the series closely, describing it as *gamda*, meaning "hardcore or intense," and the main character as *fazi'*, which means "abominable, hideous, and terrible," but also "prodigious, tremendous, and terrific," according to *Hinds and Badawy's Dictionary of Egyptian Arabic*.

Indications of the show's popularity beyond my direct fieldwork experience were numerous. The main actors graced the covers of *People*-like magazines at almost every newsstand, and for much of the summer, four- or five-story-high images of Mohammed Ramadan, advertising his play *Ahlan Ramadan*, were put up in several places around the city. *Satellite Magazine* ranked it the most popular *musalsal* (series) of the year according to social media surveys, and to give just one example of this, selfies of people imitating the main character's distinctive hair and beard style began to trend on social media, aggregated with hashtags. In Hurriya Bar in Bab Al-Luq on the night of July 8, I bumped into

Figure 2.1: Café in Manshiet Nasser while *Al-Ustura*
was on, Ramadan 2016. © Jamie Furniss

a Sudanese friend of a friend with an *Ustura*-style beard. We got on the band-
wagon and asked whether we could take his picture. He joked that since he had
gotten the haircut earlier that day, everyone wanted his picture; he had already
had five similar requests. I was eager to ask him about this copycatting, but his
answer did not provide the illumination I hoped for: "I told the barber I wasn't
sure what I wanted, and he said, 'I know just the thing for you!'"

Other ephemera and cultural practices such as *Ustura* T-shirts also prolifer-
ated. Judging by photos on Facebook, these appeared to be more common in
Upper Egypt than Cairo, but I was able to find them being sold on sidewalks
downtown and eventually bought one through a wanted ad on Facebook, which
received several responses. Wearing it produced a variety of reactions, ranging
from surprise and approval from guards at the American University's Falaki
Street site, who thought it was so funny that they called their manager so he
could have a laugh with them at the spectacle of a foreigner who was a fan of the
show, to disapproval from a female check-in agent at Etihad Airlines and questions from her male colleague about whether I was "really" Canadian. On both

Figure 2.2: *Al-Ustura* T-shirts for sale from a sidewalk
vendor in downtown Cairo. © Jamie Furniss

of those occasions, I also showed a photo of myself with Mohammed Ramadan
taken backstage at his play *Ahlan Ramadan*. The airline check-in agents reacted
in disbelief and vague disgust that a foreigner could appreciate Mohammed
Ramadan's "artistic" production. But with the security guards, the photo re-
doubled their wisecracks and got me high fives (a common masculine exchange
in Egypt) all around. A research assistant reckoned the photo was "worth more
than all the research permits we could ever get!" He advised that if ever we were
in a pinch, showing it would be sure to get a laugh and ease tensions or create
goodwill.

   In Manshiet Nasser and Ezbet Abu Hashish, *Al-Ustura* played on the screens
of every café, with the only exception being some channel flipping during the
advertisements to check the score of the soccer game. One night while I was
watching the musalsal with Hassan, a client came in asking to watch the game.

Figure 2.3: Café in Ezbet Abu Hashish
while *Al-Ustura* was playing. © Jamie Furniss

People stared at him as if to say, "Who is this guy? Why is he so completely out of it?" He beat a hasty retreat.

"Could he find another café to watch it in?" I asked.

"Nah. He's going to go home. All the cafés here play the musalsal," as Hassan referred to it. "During the time of the musalsal, the cafés are all full. At Lamuna [another café we sometimes went to], you couldn't even find a seat right now," he added. However, as soon as *Al-Ustura* was over, the place completely emptied out as the next show, *Al-kif* (about hashish), came on. Hassan did not comment much on the musalsal while we were watching it, except for some occasional exclamations. For example, when Nasser goes into his vault to get some US dollars, Hassan's face glowed with an almost embarrassed smile, and he turned to me and said, "*Dolarat, ya Jamie. Dolarat!*"

DISAPPROVAL OF THE MUSALSAL

Given the show's popularity with young, lower-class men and their identification with its main character, we might expect Mohammed Ramadan to be heralded as a working-class hero. In fact, as I began discussing the show more

Figure 2.4: Five minutes later in the café,
when *Al-kif* came on. © Jamie Furniss

widely, reading about it in the press, listening to archived talk-show interviews
and debates online, and so forth, I discovered that the series and Mohammed
Ramadan produced as much anxiety and aversion as they did excitement and
identification. This section explores those who condemned the series and their
reasons for doing so. In fact, for many upper-class Egyptians, the show's protagonist was a *baltagi* (thug) rather than a *batal sha'abi* (folk hero).

In an article about precisely this issue of how to categorize Mohammed Ramadan, in the weekly magazine *Rūz Al-Yūssif*, a film critic described the "folk hero"
as follows: "The folk hero [batal sha'abi] or the one with movie-like courage [*shagi'*
al-sima] is a title bestowed by the audience upon only the stars who . . . really connect with viewers, especially when it concerns the people's problems, burdens,
and causes, which are the factors through which an actor could gain the seal of
approval and trust as a folk hero. Achieving the title of 'folk hero,' whom the *tirsu*
[cheap seats] audience refer to as the shagi' al-sima, is not easy, but requires [that
the actor] become near to the hearts of those he represents" (Abd Al-Hādī 2016).[1]

However, after envisaging a lineage of folk heroes running through Farid
Shawqy, Al-Za'im ("the leader," referring to Adel Imam), Ahmed Al-Saqqa,

and culminating in Mohammed Ramadan, the author concludes that with the latter, "the scales got out of balance" in the continuum between *gad'anet aw-lad al-balad* (approximate translation: "the chivalry of real men") and baltaga. Although some viewers identify with Mohammed Ramadan the way they did with these other actors, Ramadan "imprinted on the minds of the audience that a folk hero is a baltagi and not a respectable defender of the unjustly treated . . . [and that] society has become a jungle where a person gets his rights using his own arms [*yakhud haquh bi-dira'uh*] in the absence of the rule of law" (Abd Al-Hādī 2016). Thus, he argues that Mohammed Ramadan has "become an example for our youth to follow," contributing to the present state of society, which is "an ethical mess that endangers the institution of values, principles, good examples, and morals." After acknowledging that widespread corruption, the systematic violation of rights, and the condescension of the rich might also have something to do with it, the author returns to his main point, which is to blame the actor for spreading baltaga: "A folk hero or shagi' al-sima is not muscular, or someone whose heart is filled with violence, evil, and vengeance. He must be a healthy example of an *ibn al-balad* [authentic, lower-class but positively connoted figure], who defends right and does right to those who are unjustly treated if it is within his ability" (Abd Al-Hādī 2016).

A good illustration of the accusation that the show had become "an example for youth to follow" that encouraged them to "take their 'right' using their own arms" comes from an episode in which the main character, Nasser, takes revenge on a mobile phone repairman, Morsi, who posted scantily clad pictures of Nasser's wife online after finding them on her phone during a repair. Nasser storms into the shop, smashes it, beats up Morsi, and then drags him out onto the street, where he dresses him in the very same nightgown his wife was photographed in. The whole scene takes place under the neighbors' watchful eyes, and he invites them to photograph the humiliation, shouting that photos of a woman in a nightgown are normal and will soon be forgotten, "but when a *man* wears a nightgown in this neighborhood, not even the dogs will ever forget it!"

Al-Ahram's youth newsfeed (the age-specific targeting is significant) carried a story shortly after this episode entitled "The Harvest of Al-Ustura," in a "you reap what you sow" sense (Zikri 2016). It described a copycat incident that occurred in Fayoum. After a woman requested a divorce from her husband, he posted nude photos of her publicly on Facebook. Her male relatives retaliated by dressing him in a nightgown and parading him through the streets of the village while people made videos, later posted to YouTube.

Although the link between the two seemed to be, at best, of a post hoc ergo propter hoc kind, Mohammed Ramadan and the show were blamed for having "caused" the man's treatment. This and other alleged copycat events were repeatedly raised in my conversations with people who condemned the show. They also arose in the media, including in interviews with Mohammed Ramadan himself:

> Presenter: What about the idea that a violent scene in *Al-Ustura* was reenacted in reality, in which the hero makes someone wear a woman's nightgown?
>
> Mohammed Ramadan: The same thing was also depicted in the film *Harami al-'Abit* which was five years ago. Khaled Salih, they made him wear a dress in the street.
>
> Presenter: But this time it really happened, in Fayoum.
>
> Mohammed Ramadan: How is that my fault [*zambi eh?*]. Ask the guy who did it before me. It's none of my business. And Khaled Salih took the idea from reality; he definitely read it in a newspaper or something.

The controversial and very mediatized personality Murtada Mansour, a soccer club owner with no special authority on this question but a reputation for weighing in on just about any controversy in the country, gave a press interview in which he called on Egyptian president Abdel Fattah el-Sisi to clean the country of "the dirtiness of Mohammed Ramadan, the baltaga of Mohammed Ramadan." "Don't be afraid," he wailed, addressing himself directly to the president. "Clean! Clean! Disinfect the televisions, the movies, Facebook. Disinfect! . . . So that our country can once again be that of God's good people!" (Author's fieldwork notes, June 2016, Cairo).

I got a taste of these views on a more personal level from some friends who often hung out at a café just south of the French Archaeological Research Institute and Cultural Centre in Munira, where *Al-Ustura* was not played. These two men, in their midtwenties, are fluent English speakers. The first is a dentist whose family is from Heliopolis; the second, who trained as a pharmacist but now works for a foreign development agency on a gender-related project, is originally from Shubra. The neighborhoods, each with its own long history and significance in Egyptian social imaginaries, do not have identical sociological makeups or reputations, but these young men shared well-established middle-class positions in society that correspond more or less to what one would expect, given where they are from.[2]

Although the place where their friends hang out almost nightly is a street café and therefore not the kind of Starbucks knockoff preferred by the city's most elite youth today (De Koning 2009), it nevertheless cultivates a style and clientele that is educated, professional, and cosmopolitan. In the image of Shubra as a neighborhood, the café is sha'abi enough to be "authentic" but still respectable. The clientele remains predominantly young and male but is mixed-gender with a following of foreigners. One way of describing it sociologically would be through its very elaborate *sheesha* tobacco flavorings, such as "chewing gum and watermelon," which appeal to a more cosmopolitan crowd. In contrast, in Upper Egyptian and low-class parts of Manshiet Nasser, harsh, unflavored *qas*, is the only type of sheesha available. Here, flavored tobacco, let alone something as precious as "chewing gum and watermelon," is considered totally effete and could never be consumed publicly by a man (women, for their part, do not go to cafés in such areas).

Unlike those in Ibrahim and Hassan's neighborhoods, this café chose to play the Euro Cup instead of *Al-Ustura*. What a café played at 10:00 p.m. during the month of Ramadan 2016, I would realize, was a kind of litmus test of whom it catered to and what image it wanted to project. In a recorded conversation, I asked the owner—a man who sought to cultivate a habitus of modernist piety and seemed to apply an Islamic version of the Protestant ethic to the operation of his café—about this choice:

> Owner: For us, soccer is more important than the television series. We
> have a proportion of young people who like to watch soccer. We support
> England, Spain, Egypt. That's the first point. Second, as I see it, acting, it
> involves nudity [he could not mean this literally] and traditional behaviors
> [*taqalid*] that I don't want to promote to young people. The level here
> is a bit more upper-class [*raqi*]. Those other places you're referring to
> [where the series is played] are *baladi* [popular or traditional, with mixed
> connotations of authenticity and low-classness], but here is raqi. We are
> among the most upper-class of the baladi cafés. We're a street café, but
> at the same time our clients are from the French Institute, the College of
> Pharmacy. Here, we have a very high proportion of doctors.
>
> Author: Some people claim that *Al-Ustura*—perhaps *musalsalat* in general,
> but *Al-Ustura* in particular—encourage negative behaviors among youth.
>
> Owner: I'll tell you. The "Legend" is a guy named Mohammed Ramadan.
> He's the hero of the series. He is—I'm sorry to put it this way—sha'abi
> [popular, with a negative, low-class connotation here]. Mohammed
> Ramadan bet on the sha'abi style. A long time ago, in the days of my
> grandfather, we had Abdel Halim Hafez. That was a time of art, of decent
> and ethical acting [*al-tamsil al-adabi w-al-ikhlaqi*]. Farid Shawqi was an
> example of gallantry and gentlemanliness. *Al-Ustura*, the young people
> love him in that role. They imitate him. The Egyptian people, they imitate
> that actor. He plays with a metal stick? Now all the young people want
> to do the same. He gets a shave? They want the same one. Our youth
> are governed by traditions and customs. They imitate him, but without

understanding. That kind of acting gives a lesson in lifestyle, in material things, in killing.... That's why I always drink from Europe here. You feel that at this café, there is a "clean" level [*mustawa nadif*]. Everyone is from the French Institute, all the people are French. The youth here, thanks to God, that is the type of place we have created for them. *Mashallah*, the people here are doctors. A "clean" social level [mustawa nadif].

In the course of making conversation with the dentist and the pharmacist-cum-gender development worker, I commented on *Al-Ustura*'s popularity. Neither was very impressed by Mohammed Ramadan. Picking up on the same line of thought as the owner, they mocked the way young people from sha'abi neighborhoods imitated and idealized the actor. One example they gave was of how when one of his films had come out a few years earlier with a scene showing him petting a lion, it apparently inspired young men to sneak into the Giza Zoo and take their picture next to a live lion to share on social media. "[Mohammed Ramadan] used to be a really good actor, like six years ago," Ashraf was willing to say. "But once he started working with Sibki [a famous producer in Egypt, with a reputation for making low-quality but high-earning films and contributing to the commercialization and debasement of cinema], he became shit." At this time, my interest in Mohammed Ramadan was still in its infancy, and I tentatively said I might have seen one of his movies on Air Egypt on my flight into the country. They asked me to describe it, so I talked about how there were lots of shirt-off street fight scenes and a scene where he dances with a snake around his neck and fires off improvised baladi guns. "Definitely a Mohammed Ramadan film," Ashraf interrupted. "He always plays a fucking baltagi, man."

WHO IS THE BALTAGI?

The idiom of baltaga, an emic category describing certain male figures and forms of conduct, was particularly central to the way the series was condemned. Understanding the term and its use in this particular context is key to analyzing the debate over *Al-Ustura*. It provides a basis for refining our understanding of how the term is used in active processes of subject formation of both others and the self. This section explores the term's meanings, which have been the subject of extensive literature in Egypt. On its face, the term largely articulates a condemnation of violent masculine behavior, but in this context, it is principally a class-inflected moral idiom that stigmatizes through the ascription of "violentness" to certain classes of people.

What defines the baltagi—generally translated to English as "thug"—in relation to the more positively connoted *futuwwa* (often translated as "tough guy," with a Robin Hood–esque implication of honor) has been a longstanding topic of interest for sociologists, political scientists, anthropologists, historians, and literary theorists working on Egypt (El-Messiri 1977; Ghannam 2013; Haeni 2005; Hafez 2010; Ismail 2000; Jacob 2007, 2011). The baltagi has also seen renewed interest since 2011, particularly due to the term's extension to paid political mercenaries during the revolution and its rhetorical deployment to discredit certain categories of political actors (Amar 2011; Ghannam 2012; Lachenal 2011, 2014; Rommel 2016). The baltagi is a socially stigmatized male figure, and one of his salient features is his use of violence. Many of his identifying characteristics, such as visible scars (especially on the face) or carrying of weapons, are signifiers of this underlying feature. However, his stigmatization is not a blanket condemnation of male violence because there are other categories for violent males (e.g., futuwwa and qabaday) that are sometimes socially acceptable and even heroic. Thus, different perspectives interpret masculine violence differently. For example, Michael Gilsenan (1996, 201) notes how a famous qabaday's "acts of extraordinary violence," which represented the "essence of the man of honor" and embodied a "cultural paradigm" in the mountains of northern Lebanon, were "inherently parodic" to intellectuals in Beirut. What in one context was "the most striking of the many [performances] that I witnessed of the *murajul* [manliness] expected of men claiming power in 'traditional' terms, encapsulat[ing] a whole universe of male violence and hierarchy," was a grotesquely melodramatic or simply comedic stereotype of the "mustachioed wild men of the mountains and the embodiment of primitive backwardness" in another.

It is important to note that there are some arguments this chapter does not attempt to make. While acknowledging how different positionalities generate different perspectives on masculinity in general and the connection between violence and being or becoming a man in particular is essential, scholars must avoid the trap of naturalizing a socially positioned, emic discourse—which itself requires interrogation—in a way that reifies certain groups as "violent classes" (e.g., men from north Lebanon, al-Zawiya al-Hamra, Upper Egypt, or *Al-Ustura* fans), and violence as an integral part of their masculinities (rural, traditional, sha'abi, i.e., popular or working class). Because it is so difficult to detach oneself from the taboo on individual recourse to physical force—and perhaps with good reason—"violence retains its capacity to unsettle and disturb" (Spencer 2010, 707). In the end, this kind of relativism comes across as unsatisfying, despite the various avenues of apologetics that anthropology might suggest in response: they are somewhat violent, but not as much as it seems; they are violent, but understood in context, this violence is permissible or serves a function in their social structure; anti-violence is ethnocentric. Considering the way the debate over *Al-Ustura* took the shape of a class struggle (albeit in a more Bourdieusian than Marxian sense), it might be tempting to consider that the main character's violence appeals to a subaltern demographic because it "emboldens them, and restores their self-confidence," or serves to cleanse them of their "inferiority complex, of their passive and despairing attitude" (Fanon [1961] 2004, 51). Even critics of that view, who eschew the idea that one way for the wretched of the earth to "become men" is through mad rage, nevertheless appear to acknowledge a link between violence and powerlessness, affirming that it is psychologically "quite true" that impotence breeds violence (Arendt 1969, 54), and "every decrease in power is an open invitation to violence" (87). While purporting to address the attitudes and behaviors of the powerless, these theories instead help explain the unease with the show on the part of what could be called the Egyptian bourgeoisie. If you are a person who supposes that something along the lines of Arendt's or Fanon's claims holds true for the psychology and behavior of youth from the *'ashwa'iyat* (Egypt's *banlieues* or "inner city," so to speak), and *The Legend* starts sounding to you like Aimé Césaire's *Rebel* (quoted in Fanon), then it is time to panic. As to their "first order" validity, there are various political and moral reasons for caution, but this chapter avoids correlating violence and class (whether in an apologetic or celebratory mode) primarily because it is difficult to defend ethnographically.

By drawing on portions of the extant literature on the baltagi, this chapter moves in a different direction, reframing the discourse condemning *Al-Ustura* from one of objectively differing thresholds for the tolerance or practice of violence to an active, class-derived process of stigmatizing male behavior in a moral register (Lachenal 2011). In this view, it is a term that, through differing judgments with respect to masculinity and violence, makes visible how lines are drawn to "separate Cairene elites from the rest of Egyptian society" (Lachenal 2014, 60) and how, by designating an Other, those who deploy the term simultaneously and dialectically carve out a set of ideals that connote "respectability" and "middle-class normality" (Rommel 2016, 37). This is a process through which people actively seek to draw lines, project particular identities, or position themselves as subjects and bestow status on that position. A focus on violence as a way of moralizing other differences offers a different way of thinking about the baltagi. Ghannam (2013, 74), for example, claims that "when to use or avoid violence, the right context for its use or avoidance, and amount of violence to use" are "what differentiate the positive concept *gada'*, the decent man, from the negative concept baltagi, the thug," and measuring violence is an "important skill that is not mastered by all men." However, baltaga can also be considered men who are always already condemned, irrespective of when, how, or how much violence they use—if any.

CHANGING THE SUBJECT

The series *Al-Ustura* is not a documentary, and whatever association it promotes between fighting, killing, extrajudicial revenge, misogyny, and lower-class men is foremost an act of imagination on the part of the scriptwriter rather than an accurate reflection of daily realities. However, ascriptions and interpretations of violence have important class-forming and class-inflected properties that function despite and precisely through their irreality. They shape and are shaped by the very social realities they misdescribe. This section now turns to the question of how fans of the show interpreted such scenes and the relationships they saw between on-screen events and their own lived realities.

When confronted with incidents like the nightgown revenge, fans of the show sought to "change the subject" from what Žižek (2008, 1) calls "subjective violence"—"violence performed by a clearly identifiable agent"—toward the "contours of the background that generate such outbursts." By pointing to the structural factors that made the main character, they both introduced a causal exculpatory narrative and a differing notion of violence. This draws attention to how from their perspective, that is, from below, the problem of violence in Egypt is less one of physical outbursts (naked, individual acts of smashing property, beating people, and so forth) than of the forms of social or objective violence that are inherent to their reality. For them, the stigmatization of violent individual subjects merely papers over this fact.[3] In a sense, it redefines what violence actually is, where it occurs, who perpetrates it, and who suffers from it.

Hassan is from Fayoum. When I showed him the *Al-Ahram Shabab* article, he noted that it occurred about forty kilometers from his home village but had no comment or judgment to pass on the event. Surprised, I prompted him, saying that there was a controversy over *Al-Ustura* and that some people felt it was "founding a school for *baltagiya* in Egypt," as my middle-class Arabic teacher had put it, discussing the series in a class. Hassan acknowledged but dismissed this controversy, defending the musalsal as good (*kwayyis*) because Nasser had never caused injustice to anyone (*ma-zulm-sh hadd*) and because he wanted only to right the wrongs of his dead brother and "take his right," a form of expression that is common in his speech and storytelling. Hassan mentioned, in addition to the dead brother, the issue of wanting to win back a girl who refused to marry him when he was poor and passed him up for a man with money. He therefore interpreted the series in terms of justice and injustice, and he saw Nasser as a righter of wrongs, as someone innocent who had never wronged anyone undeserving.

After the series ended, I met with Ibrahim one evening at his house, and we talked about the show. I asked him whether he thought Nasser was a bad character and a poor influence on youth. He began by accepting what I had implied through this leading question, seeking to excuse it by saying, "He wasn't like that before." I completed the train of thought, offering the reasoning that Hassan had given: he became who he was because his brother was killed and to get respect from the woman who refused to marry him. However, Ibrahim said this was not the reason he became *Al-Ustura*. He then proceeded to explain how there were two ways of reading the story. The first was simply that the protagonist was bad, but the second was that he was a product of injustice. He explained to me how originally Nasser had been the top of his law class and was supposed to become a general attorney, but in the end he was refused because he was from an informal neighborhood (*mantiqa ashwa'iyya*). "The same way as if you are poor, you are Christian, you have no connection [*wasta*]; you don't know the people who can be corrupted [*bituʿ al-fasaad*]." This led Ibrahim to reflect on the Egyptian revolution, saying that if the government caused injustice to one person, then that was just an incident, but when it harms one million, ten million, or twenty million, it becomes a revolution. "They made him a beast [*wahsh*]," Ibrahim continued. "If you have the choice between being a beast and a dog, Jamie, which would you prefer to be? Which would you choose?"

Ibrahim thus placed particular emphasis on one aspect of the plot that mirrors an actual controversy in Egypt in 2013, which led to the resignation of the minister of justice, Mahfouz Saber. Saber was interviewed on television about favoritism in judicial appointments and in particular the endogamous and intergenerational nature of the profession. In response to the question, "Could a sanitation worker's son be appointed [as a judge]?" Saber demurred, explaining, "With all due respect to the cleaner, a judge needs to be from a social status commensurate with this position."[4] This incident might have been particularly significant to Ibrahim, given that he comes from a hereditary group involved in waste collection.

The resemblance is not mere coincidence: Mohammed Ramadan indicated in interviews that the plot of *Al-Ustura* was directly inspired by the minister of justice's statement. Although it led to Saber's resignation, the impression that this principle prevails with respect to judicial and attorney general appointments remains widespread. The event is well remembered in Cairo, and interestingly, people often substitute other subaltern professions to that of garbage collecting in their recounting of the incident.

CONCLUSION

Al-Ustura and its controversial place in Egypt address socially defined degrees of tolerance for violence or norms for its legitimation. For critics, they highlight processes of class formation through the ascription of violence and an idiom of moral superiority, and for supporters, they highlight differing interpretations of both the definition and causes of violence. Is Nasser a cruel and antisocial individual or an epiphenomenon of a social system? And what is violence? Young guys from poor neighborhoods getting into fights (mostly with one another) or taking matters into their own hands when the law is more likely to violate their rights than ensure they are respected? Or a collective, socially structured, and often symbolic form of exclusion, stigmatization, and denial of opportunity that is inscribed into the very functioning of society?

All of this was not in the forefront of our minds as we watched the show. It is a bit like rap music: it occasionally offers insightful social criticism and political commentary, but that is not the main reason to listen to it. For Ibrahim and Hassan, the series was a medium of pleasure and fantasy; they were more engaged by the fact that it portrayed the success of a character with whom they could identify ("*Dolarat, ya Jamie! Dolaraaat!*"), or simply that it was a slick, high-budget production, than by the way it criticized Egyptian civil service recruitment. However, when I gave the show a political complexion by suggesting that it promoted baltaga, they inverted the figure and the ground, so to speak, explaining that the social problem *Al-Ustura* principally depicted concerned powers, structures, and ideologies of domination and exclusion; these were what "made" Nasser and were the real violence. These are problems that reflect Ibrahim or Hassan's own everyday encounters with bureaucracy, police, and state power. Many, if not most, middle- and upper-class Egyptians would immediately identify Ibrahim and Hassan's neighborhoods and personal styles with baltaga on the basis of appearance and reputation, with little regard for their moral conduct or individual biographies. Therefore Ibrahim and Hassan might strangely agree that in some ways, the on-screen fictions of *Al-Ustura* imitate their reality and vice versa, but not at all in the way purported by the show's critics.

This chapter concludes with a postscript that arose after fieldwork. When I showed extracts of the series at seminars in Europe, audience members pointed out that in many places Mohammed Ramadan would be identified as Black. Someone asked me whether the soundtrack choice for the series was hip-hop, because it seemed logical given the show's aesthetic. (The answer is no.) Skin color is an aspect of embodied masculinity not often discussed in scholarly literature on Egypt, where race is not "the same structuring historical force that we see in other countries, especially the United States" (Ghannam 2013, 22). However, racial differentiation has nevertheless historically served to define the contrast with the Other in Egypt (Trout Powell 2003) and remains an important code for class and regional differences. Egyptian television shows and films are so "white" that it can be hard to find well-known Egyptian actors with skin dark enough to play the country's actual historical figures, like former Egyptian president Gamal Abdel Nasser. One of the traits that singled out Ahmed Zaki, who did play Nasser, was his dark skin. Perhaps it is not a coincidence, then, that he was also often typecast "as the poor boy trying to infiltrate the upper strata or as the social rebel" (Gordon 2000, 164).

This chapter explains how, from one perspective, the Legend is a "stigmatized figure of the criminal feared by members of society," whereas from another perspective, he is a hero, "articulating the tragic realities of urban poverty as well as the dangers, pleasures, and privileges of being male" (Ferguson 2001, 16). In another context, the title of my chapter therefore could have been "*Al-Ustura*: Gangster . . . or Gangsta."

NOTES

1. This expression is famous from the puppet show *Al-Layla al-Kabira* by Salah Jahin. In it, a corpulent and very tough male figure sings a song in which he claims to be *shagi' al-sima, abu shanab barima* (I am the brave one of the cinema, the one with a twirled moustache).

2. For more on Heliopolis, see Elyachar (2005, 54–62); on Shubra, see Bayat (2010, 195–206).

3. For a theoretical statement of this argument, see Žižek (2008, 1–2, 9–10, 206); for a contextualized application of it in the region, see Kelly (2006, 177).

4. "The Statement of the Minister of Justice," interview of Mahfouz Saber, TeN TV, May 10, 2015, video, 1:40, https://www.youtube.com/watch?v=7 H8mPdTJUWw.

BIBLIOGRAPHY

Abd Al-Hādī, Husām. 2016. "*Futuwwa al-Sīnamā Adab, 'Mush Hizz Kitāf'*" [The big screen strongman: Good behavior, "not shoulder shaking"]. *Rūz Al-Yūssif*, December 10.

Abu-Lughod, Lila. 1997. "The Interpretation of Culture(s) After Television." *Representations* 59:109–134.

Amar, Paul. 2011. "Turning the Gendered Politics of the Security State Inside Out? Charging the Police with Sexual Harassment in Egypt." *International Feminist Journal of Politics* 13, no. 3: 299–328.

Arendt, Hannah. 1969. *On Violence*. New York: Harcourt Brace Jovanovich.

Armbrust, Walter. 2000."Farid Shauqi: Tough Guy, Family Man, Cinema Star."
In *Imagined Masculinities: Male Identity and Culture in the Modern Middle East*,
edited by Mai Ghoussoub and Emma Sinclair-Webb, 199–226. London: Saqi
Books.

———. 2002. "Manly Men on a National Stage (and the Women Who Make Them
Stars)." In *Histories of the Modern Middle East: New Directions*, edited by Israel
Gershoni, Hakan Erdem, and Ursula Wokock, 247–275. Boulder, CO: Lynne
Rienner.

Bayat, Asef. 2010. *Life as Politics: How Ordinary People Change the Middle East*.
Amsterdam: Amsterdam University Press.

De Koning, Anouk. 2009. *Global Dreams: Class, Gender and Public Space in
Cosmopolitan Cairo*. Cairo: American University in Cairo Press.

El-Messiri, Sawsan. 1977. "The Changing Role of the Futuwwa in the Social
Structure of Cairo." In *Patrons and Clients in Mediterranean Societies*, edited by
Ernest Gellner and John Waterbury, 239–253. London: Duckworth.

Elyachar, Julia. 2005. *Markets of Dispossession: NGOs, Economic Development, and
the State in Cairo*. Durham, NC: Duke University Press.

Fanon, Frantz. (1961) 2004. *The Wretched of the Earth*. Translated by Richard
Philcox. New York: Grove.

Ferguson, Ann. 2001. *Bad Boys: Public Schools in the Making of Black Masculinity,
Law, Meaning, and Violence*. Ann Arbor: University of Michigan Press.

Ghannam, Farha. 2012. "Meanings and Feelings: Local Interpretations of the
Use of Violence in the Egyptian Revolution." *American Ethnologist* 39, no. 1:
32–36.

———. 2013. *Live and Die Like a Man: Gender Dynamics in Urban Egypt*. Stanford,
CA: Stanford University Press.

Ghoussoub, Mai, and Emma Sinclair-Webb, eds. 2000. *Imagined Masculinities:
Male Identity and Culture in the Middle East*. London: Saqi Books.

Gilsenan, Michael. 1996. *Lords of the Lebanese Marches: Violence and Narrative in an
Arab Society*. Berkeley: University of California Press.

Gordon, Joel. 2000. "Nasser 56/Cairo 96: Reimaging Egypt's Lost Community."
In *Mass Mediations: New Approaches to Popular Culture in the Middle East and
Beyond*, edited by Walter Armbrust, 161–181. Berkeley: University of California
Press.

Haeni, Patrick. 2005. *L'ordre des caïds. Conjurer la dissidence urbaine au Caire* [The
reign of the caids: Conjuring urban dissidence in Cairo]. Paris: Karthala/CEDEJ.

Hafez, Sabry. 2010. "The New Egyptian Novel: Urban Transformation and
Narrative Form." *New Left Review* 64:47–62.

Ismail, Salwa. 2000. "The Popular Movement Dimensions of Contemporary
Militant Islamism: Socio-Spatial Determinants in the Cairo Urban Setting."
Comparative Studies in Society and History 42, no. 2: 363–393.

Jacob, Wilson C. 2007. "Eventful Transformations: Al-Futuwwa between History and the Everyday." *Comparative Studies in Society and History* 49, no. 3: 689–712.

———. 2011. *Working Out Egypt: Effendi Masculinity and Subject Formation in Colonial Modernity, 1870–1940.* Durham, NC: Duke University Press.

Joubin, Rebecca. 2013. *The Politics of Love: Sexuality, Gender, and Marriage in Syrian Television Drama.* Lanham, MD: Lexington.

———. 2016. "The Politics of the Qabaday (Tough Man) and the Changing Father Figure in Syrian Television Drama." *Journal of Middle East Women's Studies* 12, no. 1: 50–67.

Kelly, Toby. 2006. *Law, Violence and Sovereignty Among West Bank Palestinians.* Cambridge: Cambridge University Press.

Lachenal, Perrine. 2011. *Balṭagī, Glossaire de la révolution* [Baltagi: Glossary of the revolution]. Cairo: CEDEJ. https://egrev.hypotheses.org/1237.

———. 2014. "Beauty, the Beast, and the Baseball Bat: Ethnography of Self-Defense Training for Upper-Class Women in Revolutionary Cairo (Egypt)." *Comparative Sociology* 13:58–77.

Rommel, Carl. 2016. "Troublesome Thugs or Respectable Rebels? Class, Martyrdom and Cairo's Revolutionary Ultras." *Middle East Topics and Arguments* 6:33–42.

Spencer, Jonathan. 2010. "Violence." In *The Routledge Encyclopedia of Social and Cultural Anthropology,* edited by Jonathan Spencer and Alan Barnard, 707–708. London: Routledge.

Trout Powell, Eve M. 2003. *A Different Shade of Colonialism: Egypt, Great Britain, and the Mastery of the Sudan.* Berkeley: University of California Press.

Zikri, Rami. 2016. "*Hasād al-Ustūra*" [The harvest of Al-Ustura]. *Garīda al-ʿālam al-hur,* July 2. https://fw4n.com/198779.html.

Žižek, Slavoj. 2008. *Violence.* New York: Picador.

JAMIE FURNISS is Researcher at the Research Institute on Contemporary Maghreb in Tunis, Tunisia.

THREE

—w—

AL-HOGRA—A STATE OF INJUSTICE

Portraits of Moroccan Men in Search of Dignity and Piety in the Informal Economy

HSAIN ILAHIANE

Amhaqqar n-idamnannas day tan-tutur zeek.
[Whoever shows contempt for his/her blood relatives shall be torn into shreds early.]

—Berber (Amazigh) proverb

INTRODUCTION: LIFE IN *AL-HOGRA*

In contemporary Morocco, many men have chosen to migrate to Europe, whereas others have stayed behind to fulfill their breadwinner roles in the informal sector. These marginalized Moroccan informal laborers toil amid numerous proscriptions and restrictions, within a compromised ethical and moral context known as *al-hogra*. Simply put, the concept of al-hogra means "contempt" and refers to various daily micropractices of injustice and indignation visited on the vulnerable and the powerless of society by dominant groups.

This chapter provides an ethnographic account of men-as-providers laboring within the informal sector in the pursuit of a fulfilling and decent way of life—a way of life that is often at odds with their Islamic ideals. Every day, Moroccan laborers in the informal economy struggle to earn "a piece of bread" and, in so doing, chase after dignity, decency, fulfillment, and piety amid the precarity of informality and a compromised ethical terrain.

This study is based on in-depth ethnographic research carried out between 2003 and 2012 in Casablanca, Morocco, and is part of a larger research project on mobile phones, meanings of money, and technological development (Ilahiane 2014; Ilahiane and Sherry 2008). I conducted these ethnographic interviews in Moroccan colloquial Arabic (al-darija) and translated them into English. This chapter presents the stories of two men who labor to craft digni-fied, fulfilling livelihoods and who operate in the informal sector and inside and outside the boundaries of Islamic principles of piety. One is a street vendor and deals in cell phones; the other is a plumber and runs a small plumbing shop. Their stories are emblematic of many Muslim men in the wider economy. My hope is that by analyzing their struggles in search of a dignified way of life, readers will understand the complex economic conditions in which individuals are struggling to make sense of inconsistent piety and economic marginalities.

But of course, this chapter is more than just a set of ethnographic vignettes about a few individuals in certain places. My account situates these respondents in larger debates over ethical ways of making a dignified living in a Muslim so-ciety in which the majority is trapped in multiple forms of al-hogra. Within this context of informality and men's feelings of being pushed out of the economy by government policies, I discuss the utility of the concept of al-hogra to make sense of the complicated feelings of injustice experienced by Muslim Moroccan men in their day-to-day struggles to make a living.

AL-HOGRA

The word al-hogra comes from the Arabic ihtiqaar, meaning contempt, humili-ation, and degradation. In Morocco and Algeria, al-hogra is a loaded term used in colloquial Arabic (al-darija) to express feelings of injustice, indignation, and resentment related to one's helplessness to remove injustice, a state of pow-erlessness, and a set of individualistic and collective behaviors or practices rooted in a repertoire of political, economic, legal, and administrative differ-entials. Al-hogra means many things to different people in different places and life stations, and at its core it refers to contempt and to the haughty, elitist, and discriminatory attitudes that condone abuse of power, exploitation, humilia-tion, injustice, violence, and sometimes murder against the vulnerable and the powerless of society.

Although the idea of al-hogra is common in everyday conversations, it was only in 2001 that the concept rose to national prominence, when the Algerian Democratic Movement deployed it politically to denounce the corruption of the Algerian state (Bennis 2016). Since then, it has gained widespread accep-tance in framing the public discontent and anger that sparked the uprisings of the February 20 Movement (Morocco's version of the Arab Spring) in 2011 and the ongoing protests in the north of the country. Today, the term has broadened to include a wide range of feelings of deprivation and resentment, which are rooted not only in everyday interactions among Moroccans but also in the ways in which the postcolonial government has conducted its political, social, and economic development programs.

Al-hogra occurs when some individuals feel that they or the group they belong to are deprived or disempowered vis-à-vis other groups, individuals, elites, or institutions. Because al-hogra has dynamic properties and is context specific, its manifestation cannot always be anchored in absolute materialism. It is generally triggered by feelings of being deprived of a status or robbed of a basic human right for which individuals or their social group worked hard, and to which they feel entitled to aspire, or for the lack of equal opportunity to demonstrate their worth to mold their life chances. Al-hogra also stands for dissatisfaction and frustration with the status quo and is used as a vehicle for social mobilization around overlapping human rights issues such as the right to work, to education, to health, to housing, to justice, to equality, to ethnic and linguistic diversity, to religious freedom, to potable water and electricity, to dignity and respect, and so on. Because of its capacity to sum up people's multidimensional struggles and grievances and its ubiquitous deployment in oppositional local and national politics, one can safely claim that it embodies Marcel Mauss's (1966) "total social phenomena," that is, "an activity that has implications throughout society, in the economic, legal, political and religious spheres" (Edgar and Sedgwick 2008, 76).

Furthermore, parallel to Kimberlé Crenshaw's (1989) notion of intersectionality, which describes the ways in which social identities and systems of discrimination and oppression intersect and thus cannot be examined in isolation from one another, the concept of al-hogra also brings together horizontal and vertical linkages that connect an individual, a social group, a location or region, or a behavior to larger social, political, and economic systems and to the arrangements of social and power relationships they help produce and reproduce over time. In the Moroccan context, which is riddled by extreme patterns of social, economic, and regional inequalities, the notion of al-hogra may serve as a useful lens to bring interconnected issues in need of investigation into clearer focus. The notion of al-hogra, which I define as the cumulative effect and intersection of multiple factors, is an outcome of conspicuous economic disparities, political authoritarianism and corrupt institutions, social and ethnic exclusion, and the judgment of others as inferior human beings and as unworthy of humane interactions. In a society characterized by unresolved development issues, persistent poverty and unemployment, and official neglect of the poor and the marginalized, al-hogra is a useful framework to make sense of the complexity of making a living in a Muslim setting because of the term's plasticity and ability to capture the interactions and struggles of livelihood making in the informal sector. Overlapping systems of oppression, discrimination, and rampant institutional corruption contribute to the volatility of the job market and the persistence of poverty, leading to compromised ethical value systems, which in turn condemn vulnerable populations to live and work in precarious conditions.

Mohamed Bouazizi, the Tunisian street fruit vendor who set himself on fire on December 17, 2010, in response to the confiscation of his goods and to the humiliation to which he said he was subject by Tunisian police and municipal authorities, embodies what al-hogra is and looks like in practice. Bouazizi's self-immolation against al-hogra ignited the pro-democracy uprisings of the Arab Spring, which shook the foundations of authoritarian rule and is still unleashing a vibrant process of social and political change in the region and beyond. In Morocco, starting in October 2016, the Berbers (Imazighen) of the Rif, a region on the Mediterranean coast, have been carrying out one of the lengthiest demonstrations of public discontent and rage against al-hogra since the Arab Spring in 2011. Reminiscent of Bouazizi's precarious situation and tragic end, the Rif's protests were triggered by the horrific death of thirty-one-year-old fish seller Mohcine Fikri in October 2016, who protested the impounding and destruction of his swordfish merchandise. While Fikri tried to reclaim his merchandise from the trash compactor where it had been dumped by the police, he was crushed to death. Mobile phone videos of the incident showing a crushed Fikri quickly went viral on social media, igniting a wave of public outrage and disgust inside and outside Morocco. The "grinding" of Fikri, framed by protestors as an act of martyrdom of and against al-hogra (*shaheed al-hogra* in Arabic), has produced a steady pace of unrest in the Rif and throughout Morocco, sustained by discontent and anger over corruption, human rights abuses, contempt, and social exclusion (Ilahiane 2017).

As such, the notion of al-hogra offers insight into the struggles of the powerless and underprivileged, not along isolated parts of social reality but rather through intersectionality where various social, economic, legal, political, and religious relationships overlap. Al-hogra structures power relations between the ruling political and economic elites and the vulnerable and neglected populations. It is grounded in daily micropractices of indignation and injustice visited on those bereft of power and social capital. For the vulnerable population, although al-hogra sums up and expresses the multifaceted aspects of frustration with the personal and collective consequences of botched economic development and corrupt institutions—a sort of a linguistic vessel into which people pour different meanings and experiences—it also provides a vehicle for framing issues and feelings of unworthiness and inferiority, making them emotionally comprehensible to the individual and the group and providing a path with specific courses of social mobilization and action.

THE INFORMAL SECTOR

The informal sector is defined variously as own-account firms, household-based operations, or self-employed individuals operating without formal licensing or outside regulatory purview, including street vendors or laborers operating without legal contracts and entitlements. It is a vast and highly diverse sector, mostly ignored and penalized by policymakers, accounting for some 50 percent of GDP of many developing economies and 90 percent or more of all employment. The urban informal sector of Morocco, for instance, comprises about three hundred thousand microenterprises, contributes more than 15 percent of gross domestic product, and employs more than 50 percent of the active urban population (Castells and Portes 1989; Chickering and Salahdine 1991; Hart 1973; Ilahiane and Sherry 2008).

In the 1950s and early 1960s, following the Marshall Plan's success in postwar Europe, a Western model of "economic development" affected policy and practice throughout much of the world. Conceived within the theoretical matrix of modernization, the belief was that traditional society embedded in outdated modes of economic production had to give way to modern, scientific, and bureaucratic interventions in reorganizing the environment and the populace. This development philosophy fueled state-driven economic policies that focused on large-scale, capital-intensive, and state-run enterprises as the tool of development. The move to bureaucratic industrialization not only displaced rural workers but also created an increase in urban employment. By the 1970s, its failures to deliver high standards of living were evident. Its major outcome was that it produced dual economies in the Third World: the formal economy of large enterprises subsidized by government and small-scale producers, operating outside of the formal economy and its institutions (Gardner and Lewis 2015).

During the 1980s and early 1990s, the disruptive impact of Structural Adjustment Policies of the World Bank and the International Monetary Fund on the public sector led to widespread factory closures, austerity measures, and a drastic reduction in government and parastatal employment. Economic growth rates were low or often negative, and foreign direct investment was almost nonexistent. Millions of displaced workers in these large bureaucratic projects found themselves left once again to their own devices. This pattern has been repeated in numerous other developing countries throughout the world.

ETHNOGRAPHIC PORTRAIT 1: MUSTAPHA,
THE MOBILE PHONE STREET VENDOR

Perhaps the best way to understand how al-hogra relates to economic marginality and the dynamics of the informal economy is to gain insight into the abundant supply of street vendors who operate there. In this regard, the itinerary of Mustapha, who arrived in the street market of the Old City, or *joutia*, called *swiqa* or little *suq*, is perhaps not atypical. His is a story of experimentation and diversification, of "travel east and west," as he put it.

Mustapha is now thirty-two years old and sits on a mat made from a detergent carton. He wears a short beard and is dressed in a fisherman's jacket with many pockets, a baseball cap, an "authentic" pair of Ray Ban glasses, and shiny and baggy sports sweats bearing the Bouygues Telecommunications logo. He wears a waist bag and a relatively new pair of Nikes. Placed carefully on a detergent box before him are dozens of new and used mobile phones. A pile of mobile phone parts lies on a plastic sheet on the ground: chargers, batteries, antennae, plastic panels and buttons, and leather and plastic cases, along with a new pair of New Balance running shoes. His toolkit, composed of a dozen screwdrivers of all sizes and shapes, a toothbrush, and a bottle of cleaning liquid, is making the rounds among his partners. Behind him a beautifully designed wood box showcasing new and expensive wireless phone brands hangs on the wall. "People admire the wood box, and many people wanted to buy it, but I keep it to attract the eye of the strolling shopper," he tells me. "It is my *al-ishhar*, my advertising."

Mustapha's first gainful employment was beyond the borders of his own country. In the late 1980s, "Allah's way took me to Saudi Arabia, where I worked as a plaster mason assistant for three years. Work in Saudi Arabia was all right, but I could not make much money. I was also far away from my family and relatives. It was a tough experience."

For Mustapha, like many others, the move was temporary. Unwilling to put up with the distance and limited earning potential any longer, he returned to Morocco with the money he had earned in Saudi Arabia and dabbled with his own self-employment, first by opening a car repair shop in his neighborhood in the early 1990s. The choice was never entirely satisfactory to him, primarily because of cash flow problems. According to him, "people would not pay for repairs, and even if they did, they paid very late." But there were other disadvantages. "It was filthy work," he adds. It was not until later in the 1990s and the arrival of mobile telephony that his real entrepreneurial opportunity became clear.

Street vendors such as Mustapha recognized that the artisans, farmers, plumbers, and taxi drivers, the new beneficiaries of technologies, would look to the suq or joutia as their retail outlet of choice. When he was introduced to mobile phone technology in 1998, Mustapha abandoned his auto shop and set up his stand for selling and repairing mobile phones. In this new technology, he recognized several beneficial opportunities. The primary attraction, of course, is the earning potential. "I started with one hundred dirhams [about eleven US dollars], and look where I am here. You can start with a small investment. Your capital investment does not need to be big. All you need is a good mind and a good idea to make things work," he said with an achiever's attitude. "Whatever you make, it is all profit, and there is always profit here." In the street, there are no taxes, no rent, or utilities to worry about. As a mechanic, on average he made about US$4,000 a year with sweat and trials. One year, in the early days of the mobile, he made about US$12,000.

But beyond the obvious economic reasons were carefully considered lifestyle choices. On multiple occasions, Mustapha characterized the work of mobile phone dealing as "cleaner" than the work of auto mechanic, echoing a traditional tendency for commercial activities in the Moroccan marketplace to be hierarchically ordered, with the cleaner occupations accruing more prestige and being located closest to the main mosque (others were located on the secondary streets or outside the ramparts of the Medina). Yet despite the difference, the work allowed him to apply many of the same skills. It "comes natural to me because I am a mechanic." He is a *snay'i* (skilled worker) and knows how to fix and fit parts together. "Repairing cars is about knowing what is wrong with the engine, missing or broken parts. I can apply that type of 'brain' to mobile phones," he says with a sense of confidence.

In addition, despite the occasional risks associated with operating out of sanctioned boundaries, he prefers the movement and freedom of the life of a vendor in the suq. His apparent preference for the unfettered lifestyle crystallizes when he compares his old anchored profession of a mechanic with the footloose joutia alleyway street vendor he has become. It is not simply a matter of avoiding overhead and taxes. In the street, one is in the flow of the people, relationships and earning potential that comes with being in circulation. "Why don't you work for Maroc Télécom?" I asked Mustapha one day after a tough and slow market day in the joutia. He replied, "I don't want to be a government clerical worker. It's suffocating. I want to do something I can learn from and benefit from. I want to know people. I am a people person."

Perhaps just as important, the advent of the mobile phone industry provided Mustapha and others like him the opportunity to reassert what can be viewed as either a healthy competitive drive or an act of outright political resistance. As Mustapha talks about his business, it is clear that some of his motivation lies in the desire to reassert a historically Arab/Muslim identity of mastery over technical achievement and local autonomy in the pursuit of economic goals. In many ways, the appropriation of foreign imported goods is as much a political as an economic strategy.

This is best illustrated in the following brief exchange. During one conversation, the topic of goods from "the North" was broached, which I assumed to refer to a specific geographical location. Mustapha, sensing my misunderstanding, posed me a Socratic style challenge. "What is 'the North'?"

I responded, "It's a geographical place, where contraband comes from . . . the Spanish enclaves."

"No, you're wrong," replied Mustapha. "The North is where better quality products come from." This underscores a popular belief, if not an article of faith or fact for Moroccans: higher and better-quality products come from the North and outside Morocco. When talking about product quality, Mustapha distinguishes between what he calls the "interior of Morocco" and the North. The interior refers to Casablanca products, and the North means European, Asian, or foreign-made products.

According to Mustapha, Moroccan-made goods "do not have al-'ilem [science]. Moroccans do not make things or create them. Products need specific studies." Mustapha's choice of classical Arabic to offer this explanation to the ethnographer is not meant merely to impress, but to invoke the long history of Arab mastery of technical expertise and knowledge. The Arabs in the golden age of Islam, after all, provided the world with major contributions to the fields of mathematics, geometry, astronomy, and medicine. This classical Arab technical mastery is distinguished from the substandard contributions of the closely held systems of production currently in place in Moroccan society. "They [Moroccan firms] are thieves. They are careless, and they don't know what they're doing. Local products are corrupt. They're about tobacco, alcohol, lies, and corruption." Northern products, associated with the smuggling circuits, are framed in terms d'origine products (the real thing), whereas locally manufactured goods distributed throughout Morocco are considered second rate, corrupt, or simply Casablanca made—that is, ordinaire.

It has been more than four decades since anthropologist Clifford Geertz (1979) characterized the bazaar economy of Morocco as a "mosaic" of relationships, in which one's occupation correlated closely with a complex array of ethnic, tribal, religious, and other delineations. This complex ordering—sufficiently accessible to insiders—enabled tremendous fluidity in the conduct of commercial trade (distinctions between buyers and sellers were not made) and permitted various institutions in support of the traditional suq economy, such as the organizational framework of the caravanserai, credit arrangements or *qirad*, security agreements, and Sufi brotherhoods (Geertz 1979). Yet in many cases, Geertz's insights still ring true. In the suq economy, the flow of commerce is fragmented into several unrelated, face-to-face transactions. There are competitive goods and services traders, and the system can absorb many people, but at the risk of turning away businessmen from economies of scale and the development of markets toward petty peddling and hawking. Within this context, street vendors capitalize on opportunistic moves and tend to adopt a "*carpe diem* attitude towards commerce" (Geertz 1963, 36).

It is not as explicitly competitive as the analysis portrays it, however. In his dealings and movements, Mustapha "bedazzles and enchants" buyers with information—he creates all sorts of stories. He seems always to be building a montage for his scene. He is smooth; he uses this to gain the trust of shoppers and vendors. Cellular store customers in the modern district are never invited behind the counter. But in joutia, vendors will sit down with their customers, show them how to navigate the interface, and discuss the relative merits of various technologies. Mustapha and his associates spend an average of thirty to forty minutes with potential buyers: "We provide free services here and there so that we can build trust; people are illiterate, and we explain to them the functions and the basics of mobile phones. All they need to know is how to use the phone for talking. That is how we do our advertisement. Good works [*a'maal hasana*] and good words [*kalimat tayyeba*] lead to social networks; people come from all over, even people from the Moroccan Radio and Television, to search for Mustapha."

In short, successful traders in the suq bear all the hallmarks of master salesmen everywhere. For Mustapha, selling and buying in joutia is

> about people. You really have to know how to deal with them. People come from the bureaucracy [government employees]; you must know how to deal with them. They are spoiled and selfish. But don't be afraid of them; be afraid of Allah only. You must deal with them fairly. You've got to deal with them in good faith. Don't let their pompousness get in the way. If you deal this way, you gain rewards from Allah. Some of them are short in terms of reasoning or thinking. You've got to have this profession in your blood. You've got to have the tongue—it really brings down walls.

Equally important in shaping conduct in the suq is the role of Islam as an ethical and cultural force. The anthropological literature tells us that in the traditional suq economy, the most successful entrepreneurs are traders combining commercial frugality with religious principles of asceticism (Geertz 1963, 1979). Mustapha talks about ways in which Islamic ethics have shaped his attitude toward commerce: "This is what our religion says—it's how you deal with people. It's not in the diploma you have; it's in the type of mind you have. You know, the Prophet Muhammad, peace be upon him, told us to teach our children trade. You know, the Prophet was a trader. Trade teaches you how to deal with people, teaches you character, and teaches you morality. That's what it's all about." Furthermore, he adds,

> Joutia is a sacred place. This spot here is my mosque. It is a gift from Allah that I can do this. The prophet gave us trade. This is a holy place. I come here to pray. This place is imbued with *baraka* [divine power]. Use your tongue— give people time and advice. No need to rush them. You want to possess them. I have kids. I want to take *halal*—honestly made and lawful money to them. I don't want to take *haram* [illicit money, or the forbidden] to them. I don't want to be one of those people who is cursed by his parents [*maskhoot al-walidin*]. I want the blessings of my parents [*rdat al-walidin*].

Parents are vested with the power of the curse and the blessing, *ssakht wa rdah,* granted to them by God. The term *ssakht* literally means "anger" or "wrath," and the son or daughter who has been cast the curse is believed to be maskhoot(a) al-walidin. Once cursed, they are said to have a future in which whatever they plant will not reap. Furthermore, wrath and misfortune await them ahead. A cursed person will always be a loser and unlucky, and in being a loser he is ostracized by the community. Any deals or activities involving a cursed person are believed to be contagious and imbued with ssakht and lack the baraka, a critical element for the blessing of human relationships and economic production. An old man nicely and succinctly conveyed the essentials of ssakht to me, stating it is "like SIDA [the French word for HIV/AIDS], when thrown on someone they will wear it to the grave and the after-life." Only *tawba* (repentance) in the presence of a holy man and *taa'a* (obedience) of Allah and parents can expunge the curse.

However, Mustapha is not alone with his wits in the competition for customers. Another social and spatial dimension of order in the street market value chains deals with the role of what the street vendors call *al-nasaaba*, or trappers. At the peak of heavy trading, usually at dusk, a line of about thirty to forty young men standing and peddling all sorts of mobile phones forms in the middle of the street, just a few feet from the main street vendors. The trappers dress very well in contraband clothing with European and American labels: Spanish sweatshirts, Nike shoes, and Levis, with Ray Bans resting on their heads. These young men, or what Mustapha calls "the unemployed and young retired cadres of Morocco," are there in the line one day but disappear the next.

For his part, Mustapha was critical of the al-nasaaba: "These people just sell to make one hundred dirhams or so to go get drunk or get high. Make their one hundred dirhams [about eleven US dollars] and go. They are 'Satans.' They dress nicely so they can gain people's trust." Like other vendors, he claims that the al-nasaaba are ruining the reputation of the market. "Don't buy from those guys; they will rip you off. Buy from us." But in fact, like other vendors, he works closely with them. The al-nasaaba work as loosely affiliated contractors, engaged to sell the lemons, the stuff the street vendors themselves cannot move. Besides the often downplayed relationships with the al-nasaaba are relationships with the joutia shopkeepers themselves. Regarding relations with the shopkeepers, Mustapha says, "Yes, they are legitimate, but they are greedy. They're never satisfied with how much money they make because they must pay some to the state. As for me, I'm itinerant. If I make fifty dirhams in a day, that's great. That's the mercy of Allah." In his eyes, he is a peer of the men who own the joutia shops. "You have to be professional and skilled" in dealing with them. "I get parts from them; I give the store owners publicity. Their stuff is expensive because of taxes, overhead, et cetera. I bring people to them, I bring them business, I bring activity." Mustapha gets a discount on parts (below what ordinary consumers would pay) at the shops. The owner of the store also lets him use the electrical outlet to test chargers, mobile phones, and other elements.

Street vendors thus maintain crosscutting patterns of information sharing and services with anchored shopkeepers of joutia. By virtue of their place and function, street vendors appear to constitute a restless community as they move between the standing al-nasaaba and shopkeepers. This sense of commuting between al-nasaaba and shopkeepers reinforces joutia's agile and flexible social patterns in the sense that "no one in the bazaar can afford to remain immobile. It is a scrambler's life" (Geertz 1979, 187). This mobility, like his "power of the tongue," is what gives Mustapha his edge. "Store owners must also respect me," he says. "They sell some of the contraband that I supply to them. I have the connections with people in *the North*."

ETHNOGRAPHIC PORTRAIT 2: RASHID, THE PLUMBER AND STORE MANAGER

If the foregoing section provided a portrayal of Mustapha's struggles to make a halal living in the suq, the following shows the story of an individual who operates inside and outside the boundaries of conventional and Islamic banking principles. His account highlights the larger debate over *riba* (usury), which explains his ambivalent and pragmatic embrace of on-the-ground economic realities.

Rashid is a plumber, store owner, entrepreneur, and shantytown dweller. He is thirty-five years old and married with a three-year-old child. He shares his shantytown dwelling with his two brothers, one a plumber and the other a livestock trader. He is a practicing Muslim, and his financial situation provides an interesting and complex set of social relationships informed by Islamic ideals and the pragmatics of everyday life and business practices of a working-class environment. Although he is highly conscious of the emotional and spiritual cost of interest charging banks (*al-abnaak al-ribawiyya*), he has a bank account, a *carnet blue* (deposits and savings book), and an Automatic Teller Machine card for personal use. At the same time, he has yet to open a business account for his plumbing store, which has an estimated inventory of about US$3,000–5,000. In addition, although he is a member of a microfinance group loan, he also taps into his siblings' financial assets. One of the reasons behind one of his brothers' (the livestock trader) reluctance to open a bank account is to make sure his cash resources are available and accessible to household members. Money, especially cash in this instance, ties the family together. In the case of Rashid, it reinforces the sense of brotherhood in this world and in the hereafter, augmenting ways of being a Muslim in a non-shari'a-compliant banking environment.

Three years ago, Rashid bought a piece of property in his neighborhood and turned it into a preschool where two of his sisters teach about thirty students. When pressed whether this purchase was an investment, he flatly and in no uncertain terms replied that it was not. If it was, he would have hired a stranger to the family to run and manage it. Even though he receives a monthly share or divides the revenue of the school among his sisters and himself, he still thinks of this project as helping his sisters as well as others indirectly in the wider community, especially the other plumber brother, who is in urgent need of a certain amount of money to obtain a working contract overseas. Rashid also made sure that I understood his project was not an act of charity by saying, "This is not *sadaqa* [voluntary charity]; these are my brothers and sisters; I must help them. It is obligatory, and this is all *ajr* [rewards from Allah] and blessings from my parents [rdat al-walidin]."

Rashid pays government taxes on his store and zakat dues on his entire inventory and monetary assets. Paying zakat (obligatory charity), he insisted, should not go to any members of the family and must be donated to others; in his case, his zakat donations are given to nonrelatives and to his acquaintances in the neighborhood. As for zakat payments, he pays 2.5 percent of his entire store and monetary assets. "If you don't do zakat, usually something bad will happen to you [zakat katban fi-bnadam]," he says with a serious face. Rashid also stresses the fact that zakat takes away or washes away riba or interest on money; it purifies one's polluted money (flus al-haram), and that purification is the sustenance of other people (the needy, widows, orphans, the elderly, and so on). In addition to his occasional and daily charity donations to street beggars, he donates ten dirhams to the imam fund of his shantytown's mosque. Although they are common financial practices in his neighborhood, Rashid does not participate in informal rotating credit and saving associations, called locally daret. He deems these types of financial associations not only haram or illicit because money received in these transactions is a result of pure luck rather than hard work, but also because they operate on lottery or gambling (al-qimar) principles, which are also haram.

Despite striving to lead an ideal Muslim way of life, Rashid took a small loan of about US$1,000 as a member of a microcredit group from a conventional bank. The loan came with a rate of interest of 10 percent. On recognizing the inconsistency between his ideal construction of what a Muslim way of life should be and the daily economic pressures in a resource-poor environment, Rashid, with his head leaning down and his right hand holding his forehead, mumbled that, "Allah understands, and what else can one do in a place like this where there is no Islamic banking or support for the poor like us?" As if to recover from this gap between the ideal and the real, he quickly moved on to say, "Being able to borrow money makes a person more responsible and being responsible means knowing the limits of one's budget. Taking bank loans with interest [faa'ida] for the ram of the Day of Sacrifice [eid al-adha], however, is haram. The ram should be bought from the sweat of one's labor, not by a bank loan. If one does not have money for the purchase of a ram, one must not force himself to borrow money and become indebted."

For Rashid, it seems that money matters and transactions require diverse and entangled sets of family, community, and business ties. He works as a plumber and store owner, takes a loan with interest from the bank with four cosigners from his community, "invests" in a school, and taps into community and family funds. From the perspective of Rashid, who is trying to put his Islamic ideals into practice and augment his Islamic credentials in a secular banking milieu, the idea of borrowing money is ironically believed to provide him with a built-in discipline to incite him to save and explore potential commercial opportunities. Bank loans are viewed as yet another quick mechanism to save money in a resource limited environment. Rashid is constantly cultivating and leveraging personal and family obligations. Besides his uncomfortable awareness and recognition, he is constantly trading purification or Islamic ideals of avoiding riba and interest on financial transactions for practical results. In sum, Rashid's financial map illustrates a kind of bricoleur mode of operation by which he skillfully assembles and makes sense of fragmented and irreconcilable elements of personal finance management. Not only is Rashid compelled to bring together different formal and informal financial strategies to bear on his difficult circumstances, but he is also forced to compromise his religious ideals to meet the real and daily demands of making a living in the informal economy.

ETHICAL LIVING IN PRECARITY

The preceding sections describe the ways in which narratives about seeking the halal, or the licit, as a means of obtaining parental blessings and leading a holy living underscore the necessity for attentiveness about the ethical and devotional uprightness of the faithful. The passionate debate over the right and halal way of life appears to create a state of anxiety expressed in defining and reframing what constitutes proper and halal behavior, resulting in a complex set of commercial and financial assemblage. These commercial and financial arrangements consist of a bricoleur strategy, in which individuals like Mustapha and Rashid make use of formal and informal commercial practices and financial products and relationships. Because of the desire and necessity to adjust to economic requirements, they have constructed ambiguous livelihood strategies that contravene the religious injunctions of halal living and the prohibition of riba. Although these individuals appear to successfully weave a dignified way of life in the informal sector, they continue to live under incessant questioning of their daily actions—actions that have qualms and doubts about riba because, as Rashid states,

> I know it is not entirely Islamic what we do. I pray. I fast Ramadan. I give charity. I am kind, and one day I will go on pilgrimage. But this thing of the riba is, as you know, *Allah ghalab* [Allah is great, and we are helpless and vulnerable], and there is no God but God. He is compassionate, and He will look, God willing, in what is in our hearts and the conditions that have led us to doing or getting involved in riba and what looks like riba. I ask God for forgiveness, and I seek refuge in Him from Satan. God knows I am trying to make ends meet. We are poor. As you know, we live in misery. God willing, I will go on pilgrimage and wash away all these contraventions.

Grudgingly, with a certain sense of agony, Rashid admitted, "The punishments and reward for zakat and riba are the same [*kif-kif*]. If you don't pay your zakat dues, harm and failure will come your way [*musiba*]. The harmful things occur when one is practicing riba and declaring war on Allah. Bad things and accidents happen to you and these are signs from Allah to let you know that He is not pleased with the path you have taken."

Rashid continued. "Let me show you the evidence of what I am saying." He rolled up the sleeves of his right arm and said, "See this mark near my wrist? I almost broke my hand wrist when playing kickboxing. It still hurts. This happened to me just a few days after I took a microcredit loan from the bank. Riba caused me this accident, and I believe that this is a sign from Allah to warn me to stay away from flus al-haram or riba bearing money. *Wakkal al-haram wa al-haram kay khraj 'ala mulah* [misfortune will occur to those who eat the illicit]."

Like Mustapha's pursuit of a halal lifestyle and livelihood, Rashid's tormented concerns about his health and fate in this world and in the hereafter are rooted in the fear of nullifying parental blessings and the scriptural injunction of halal living. Closely related to this nagging unease, a salient issue is the ambiguity that arises when the faithful is required, on one hand, to lead a pious and holy life and, on the other hand, to carry on with the pragmatism and flexibility dictated by the force of circumstances that produce a partial spiritual system.

CONCLUSION

How can we make sense of the persistence of Muslim men at hard work and the pursuit of dignity and fulfillment in conditions filled with religious, economic, and political contradictions? Political theorist and historian Achille Mbembe (2017) uses the notion of a "negative moment" to analyze the disquieting economic and political malaise of postcolonial African societies. A negative moment is an instance "when new antagonisms emerge while old ones remain unresolved. It is a moment when contradictory forces—inchoate, fractured, fragmented—are at work but what might come out of their interaction is anything but certain. It is also a moment when multiple old and recent unresolved crises seem to be on the path towards a collision" (Mbembe 2017, 2). In postcolonial Morocco, the enduring al-hogra is a model of a negative moment with respect to the unresolved interplay between postcolonial political formations and economic neoliberalism. Remember Rashid's quote above in which he states "Allah ghalab," meaning that Allah is the mightiest and Rashid is helpless and vulnerable before the will of Allah. Rashid's feelings of precarity and helplessness appear to illustrate the situation of al-hogra and to speak to a sequence of disappointments and setbacks visited on the vulnerable by the powerful who produced and still reproduce the state of al-hogra. My respondents, as quoted below, thus use the concept of al-hogra to describe themselves and their life chances.

Evocative of Frantz Fanon's (1963) biting critique of the betrayals of postcolonial African middle classes in *Wretched of the Earth*, these struggling informal sector Muslim men tend to have similar views of the Moroccan elite for its failure to modernize the country, for squandering opportunities to lift its population from poverty and precarity, and for putting them in material and spiritual danger. Said a tired Rashid one afternoon after Friday prayer,

> They [Moroccan elites] are thieves, looters; they are *mufsideen* on Allah's earth [corrupt people]. All they care about is their pockets, their families, and their friends. . . . Us, we have Allah. And for us is the street and no education, no, no health, no housing, no human rights, no Islamic banks. For us, shantytowns and living the life of flies on a dead animal skin [referencing a well-known 1970s anti-establishment song by Nass Al Ghiwane]. . . . They made our parents poor and us poor; we will not forgive them. Can you imagine that we have been living in shantytowns for forty years? We will never get out of poverty and al-hogra. *Hna mahgureen* [we are humiliated and oppressed].

These two Muslim men find themselves in a double "negative moment": humiliated and denied basic economic and political rights by their national elites. However, their stories speak at once to the ethics of hard work undertaken to care and provide for themselves and for their families in a compromised context and to their sheer tenacity to leverage Islamic ethics and creative entrepreneurial agency to mold a piece of bread and a meaningful, dignified, and fulfilling life. In the process, these men are not only piecing together a decent and normal life against all odds but are also telling their stories of being and acting as good Muslim men in the world.

BIBLIOGRAPHY

Bennis, Samir. 2016. "*Al-hogra fi al-hirak al-maghribi* [Al-hogra in Moroccan protests]." *Bayan al-Yaoum* (Rabat, Morocco), November 15.

Castells, Manuel, and Alejandro Portes, eds. 1989. "World Underneath: The Origins, Dynamics, and Effects of the Informal Economy." In *The Informal Economy*, edited by Manuel Castells and Alejandro Portes, 11–17. Baltimore: Johns Hopkins University Press.

Chickering, Lawrence A., and Mohamed Salahdine, eds. 1991. *The Silent Revolution: The Informal Sector in Five Asian and Near Eastern Countries*. San Francisco: ICS.

Crenshaw, Kimberlé. 1989. "Demarginalizing the Intersection of Race and Sex: A Black Feminist Critique of Antidiscrimination Doctrine, Feminist Theory, and Antiracist Politics." *University of Chicago Legal Forum* 1:139–167.

Edgar, Andrew, and Peter Sedgwick, eds. 2008. *Cultural Theory: The Key Concepts.* New York: Routledge.

Fanon, Frantz. 1963. *The Wretched of the Earth.* New York: Grove.

Gardner, Katy, and David Lewis. 2015. *Anthropology and Development.* London: Pluto.

Geertz, Clifford. 1963. *Peddlers and Princes: Social Development and Economic Change in Two Indonesian Towns.* Chicago: University of Chicago Press.

———. 1979. "Suq: The Bazaar Economy in Sefrou." In *Meaning and Order in Contemporary Morocco: Three Essays in Cultural Anthropology,* edited by Clifford Geertz, Hildred Geertz, and Lawrence Rosen, 123–225. New York: Cambridge University Press.

Hart, Keith. 1973. "Informal Economy Opportunities and the Urban Employment in Ghana." *Journal of Modern African Studies* 11, no. 1: 61–89.

Ilahiane, Hsain. 2014. "Mediating Purity: Money, Usury and Interest, and Ethical Anxiety in Morocco." *Human Organization* 73, no. 4: 315–325.

———. 2017. "Morocco's Rif Revolt: Only a Democratic Response is Sufficient." Informed Comment, July 21. https://www.juancole.com/2017/07/moroccos-democratic-sufficient.html.

Ilahiane, Hsain, and John W. Sherry. 2008. "Joutia: Street Vendor Entrepreneurship and the Informal Economy of Information and Communication Technologies in Morocco." *Journal of North African Studies* 13, no. 2: 243–255.

Mauss, Marcel. 1996. *The Gift.* London: Cohen and West.

Mbembe, Achille. 2017. "Decolonizing Knowledge and the Question of the Archive." http://wiser.wits.ac.za/system/files/Achille%20Mbembe%20-%20Decolonizing%20Knowledge%20and%20the%20Question%20of%20the%20Archive.pdf.

HSAIN ILAHIANE is Professor of Anthropology at Mississippi State University. He is author of *Ethnicities, Community Making, and Agrarian Change: The Political Ecology of a Moroccan Oasis* and of *Historical Dictionary of the Berbers (Imazighen).*

PART II

MASCULINITY AND DISPLACEMENT: MOVING, SETTLING, AND QUESTIONS OF BELONGING

REPEATING MANHOOD

Migration and the Unmaking of
Men in Morocco

ALICE ELLIOT

INTRODUCTION

"He sits like a woman," Rashida muttered bitterly to me, nodding in the direction of her husband, Samir, who was watching television in the other room. Samir, an emigrant in Italy for many years, had been back in his hometown in central Morocco for about three weeks, and the atmosphere in the Ghzaouli family was becoming increasingly tense. His first days back home had been marked by intense activity—receiving guests, visiting relatives, distributing gifts and money *men l-brra* (from "the outside"), telling stories about *temma* (there).[1] Following this short burst of activity, Samir had started spending increasing amounts of time at home, watching television, mending little things around the house, playing with his children, drawing sketches of the extra story he was planning to build on the family home, and taking very long naps. The whole household, after a festive interlude for Samir's return, had returned to its daily rhythms of cooking, going to school and the marketplace, and working on night shifts or building sites. Amid this web of activities and routines, Samir was still, "sitting," doing nothing.[2]

Samir had been unemployed in Italy for a long time and did not have the resources to "move" (act, plan, buy, busy himself) as an emigrant man is expected to do when he returns to Morocco for a visit. Samir could not build a new house, could not plan and pay for the wedding of one of his younger brothers, and could not sponsor the building of a new mosque in the neighborhood. He did not have the resources to engage in any kind of activity that would shift him from the precarious stasis his wife identified with her acerbic comment: "He sits like a woman."

His prolonged sitting in a domestic space—a space that, in the working-class neighborhood where the Ghzaouli family lives, is considered a female sphere in the daytime—created palpable tensions in the household. Samir's children (a girl aged ten and a boy aged twelve at the time), after a period of obeying their father to the letter and taking pains to show him their loving respect, had gone back to their usual way of behaving. This included treating their uncles—their father's brothers—as the figures of authority in the house, as if Samir's presence was quickly dwindling to the point of becoming invisible. Samir's wife had started complaining about how he would hover around her in the house, telling her how to do her chores and interfering with her domestic routine, something she found both highly annoying and thoroughly inappropriate for a man. Samir's sitting when he returned home seemed to be questioning his qualities not only as a migrant man but also, as a man.

Taking Samir Ghzaouli's tense homecoming as ethnographic starting point, this chapter focuses on the ways in which migration simultaneously shapes and questions—or makes and unmakes—men in Morocco. It traces how migration becomes a fundamental component of masculinity in Moroccan emigrant areas, and how gendered expectations intersect with expectations of *l-brra*—literally "the outside" in Moroccan Arabic, and the term used to refer to Europe or "the West" (Elliot 2021). Rather than focusing on the ways in which migration is a gendered act and often instantiates a transition from boyhood to manhood, a topic dealt with extensively in the migration literature (e.g., Ali 2007; Jónsson 2008; Kandel and Massey 2002; Menin 2016; Pandolfo 2007), this chapter focuses on the work required of emigrant men to remain men despite all odds and traces the specific ways in which l-brra makes gender a particularly precarious achievement. Indeed, while the migration scholarship tends to frame migration as a strategic move to acquire locally idealized masculinities, this chapter argues that contact with l-brra becomes itself a specific and distinct form of manhood—one that needs to be continually reiterated, and a reiteration that is not without (gendered) risks (Butler 1990).

I address this complex gendered reiteration by tracing the kinds of idealized, at times even stylized expectations that are put on those identified, and who identify themselves, as emigrant men when they return home to central Morocco. My sense is that only by considering the intersection of gendered and migratory expectations can we begin to understand why Rashida's comment about her husband, "he sits like a woman," is so important and effective. As we shall see, taking seriously normative models of femininity and masculinity does not mean assuming that life in Morocco—or anywhere else for that matter—is straightforwardly lived as, or in any straightforward sense looks like, these gendered ideals. Rather, it means attending to the complex workings of gendered ideals and abstractions on specific people, bodies, and relations. The fact that these are ideal types and abstract expectations of "men" and "women" does not diminish their purchase and power in everyday life—if anything, it heightens it, particularly, as we shall see, when migration is involved.

I begin by looking at conceptualizations of sitting in the Ghzaouli neighborhood and their gendered implications for emigrant men. I then trace the ways in which emigrant men are expected to move in specific ways when they return home, and the key role l-brra plays in what Farha Ghannam (2013) has termed the "materialization of masculinity." Finally, I trace why the repetition of migratory movement becomes so crucial and so dangerous for emigrants, at once generative and corrosive of specific kinds of men.

FIELD AND METHOD

My exploration of migration and masculinity draws on seventeen months of fieldwork in 2009–10 in rural emigrant areas of central Morocco, and on regular research visits paid to the region throughout the following decade. These rural and mountainous areas have become one of Morocco's main departure centers for emigration to southern Europe. Although migration in the region gained momentum later than in other areas of Morocco such as the northeastern Rif region, since the late 1970s the area has seen impressive levels of transnational movement, particularly toward Italy and Spain (De Haas 2007). Today, it is near impossible to encounter a household in the region that does not have at least one family member living abroad, and migration has become one of central Morocco's defining characteristics. The region is also sometimes referred to in Morocco as "the triangle of death"—a chilling reminder of the incessant deaths in the Mediterranean Sea of young people from the area produced by European migratory regimes (Smythe 2018), and a chilling testimony to the role migration has assumed in the administering of life and death in the region.

Migration in this area is still largely (though by no means uniquely; see Salih 2003) a male affair, and it is predominantly men who leave, and who leave first. Men in the region generally emigrate as young *drari* (boys), often marrying young women from their hometowns and villages during return visits (Elliot 2016b). In many ways, emigrant men are the ones who sustain the area's migratory cosmology, the human conduits between home and l-brra. Emigrant men are a conspicuous "absent presence" throughout my work, because they are, by definition, mostly physically absent from the areas where I do fieldwork but also crucial figures in the unfolding of everyday life.

In this chapter, however, I attend to those moments when emigrants are physically present in Morocco, when they return home from l-brra to visit their families. I use the complex, tense negotiations that emerge on their returns to reflect on the ways in which migration nurtures and questions specific forms of gender, making and unmaking specific kinds of men.

THE GENDER OF SITTING

By accusing her husband, Samir, of "sitting like a woman," Rashida was drawing on a specific gendered understanding of sitting and using it to frame her emigrant husband's behavior in explicitly gendered terms. In rural central Morocco, the house is not a place where men are expected to spend excessive amounts of time. In the Ghzaoulis' neighborhood, men and older boys are out of the house most of the day—working in the surrounding fields or in construction, looking for jobs, sitting in coffeehouses, clearing up bureaucratic matters with public officials, secretly meeting girlfriends, hanging around with friends, and so on.

In the Ghzaoulis' neighborhood, then, men are generally "moving" and "doing," whereas "sitting" is theoretically a women's affair. Importantly, when the term *sitting* (*galsa*) is used for women, it is not meant to describe a static body. Indeed, women never actually idly sit for long periods of time in rural Morocco and are generally performing demanding domestic and nondomestic activities throughout the day (Mernissi 1988). Sitting refers more to a certain type of (female) person, implying a moral disposition rather than an actual immobile body.

Sitting, however, has different connotations for men. Sitting (*gales*) can mean that the man in question is unemployed, temporarily out of a job. But gales does not refer solely to one's working situation and can also (just as for women) refer to a person's gendered predisposition. "*Dima gales*" (he always sits/he's always sitting around), is a telling comment that regards not only the inactivity of a body but also the sort of person someone is. In this sense, not to sit is considered a proper state of being for a man. Importantly, sitting acquires different meanings in different contexts. A man sitting at a café for too long can be directly and indirectly criticized for his inactivity, laziness, or negligence toward *daru* (his home). But the stakes become much higher for a man who sits in the house for too long, something that is not only ridiculed but also calls into question claims to male adulthood.

Another crucial element that affects the evaluation of (domestic and non-domestic) sitting is, of course, status, as well as age.[3] A man may sit for longer periods of time than others because he can afford to: he may have the money to pay someone to work his land, he may be receiving a generous pension after early retirement from state employment, or he may be simply part of a wealthier (and luckier) lineage.[4] In this context, sitting can even be a source of prestige and power (Gaibazzi 2015).

However, sitting because one can afford to—for example, having the resources to delegate physical labor to others, or being part of an intellectual elite—differs fundamentally from sitting because one cannot afford, is unable, or does not want to move. And in the Ghzaoulis' neighborhood, men who spend too much time "just sitting in the house" are seen as failing to comply with basic male requirements and qualities: those of moving and doing.

Within this context, it may be clearer why Samir's stasis in the Ghzaouli household was problematic in a gendered sense. Samir was not of the right gender, status, or age to be spending prolonged amounts of time "sitting and doing nothing" at home. But most important, Samir was the wrong type of man. His connection with l-brra, the fact that he was "a man who goes" (*rajel lli kaimshi*), made his domestic stillness all the more powerful in the questioning of his gendered personhood. Indeed, my sense is that Samir's "domestic stillness" was particularly problematic precisely because his masculinity was grounded in his connection with l-brra, whereas this defining connection was expected to actualize itself back home through specific gendered movements and doings.

MOVING LIKE A MIGRANT, MOVING LIKE A MAN

When emigrants return to Morocco from l-brra, they are expected to move, and in a sense excessively so. If doing and not sitting are expected of all men, these expectations are infinitely multiplied when it comes to emigrant men. "The outside" becomes a human quality as much as a geographical destination, and this quality is observed and evaluated in specific ways when an emigrant returns home. Energetic doings are seen as the inevitable consequence of one's contact with "the outside." In a way, a man becomes a rajel lli kaimshi (a man who goes) through his behaviors and attitudes during his visits home: the way he walks confidently down the street, the way he beckons the waiter from across the bar, the way he approaches a young woman, the choice of decoration on his newly built house. Recalling Michael Herzfeld's (1985, 25) point about the value positioned on the "conventionalized unconventionality" of men's behavior in the Cretan mountain village of Glendi, emigrant men in central Morocco are expected not just to stick to conventional male behaviors but also to stick to them with originality, excess, and even eccentricity. As Herzfeld shows for Glendi men, the essential thing for an action is that it both confirms stereotypical expectations of malehood and skillfully and inventively manipulates these expectations.

I suggest that the "conventionalized unconventionality" expected of emigrant men is linked to the fact that to be a man, for an emigrant, means being an emigrant man. This is more than a simple play on words. The fact that the social personhood of emigrants is rooted in their movement to l-brra means that people's expectations of emigrants are inseparable from their expectations of l-brra itself. "The outside" contributes to produce specific kinds of men, and these men in turn respond to specific kinds of requirements and expectations. With this, I do not mean to imply that the expectations are static, nor that adherence to them is expected to be mechanistic. As anthropological work on Arab and Muslim masculinities has richly argued—in an explicit effort to subvert the scholarly trend to depict the figure of the "Arab man" (whoever and whatever that is) as "rigid, inflexible, and defined within unchanging codes of honor and systems of 'patriarchy'" (Marsden 2007, 475; see also, e.g., Amar 2011; Ghannam 2013; Inhorn and Naguib 2018; Schielke 2015)—the gendered expectations of migrants returning to Morocco are extremely varied, sometimes profoundly contradictory, and continually reconfigured.

These continual reconfigurations are related not only to the social changes taking place in Morocco itself—most notably perhaps the steadily increasing schooling and employment of women and its gendered implications (Elliot 2016a)—but also to the complex, shifting, and contradicting perceptions of what "the outside" is, does, and offers. Indeed, the conundrum facing many emigrant returnees is precisely the indeterminacy and boundlessness that characterizes people's imagination of l-brra. These imaginations translate into complex expectations and requests of those who have been there, often expressed (crucially so) through a normative gendered language of male worth and male duties.

This makes emigrants' return visits fundamental moments of gender performativity—or indeed of "gender materialization" as Ghannam (2013) defines the struggles, challenges, and emotional and physical pressures of becoming a man in her work on masculinity in urban Egypt. Whether a man is "good at being a man," as Herzfeld (1985, 16) puts it, is subject to scrutiny during return visits.

One key area where the gendered personhood of emigrant men is assessed and reinstated is in the construction of houses. To illustrate this and to trace the relationship between migrant house-making and gendered personhood, let me return to Samir and his "domestic sitting."

BUILDING MANHOOD

Samir filled the many hours he spent sitting at home sketching the extra story he was planning to build on the Ghzaouli house. This extra story, Samir told me, had always been in his imagination of "*dari*" (my house) from the very day he had bought the land where his one-story house now stood. The plan for the extra story was evident in the material nature of the house itself. Its upper part stood visibly unfinished and unpainted, rebars were still sticking out vertically from the main walls, and the flat roof was treated by all members of the household, as is common in the area, as something halfway between a roof and a future floor.

For nearly ten years, the Ghzaouli family had lived in a house that incorporated the visible intention of its expansion. This expansion had yet to be actualized, but Samir dedicated to it most of his energy on his returns, and possibly many of his thoughts while he was in Italy. After dinner, when watching television, and while sitting on a plastic chair outside the house in the evening breeze and waiting for tea to be served, Samir would take out a pen and a worn piece of paper from the pocket of his jeans and start sketching over older sketches of his future home. He would change the size of the rooms, calculate the height of the walls, plan where the various members of the family would have their rooms, and make other little alterations. After sketching and thinking for a while, he would fold up the piece of paper and put it back in his jeans pocket. This ritual would be repeated several times over the course of the day, and Samir always kept this ever-evolving house plan with him. This carefully stored and worn piece of paper reminded me of a *hjuba*, the tiny piece of paper with phrases from the Qur'an written by local Muslim clerics and kept in amulets or tucked into clothes for protection—for example, during a dangerous crossing of the Mediterranean.

In many ways, this piece of scribbled-on paper did provide protection for Samir. First of all, it was a protection against insanity. When I would sit next to him observing his architectural imaginings, Samir would tell me that if he did not plan his house, he would go mad (*hmeq*). It was difficult for me to discern whether he was referring to the tensions perceptibly rising in the household, to the sense of unmet expectation emanating from those around him, or to a more subtle existential need. Whatever the reason, Samir would pat the jeans pocket where he stored his house plan and tell me, "Without this, I'm going to implode [*ntartaq*]."

Together with insanity and implosion, and strongly linked to these, the piece of paper also protected Samir against stillness and inactivity. Drawing, planning, and talking about the extra story of the house was what anchored Samir to the image he had of himself of an emigrant man. It was what protected him, from his perspective at least, against inactive stasis in his own home. Indeed, Samir saw this extra story as his main commitment when he was in Morocco: drawing, planning, reimagining, and discussing the house was in fact what he mostly did during his visits.

By immersing himself in sketching out the future development of his house, Samir was paralleling what most emigrant men do and are expected to do when they return to Morocco: house-making. As has been observed time and again in a variety of ethnographic settings (e.g., Chu 2010; Dalakoglou 2010; Lopez 2015), one of the main activities that occupy emigrants during their visits to Morocco is the building of houses. In many ways, the whole migratory project is oriented toward "doing a house" back home. "Doing a house" goes beyond the concrete function of providing a shelter, acquiring specific significance and meaning in the context of migration. In Morocco, this is not only linked to the "socio-economy of symbols" and the need to have tangible signs of both success in the outside and enduring belonging to *le-bled*, or one's country/land (McMurray 2001). It is also linked to the fact that when emigrant men return home, they are expected to actualize their precious connection with "the outside" through constant doings. "Doing a house" is in many ways the generative matrix for other subject-defining doings, such as "doing a wedding" and "doing children."

Indeed, the process of construction is as essential as the final, built house, and this is confirmed by the fact that the building process never really comes to a halt. Houses are continually being expanded, embellished, and changed every time emigrants return. New stories and rooms are added, internal furnishings are upgraded, and new covers for the long couches are bought and fitted. Depending on one's financial abilities, the foundations for a completely new house—and in some cases, even those for a mosque—may be laid. A person's quality as someone who *kaimshi brra* (goes [to the] outside) is thus always in excess of a first, completed house, so the process of building or thinking about building never really comes to a halt. Indeed, I would say that this process cannot stop, because an emigrant's personhood pivots around the ability to move, and the building of houses is the most important and tangible expression of this. Were this movement to cease, the ability of an emigrant man to "move" rapidly becomes questioned. This is precisely what was happening with Samir.

From Samir's perspective, by sketching the future development of his house, he was doing exactly what other emigrants do when they return home: he was building. For the time being, he was building on a piece of paper, but it was the building of an indisputable future reality rather than daydreaming or a fantasy. It could not be otherwise, because he conceived of himself as someone who moves and does, not someone who sits and waits. He did not have enough resources to add the new story to the house for the time being. But the preparatory work for its building (planning, imagining, sketching, worrying, fixing) was taking place constantly. For Samir, its execution was imminent.

His wife, Rashida, out of earshot of her in-laws, would tell me that the only thing imminent was Samir's madness: "He's been scribbling on that piece of paper for years," she would tell me. "Don't believe him when he says he'll build on the top; *makaynsh la flus la walu* [there is no money no nothing], and he's just going mad." What Samir did in order to avoid madness, building on paper, was seen by his wife precisely as the sign of impeding madness. And though his architectural imaginings kept him anchored to his self-conceptualization as a moral male subject who provided for his family, these imaginings were not enough to prove to those around him that he was worthy of this personhood. For those around him, starting from his own wife, Samir was problematically inactive and behaving *"bhal shi mra"* (like some woman). Indeed, the fact that the house stood unfinished was material proof, for his wife, of Samir's difficulty in acting as a man when he returned home.

CRISIS

Samir's returns home had not always been typified by sitting and the absence of house-making activities. Throughout his first decade of migration, Samir had in many ways successfully complied with the complex expectations placed on "men who go." He had married a young woman the first time he returned, and a son was born about a year later. On his second visit, he bought a piece of land on the outskirts of a big rural town, and he paid laborers to lay the foundations and put up the supporting pillars for a house. On his third visit home, the walls and roof of the first floor of the house were built, and his wife, his now two children, his mother and father, his two brothers, and one sister moved in to live there. In the years that followed, he continued "doing" the house, and every time he returned, he picked up from where he had left off on his previous visit.

It was only since the early 2010s that Samir's house doings had dwindled, his sitting in Morocco temporally coinciding with his unemployment in Italy. I had been told about Samir's bleak work situation long before the problematic return of this chapter. Samir's relatives had told me that he had been sitting for a long time in Italy. Sitting, here, was used in the general sense of being unemployed and did not necessarily carry moral or gendered implications.

The Italian factory where he had worked for nearly a decade had closed, and opportunities for manual labor in the fields, where he had worked in the past to subsidize his factory income, were dwindling.

People in the area generally acknowledge that life is difficult *f l-brra* (in the outside), and since 2009, stories about the effects of *l-azma* (the crisis; i.e., the European financial crisis) on Moroccan emigrants have been increasingly circulating in the region, with both national media and local word-of-mouth often reporting how migrants are sitting (i.e., out of work) in l-brra (Elliot 2015).

However, this factual, often strikingly accurate, knowledge of the economic situation of "the outside" tends to translate neither into decreased expectations put on returnee emigrants nor into the transformation of gendered, and moral, scales through which emigrants' ability (or not) to "move" is evaluated. Although Rashida and other family members acknowledged and even discussed openly Samir's unemployment in Italy, Samir's stillness back home was still read in gendered terms and related directly to his standing as a man. In other words, knowledge of economic realities and events in "the outside" does not eclipse, or erase, other regimes of value and evaluation through which individual persons are understood and expected to be when they return home. The gendered conceptualization of sitting effectively trumps economic rationalizations, and sitting remains about gender even if the reasons behind it are understood as also economic.

The fact that gendered expectations of emigrant men are resilient to economic considerations has tangible and even physical effects on those caught up, for better or worse, in such intersecting regimes of value and valuation. Samir probably preferred spending many hours in the gendered space of the home to facing the pressing expectations positioned on emigrant men outside of it. He did not have the resources to move in the neighborhood as an emigrant man was expected to do—to leave extravagant tips, to have enough foreign-bought cigarettes to pass round at the café, and so on. Samir's sense of unease in the neighborhood manifested itself clearly in his bodily posture on those rare occasions when he did leave the house. On these increasingly rare outings, Samir had started walking in a stooped fashion, his head lowered toward the ground, his feet dragging on the street. This was a very different picture from the man who had arrived from Italy confident and radiant at the beginning of the summer. "*Mabaynsh rajel meskin* [he doesn't appear/look like a man, poor thing]," Samir's mother told me when we were looking out of the window one evening and noticed her son slowly walking toward the house.

Therefore, it was not only through his "building stasis" that Samir's gendered standing was coming under scrutiny back home. This stasis—visible in the unfinished house itself—was the palpable manifestation of his stillness in a variety of different realms. And the longer Samir stayed still in Morocco, the more problematic this sitting became. It is probably also for this reason that when Samir one day announced *"ana ghadi"* (I'm going, i.e., I'm returning to Italy), a palpable sense of relief was felt in the Ghzaouli household. Let me consider for a moment the significance of this departure and address how, for men like Samir, returning to "the outside" becomes a fundamental way to counterbalance their precarious standing in Morocco.

THE GENDER OF THE CROSSING

Like the whistling of the pressure cooker full of meat, vegetables, and spices that can be heard at lunchtime in any Moroccan alleyway, Samir's phrase "ana ghadi" (I am going) finally let the pressure whistle out of the Ghzaouli household. His mother, wife, and sister started baking sweets for Samir to take back to Italy; his brothers rushed to the weekly market to buy mint, olive oil, and olives; his children started spending more time indoors with him. The whole household got involved in packing Samir's bag. His wife washed his favorite shirts; his children helped fold his clothes. His mother took his passport out of the drawer in the kitchen where it had been locked away throughout Samir's stay, the key dangling safely from her apron. Both children sat on Samir's suitcase when it was eventually time to close it, laughing hard with their father as the three of them undertook the seemingly impossible task of closing the zipper. The whole family ended up joining them in the bedroom, everyone with different advice on how to get the bag to close and, by the end, in tears of laughter.

Samir's imminent departure had the effect of clicking a switch—the house was once again bustling with preparations, laughter, and special foods. Friends and relatives called in to say goodbye, and the house became, for about three days, full of people, tea, big meals, children running in and out the front door, music. The festive, special atmosphere that characterized Samir's arrival reappeared for his imminent departure. On both arrival and departure, Samir's position in the household was strikingly unambiguous and clear-cut. He busied himself to make sure his guests had enough to eat and that his bag was being packed correctly, had boisterous conversations with his friends, and made witty appreciative comments about his wife's beauty when she was serving them tea. Samir became transformed on these occasions. He was the proud head of the household, and all the activities and movements of food and goods and guests were centered around him. When his imminent departure was being celebrated, Samir appeared firmly "in his place." In these moments, his wife, his mother, and indeed any onlooker could not accuse him of being *"mashi rajel"* (not a man).

Once Samir left for Europe, the house changed again. The children were noisier, the arguments between mother and daughter-in-law grew harsher, the brothers took longer naps, less meat was served at mealtimes, and so on. It was as if the house had been put on hold for a couple of months, walking on tiptoes around the problematically "still" household head. Gradually, references and stories about Samir in l-brra would reemerge in family daily conversations, and Samir would be positioned once more in his proper mode of existence: that of an emigrant man in "the outside," rather than of someone "sitting like a woman" back home.

The whole family knew that what Samir was returning to in "the outside" was also stillness—the stillness of unemployment. This awareness, however, did not seem to affect the value people around Samir attached to his crossing back into Europe. The fact that he still had the ability (and indeed quality) to move in and out of l-brra made Samir's stillness in Italy virtually irrelevant. But whereas in "the outside," gales was about lack of employment, bad luck, laziness, or racism of the *nsara* (Christians/Westerners), in Morocco, gales was about personhood and, more specifically, gendered personhood.

It is in this sense that I am suggesting the performance, and indeed embodiment, of masculinity of emigrants like Samir is attached—by a thin, precarious thread—to their ability to move between Morocco and "the outside." As long as his visit remained a visit and not a stay, Samir's temporary sitting in Morocco was tense and odd but just about acceptable. If this movement between home and abroad were to be indefinitely interrupted, this would have fundamental consequences on Samir. In that case, "sitting like a woman" would become definite and definitive rather than temporary and transient. The conceptualization of "the outside" as a place of possibility, part of a cosmos where cause and effect, work and money, movement and sitting follow different kinds of logics (Elliot 2021), made Samir's inexorable return to l-brra, despite his recent bad luck there, a fundamental, undeniable quality of his personhood. Indeed, this was what anchored him to the position of being an adult man (*rajel*), despite his sporadic presences resembling more those of an unmarried girl (*bent*) "sitting at home." Samir's gendered self could be seen as being continually reformed and reinstated through the repetition of the crossing into "the outside."

I suggest that this process of continual reformation and reinstatement of gendered selves through the repetition of the crossing is true for many emigrant men in the area. Indeed, my sense is that even in the case of very successful emigrants, the gendered qualities of their personhood are deeply engrained in their movements to and from "the outside." Samir's wealthy emigrant neighbor, Hajj Khalid, provides a good example of this, and though I run the risk of simplifying his story because I can only touch on it briefly here, his case does reveal how wealthy emigrants can also see their personhood questioned in gendered terms when they return home.

Hajj Khalid's five-story, detached house was just a few streets away from the Ghzaouli household. Hajj Khalid's imposing house reflected the success of his migratory trajectory. He had left for Italy in the mid-1980s and always found ways to earn money there. Throughout his years as an emigrant, Khalid had built five houses in his hometown and its outskirts, each with several apartments. He had also been on two Mecca pilgrimages (an extremely costly and prestigious venture), married three women (and divorced one), and had seven children, all but one of whom now lived in Italy. Whenever he returned to Morocco, Hajj Khalid engaged in multiple doings: he would start building a new house, enrich the decorations of his older houses, pay for a lavish wedding for one of his relatives, and organize big meals to celebrate the victory of a local politician he had sponsored in the latest elections. When I first met him in the summer of 2009, Hajj Khalid was in the middle of prolonged, and animated, negotiations about the price of a piece of land behind one of his houses. His plan was to build a mosque—it would be, he told me, an offering to God, and a gift to the neighborhood where he grew up.

To my surprise, the neighborhood was not as enthusiastic as Hajj Khalid about the building of the mosque. Indeed, the people I knew in the neighborhood were not particularly enthusiastic about anything that Hajj Khalid had done throughout his three decades of migration. Most people in the neighborhood spoke of Hajj Khalid with contempt. Although I was accustomed to the criticisms and mocking of emigrants, I was surprised that this criticism was directed specifically at Hajj Khalid's masculinity. It was the emphasis people put on Hajj Khalid's failure to behave like a man that brought to my attention how gendered scrutiny was directed not only to those men who failed to "move" like Samir, but also to other, more successful, and definitely more "active" migrants. "He's not a man, he's a princess [*princesse*, in French]," people would tell me when I asked about Hajj Khalid. "He just wants, wants, wants [*bgha bgha*] and buys everything, without measure."

These comments could be read simply as expressions of envy on the part of Hajj Khalid's less wealthy neighbors, and undoubtedly they did contain elements of this. However, they also refer just as significantly to another key element: the lack of measure in Hajj Khalid's behavior. Hajj Khalid's excessiveness in things that signify and generate "men" in the area (marriage, pilgrimage, house-making) was calling into question, rather than enhancing, his gendered standing. In the eyes of neighbors and even relatives, this excess risked becoming a parody of manhood rather than an inventive reiteration of it. A *"rajel bla qyas"* (man without measure) was not necessarily more of a man than one who did not have the resources to move at all (cf. Gilsenan 1996; Osella and Osella 2000). By failing to attune his emigrant success to the neighborhood requirements, Hajj Khalid, like Samir, had made the place he occupied at home controversial. It was his repeated crossings to "the outside," and his prolonged absences, that somehow counterbalanced the tensions and questioning that his brief and intense appearances produced. If men like Samir or Hajj Khalid were somehow to "protect" the gendered personhoods they had acquired by originally emigrating, it was not acceptable for either of them to spend extensive amounts of time back home. The "double absence" of migrants discussed by Abdelmalek Sayad (1999) in his opus on Algerian migrations takes on palpable, even necessary properties.

I have come across few cases of men who have made one initial crossing to "the outside" and then settled indefinitely back in the area being spoken of with respect and admiration. Rather, I would say that a parallel is drawn between their interrupted interaction with "the outside" and a precarious interruption of their *rejla* (masculinity/manhood). Many of the younger men who have returned to live in Morocco did not come back of their own free will but because they were deported—put on a boat or plane by the Spanish or Italian border police and handed over to the Moroccan authorities. *"Kharjouh"* (they exited him), someone will mutter quietly to me, nodding toward a man passing us in the street. Deportation often occurs when emigrants have not yet accumulated, or have lost, resources and status to embody the kinds of migratory and gendered qualities expected back home; in Italy, especially, policies of *rimpatrio* (deportation) generally target migrants who are most socially and economically vulnerable. This makes those men who have been to "the outside" but can no longer return a particular type, and their behaviors and attitudes are often described by onlookers as being womanlike: they spend most hours of the day in the house, walk quickly in the street while keeping their eyes to the ground, rarely show their faces in coffee bars, and stop to talk only with older women from the neighborhood. It takes a lot of resources, guts, and inventiveness to convey a sense of "complete manhood" when the emigrant component has disappeared from one's personhood. This means that most men who have been to l-brra keep repeating "the crossing" throughout their lives if they can.

REPEATING MANHOOD

The repeated, lifelong crossing between home and "the outside" of emigrant men testifies to the deeply precarious nature of what Ghannam (2013) calls "gender materialization." This materialization is precarious because, as we have seen, it can be called into question at any moment—when a house is left "undone" for too long, when a body sits idle at the wrong time and in the wrong place, or even when a global financial crisis limits an emigrant's "doing" abilities. But emigrants' materialization of masculinity is also precarious in the sense that it is not permanent and instead needs to be reiterated and reinstated throughout a lifetime. In other words, for men like Samir, gender trajectories are not settled with their original crossing into Europe. As much of the migration literature testifies, one's first crossing—generally a clandestine and dangerous passage—is framed as a gendered act and often as an explicit passage into male adulthood: "*wulla rajel temma*" (he became a man there), mothers tell me of their migrant sons. But in order to remain men, emigrants need to sustain, in time and in space, their constitutive relationship with "the outside" inaugurated with their first crossing.

This sustainment pivots around different kinds of movements on different kinds of scales—from intimate movements of the body in the domestic sphere to the transnational movement of remittances. However, it is the repetition of the crossing between home and abroad that anchors emigrant men most firmly to a recognized and recognizable gendered existence. This repetition is what makes an emigrant man a man, or a man an emigrant man—here, crucially, one and the same.

This repetition is not without consequences. A few years ago, I was sitting with my friend Zahra in front of her house, enjoying the evening breeze. Zahra was telling me a story I have heard time and again from wives of emigrants in Morocco. She was describing to me how her husband looked worse, different, and changed every time he returned home from Italy. On this particular visit, she said, he looked worse than ever. "It's as if he isn't here," she whispered to me. "His head and his spirit are broken/ruined [*khessru*]." While speaking, she gestured toward me for a coin and started rubbing it on a paper tissue she had opened on her lap. After a few strokes, the tissue tore. Zahra lifted the tissue to look through the rip in the dimming evening light. "Repeat [*'awed*], repeat too many times and it will tear," she murmured.

I have argued in this chapter that repetition of "the crossing" anchors emigrant men to a recognized and recognizable existence in Morocco. But while repetitive contact with l-brra makes certain strands of social, and gendered, existence possible, it also fundamentally threatens others. This is because the gendered subjects who emerge through a repeated contact with "the outside" are of a specific kind. As we have seen in this chapter, it is not only the case that through their repeated crossings into Europe emigrants become the adult, and at times wealthy, selves that they (are) expected to become. Emigrants' personhood comes to be inextricably linked to "the outside," which in turn becomes a personal quality as much as a geographical location. Emigrants are seen as fundamentally transformed—and not necessarily in good ways—by "the outside." "The outside" is at times attributed with the ability to "*dkhel f bnadem*" (enter into people/humans) and even the power to "fill in," or perhaps "hollow out," emigrants completely, making them near invisible when at home, just as the Algerian emigrants of the mid-twentieth century described by Sayad (1999) were nonexistent in France and back home.

In short, it is common knowledge in emigrant areas of central Morocco that repeated contact with "the outside" produces deep, nonnegotiable difference. This difference is at once enthralling and tragic. It is enthralling because "the outside" adds *shi haja* (something) to one's person, and this shi haja puts a migrant on a different scale to nonmigrants. Whether it is because of the economic success that, at times, results from their venture, because of l-brra's quasi-cosmological powers intruding into emigrants' bodies, or because they embody the legal as well as imaginative possibility of transnational movement for others, "the outside" makes emigrants special kinds of men.

Specialness, however, contains within it the potential for strangeness and estrangement—and often emigrant men return home only to be treated as awkward subjects. I identify this as the tragic side of l-brra's involvement in the formation of gendered subjects because, if on the one hand migration is grounded in a desire for difference, then on the other it is grounded in a desire for what could be conceived as a form of sameness.

In central Morocco, while on the one hand one leaves for "the outside" to change, on the other hand one leaves to stay the same (cf. Pedersen 2007). One leaves to become different, independent, and special. Yet there is also a deep desire for repetition underlining the movement of young men in particular: one moves in order to stay the same, hoping to become the man one is expected to be, to be the father one's father was, to have the means and the possibilities to offer sameness to one's family. Something goes "wrong" with migration, however, or maybe something goes "too right." Either way, repetitive crossing into l-brra throughout a lifetime makes repetition at other scales difficult, if not impossible.

The repeated movement between home and abroad is what enables men to remain men. However, the difference produced through this repetition is also what ultimately erodes the very gendered and relational projects that migration is imagined to nurture. As Zahra showed me with a coin, repetition of the crossing can wear people out—physically, emotionally, and relationally—until they may even tear.

NOTES

1. This chapter draws on research conducted in Darija, Moroccan Arabic. Words and quotes have been translated into English by the author. All personal names have been changed.
2. This chapter is based on a section of my monograph *The Outside: Migration as Life in Morocco* (IUP, 2021).
3. See Gabriele Vom Bruck's (1997) critical engagement with Pierre Bourdieu's (1977) essay *The Kabyle House*, where she interrogates the classic homologies man:woman/public:private/outside:inside—prevalent in popular analyses of the Muslim world—by bringing into the picture status, age, and the nested and relational gendering of space.
4. See David Crawford's (2008) study of the distinctly political value of "empty time" in a High Atlas Amazigh village.

BIBLIOGRAPHY

Ali, Syed. 2007. "'Go West Young Man': The Culture of Migration among Muslims in Hyderabad, India." *Journal of Ethnic and Migration Studies* 33, no. 1: 37–58.

Amar, Paul. 2011. "Middle East Masculinity Studies: Discourses of 'Men in Crisis,' Industries of Gender in Revolution." *Journal of Middle East Women's Studies* 6, no. 3: 36–70.

Bourdieu, Pierre. 1977. "The Kabyle House and the World Reversed." In *Outline of a Theory of Practice*, 271–283. Cambridge: Cambridge University Press.

Butler, Judith. 1990. *Gender Trouble: Gender and the Subversion of Identity*. New York: Routledge.

Chu, Julie Y. 2010. *Cosmologies of Credit: Transnational Mobility and the Politics of Destination in China*. Durham, NC: Duke University Press.

Crawford, David. 2008. *Moroccan Households in the World Economy: Labour and Inequality in a Berber Village*. Baton Rouge: Louisiana State University Press.

Dalakoglou, Dimitris. 2010. "Migrating-Remitting-'Building'-Dwelling: House Making as 'Proxy' Presence in Postsocialist Albania." *Journal of the Royal Anthropological Institute* 16:761–777.

De Haas, Hein. 2007. "Morocco's Migration Experience: A Transitional Perspective." *International Migration* 45:39–70.

Elliot, Alice. 2015. "Crisis on the Opposite Shore: Notes from the Field on Crisis, Revolution, and the Possible." *Allegra Laboratory*, August 20.

———. 2016a. "The Makeup of Destiny: Predestination and the Labor of Hope in a Moroccan Emigrant Town." *American Ethnologist* 43(3): 489–499.

———. 2016b. "Paused Subjects: Waiting for Migration in North Africa." *Time and Society* 25, no. 1: 102–116.

———. 2021. *The Outside: Migration as Life in Morocco.* Bloomington: Indiana University Press.

Gaibazzi, Paolo. 2015. *Bush Bound: Young Men and Rural Permanence in Migrant West Africa.* New York: Berghahn Books.

Ghannam, Farha. 2013. *Live and Die Like a Man: Gender Dynamics in Urban Egypt.* Stanford, CA: Stanford University Press.

Gilsenan, Michael. 1996. *Lords of the Lebanese Marches: Violence and Narrative in an Arab Society.* London: I. B. Tauris.

Herzfeld, Michael. 1985. *The Poetics of Manhood: Contest and Identity in a Cretan Mountain Village.* Princeton, NJ: Princeton University Press.

Inhorn, Marcia C., and Nefissa Naguib, eds. 2018. *Reconceiving Muslim Men: Love and Marriage, Family and Care in Precarious Times.* New York: Berghahn Books.

Jónsson, Gunvor. 2008. "Migration Aspirations and Immobility in a Malian Soninke Village." International Migration Institute Working Paper 10.

Kandel, William, and Douglas S. Massey. 2002. "The Culture of Mexican Migration: A Theoretical and Empirical Analysis." *Social Forces* 80, no. 3: 981–1004.

Lopez, Sarah Lynn. 2015. *The Remittance Landscape: Spaces of Migration in Rural Mexico and Urban USA.* Chicago: Chicago University Press.

Marsden, Magnus. 2007. "All-Male Sonic Gatherings, Islamic Reform, and Masculinity in Northern Pakistan." *American Ethnologist* 34, no. 3: 473–490.

McMurray, David A. 2001. *In and Out of Morocco: Smuggling and Migration in a Frontier Boomtown.* Minneapolis: University of Minnesota Press.

Menin, Laura. 2016. "Men Do Not Get Scared! (*rjjala mā tāy-khāfūsh*): Luck, Destiny and the Gendered Vocabularies of Clandestine Migration in Central Morocco." *Archivio Antropologico Mediterraneo* 18, no. 1: 25–36.

Mernissi, Fatima. 1988. *Doing Daily Battle: Interviews with Moroccan Women.* London: Women's Press.

Osella, Filippo, and Caroline Osella. 2000. "Migration, Money and Masculinity in Kerala." *Journal of the Royal Anthropological Institute* 6:117–133.

Pandolfo, Stefania. 2007. "The Burning: Finitude and the Politico-Theological Imagination of Illegal Migration." *Anthropological Theory* 7, no. 3: 329–363.

Pedersen, Morten Axel. 2007. "Multiplicity without Myth: Theorising Darhad Perspectivism." *Inner Asia* 9, no. 2: 311–328.

Salih, Ruba. 2003. *Gender in Transnationalism: Home, Longing and Belonging among Moroccan Migrant Women*. London: Routledge.

Sayad, Abdelmalek. 1999. *La Double Absence. Des Illusions de l'Émigré aux Souffrances de l'Immigré* [The double absence: From the illusions of the emigrant to the suffering of the immigrant]. Paris: Le Seuil.

Schielke, Samuli. 2015. *Egypt in the Future Tense: Hope, Frustration and Ambivalence before and after 2011*. Bloomington: Indiana University Press.

Smythe, SA. 2018. "The Black Mediterranean and the Politics of Imagination." *Middle East Report: Suffering and the Limits of Relief* 286:3–9.

Vom Bruck, Gabriele. 1997. "A House Turned Inside Out: Inhabiting Space in a Yemeni City." *Journal of Material Culture* 2, no. 2: 139–172.

ALICE ELLIOT is Lecturer in the Department of Anthropology at Goldsmiths, University of London. She is author of *The Outside: Migration as Life in Morocco* and coeditor of *Methodologies of Mobility: Ethnography and Experiment*.

"I AM A GOOD MAN—I'M A GARDENER!"

Arab Migrant Fathers' Reactions to Mistrusted Masculinity in Denmark

ANNE HOVGAARD JØRGENSEN

INTRODUCTION

The Danish society has contributed to a marginalization of the [refugee] father and his role and position in the family.... There is a need to do things differently ... also in relation to home-school cooperation, right? Because, if the teachers keep having the idea, that [the refugee father] is dangerous and violent, and therefore do not tell him what is going on in school . . . the father loses his position in the family.

These are the words of Alim, now a father, who was born in Lebanon as a Palestinian refugee and then fled to Denmark with his parents as a child. In this chapter, we meet Arab migrant fathers, such as Alim, who face a particular set of intersubjective experiences concerning mistrust in their encounters with teachers, *pædagoger*,[1] and social workers. These fathers were born in Arab countries such as Lebanon, Morocco, and Palestine and have, at some point in their lives, immigrated or fled to Denmark, where they later became fathers. The chapter shows how these fathers were engaged actors, individually governing their own lives; they were complicit in their own fates and not simply insignificant and impotent creatures of circumstances (Jackson 2013, 15). It analyzes how these Arab fathers' encounters with school professionals were affected by power relations and by their own abilities to navigate the school context. In addition, it analyzes how a sentiment of mistrust toward their "Arab masculinity" is entangled in these fathers' lifeworlds in various ways. I suggest the concept of "mistrusted masculinity" (Jørgensen 2017) as an etic concept to capture this phenomenon of mistrust, which I discovered as I listened and learned from these Arab fathers during my fieldwork.[2] As such, this chapter asks how Arab migrant fathers experience and react to school professionals' distrust of them as caring fathers.

FIELDWORK AND METHODS

This chapter focuses on three Arab fathers' narratives, which portray various positions, challenges, and strategies in the context of the Danish state school and welfare state. The narratives are part of my broader fieldwork on migrant fathers' experiences with and navigation of home-school cooperation (Jørgensen 2019). The ethnographic material is collected from five months of fieldwork at the Rosendal School, a Danish state school. The Danish state school system (*folkeskole*) is responsible for the basic education of the vast majority of the new generation of Danish children; in 2015, it educated 81 percent of Danish children (Gilliam 2017, 99). Over a five-month period in 2015, I participated in everyday life at the school, observed fifty parent-teacher conferences and other parent events at the school, and visited families in their homes and in the community center at the housing project, where some of the families lived (Jørgensen 2019). I also conducted participant observation and interviews in so-called fathers' groups in Danish, or in the father's first language with help from an interpreter. These fathers' groups had various structures, but the two fathers' groups presented in this chapter were part of a nationwide "community regeneration master plan initiative" (*boligsociale helhedsplaner*). The goal was to create positive developments in deprived and marginalized social housing estates through initiatives focusing on empowering, counseling, and crime-prevention programs (Andersen et al. 2014). My informants have all been provided with new names, and their personal information has been slightly changed to protect anonymity. My research followed the ethical standards defined by the American Anthropological Association (2012).

THE "ETHNIC OTHER"

It is important to describe the context of being an immigrant or refugee in Denmark. In Denmark, political debates on migrants have ensued since the first so-called guest workers came to Denmark in the late 1960s (Dindler and Olsen 1988; Pedersen and Selmer 1991). Hereafter, historical and political events have caused heated debates between political actors around issues of integration, nationality, democracy, and "Danishness." During these debates, the categories used to describe migrants are many, often referring to the "ethnic Other."

As such, people with "another ethnic background" or "non-ethnic Danes" are categories constructed in opposition to "ethnic Danes" (Jørgensen 2019). Such terms often refer to immigrants and refugees from the Global South, and in recent years this tendency has strengthened, with the category of "non-Western immigrants, refugees and their descendants."[3] This category has moved from statistical research into political debate and law, where this specific type of migrant is often constructed as the most problematic migrant (Gilliam 2018; Jørgensen 2019, 13). This tendency has been intensified by neonationalist streams in Denmark and throughout Europe, entangled in the recent refugee crises caused by the Syrian Civil War and by intensifying political tensions concerning migration and Islam (Jørgensen 2019, 13–14; Pedersen and Rytter 2011). This construction of the "non-Western person" is embedded in certain political and historical processes of Islamophobia and an Orientalist discourse. Here, the West is constituted as comprised of the "civilized nations" in opposition to "the rest," the "non-West" (see, e.g., Christensen, Larsen, and Jensen 2017; Gilliam 2018; Inhorn 2012; Said 1986). In this way, categories such as the "ethnic Other" or "non-Western immigrant" function to both Other and essentialize Arab migrant fathers in media and political rhetoric.

A "RACE-BLIND IDEOLOGY"

Many of my interlocutors felt that their foreign background meant something (also see Jensen 2010). The characteristics of physical appearance, such as brown skin color and black hair, less-than-perfect Danish, an Arab name, or being Muslim, especially in combination, seemed to acquire salience in their everyday lives. In his study of how these characteristics acquire various meanings, anthropologist Peter Hervik (2015, 31) argues that there is a "race-blind ideology" in Denmark in line with the general idea that physical differences do not mean "anything." He argues that in the Scandinavian countries, the term *race* is seen as referring to the racist German Nazi ideology, the oppression of African Americans in the United States, and the apartheid system of South Africa. Hervik's argument is that the relative underemphasis on racism is reinforced by the general egalitarian philosophy of the Scandinavian welfare model and the core value of equality in the Danish "self-identity." According to anthropologist Laura Gilliam (2009, 244), this "color blindness" is reinforced by the fact that until approximately fifty years ago, Denmark had no large population that could be termed Black and could thus articulate Danish "whiteness" as a racial characteristic rather than just the norm. This stands in contrast to the American context, for example, where race and color are more openly discussed (Hervik 2015). Following the argument of a "race-blind ideology," it has been argued that racism is still an undercurrent in the strong nationalist discourse in which physical color differences are not directly mentioned, but nevertheless it is granted significance through essentialist notions of specific ethnicities/cultures as incompatible with "Danish culture or nationality" (Hervik 2015, 46; Jensen 2010, 7).

Some of my interlocutors told me that their children had begun to claim that they were Danish, too. This might point to the emerging possibilities for new identity formations among new generations, as previous studies have found that so-called ethnic-minority children and youth tend to refrain from identifying themselves as Danes (Gilliam 2009, 239; Gitz-Johansen 2006; Jensen 2010). Belonging as they did to an older generation and not born in Denmark, the fathers in my study did not define themselves as Danish. They tended to use words like "foreigner," "refugee," or "immigrant" to describe themselves and "people like them" from other Arab, Middle Eastern, or Muslim countries. When we talked about their own childhoods and their own fathers, their original nationalities became important, but in discussing everyday encounters with school professionals in Denmark, the Arab fathers would often categorize themselves as "foreigners" or "immigrants." This categorization may be a product of the simplifying dichotomy of the Danes versus not-ethnic-Danes discourse mentioned earlier, a discourse that renders differences within the non-ethnic-Danes category less visible. Moreover, the category "Arab" is not much used in Danish everyday language, and if it is used, it is sometimes incorrectly used to mean "Muslims in Denmark" or to include people with an origin in other common migrant-sending countries such as Pakistan, Iran, or Turkey.

LINES OF BECOMING

The idea of intersubjectivity originates from phenomenological thoughts about how the human being is situated in an already existing world that is loaded with meaning and how this meaning is shared in interexperiences (Jackson 1996, 27). In this way, our understandings of the world are structured in accordance with the intersubjective handing over of preunderstanding and patterns into which we are socialized and that exist in an already shaped history (Rasmussen 2017, 67). Within phenomenologically inspired anthropology, scholars have discussed whether the prefix *inter-* in *intersubjectivity* successfully reproduces the dualistic separation of two subjects (Rasmussen 2017, 72–73). Following this, anthropologist Tim Ingold (2012, 2015) has used the metaphor of *lines of becoming* to argue that a frame of mind, a sentiment, or whatever social phenomenon is concerned is a product of the existence and entanglement of multiple objects and subjects. I use Ingold's term in a broad sense, viewing these lines as constituted by humans, things, histories, and discourses. While navigating life, people are constantly being influenced by various lines that affect their being in the world (also see Rasmussen 2017).

Following Ingold, we are placed in—or inhabit—a world that is already full of interweaving lines, and our intersubjective encounters can be seen as a kind of meshwork of these lines' entanglement (Ingold 2012, 49). This chapter argues that the intersubjective encounters between Arab fathers and Danish teachers can be seen as social happenings comprised of multiple lines of becoming, including mistrust. This chapter shows how this line of mistrust operated on different scales. First, I present how this line of becoming operated on a macro scale as in media and political rhetoric. Then I analyze how this line became entangled in the small-scale intersubjective encounters between Arab fathers and school professionals.

MISTRUSTED MASCULINITY

Professor of communications Rikke Andreasen has studied media discourses, and her analysis of the Danish media's representation of the Muslim man finds that there is a tendency to portray the Muslim man as dangerous and aggressive and the Muslim woman as vulnerable to violence and forced marriage (Andreasen 2007, 237; also see Seidenfaden 2010). The same tendency is seen in other European countries. Anthropologist Katherine Pratt Ewing (2008) argues that Muslim masculinity in Germany has experienced a stigmatization produced through the practice of governmentality, public debates, and the media. This phenomenon is the manifestation of a structure of social fantasy that underlines a German national imaginary, resting on the foundation of the abjection of a social Other (Ewing 2008, 20). Anthropologist Marcia C. Inhorn (2012, 51) suggests an era of "new Orientalism" in post–September 11 representations of the Middle East masculinity (also see Dalgaard 2016; Ewing 2008, 27–28) in Western popular culture. In this new Orientalism, the Muslim man exists as the Other, representing the antithesis of modern and enlightenment values. Here, the values of democracy are seen as the universal goal and as belonging to the West, and within the celebration of democracy, "traditional" gender roles are perceived as a Middle Eastern, underdeveloped cultural element contrary to Western egalitarian values (Ewing 2008, 28–29; also see Haga 2015, 40). The concept of gender equality also becomes a core value of the modern democratic family. Some of my interlocutors did believe that specific tasks were connected more to one gender than the other, which in the Danish debate on gender equality could be perceived as "traditional gender roles." I generally got the impression that this division of tasks was by mutual agreement (also see Elliot, this volume) and was based on the idea of men as closer to the role of the bread-winner and women as more involved in childcare (also see Liversage 2016),[4] although nearly all the mothers participated in the labor market.

By looking at the integration projects launched by the Danish welfare state, we see another indicator of marginalization of Arab masculinity. Sociologist Line Seidenfaden (2010) has conducted a thorough review of the Danish government's "Experience Database," containing five hundred integration projects launched between 2005 and 2011. Integration projects should here be understood as social empowerment projects with the purpose of helping immigrants and refugees to "integrate" into Danish society. Of the 500 projects, 105 were gender specific. Approximately two-thirds of these projects had an explicit gender perspective targeting adult women; just as many projects (15 percent) targeted girls/young women and boys/young men, whereas only 3 percent of the projects targeted adult men, and 2 percent targeted both men and boys. The survey thus shows a clear preponderance of projects targeting women (Seidenfaden 2010, 45). Of projects specifically concerning parenting, most were directed at mothers, whereas the few projects for men were focused on sports and on crime prevention (Seidenfaden 2010, 45).[5] Generally, Seidenfaden (2010) concludes, there has been a marginal focus on "men with ethnic minority background" as fathers, which points to a lack of interest in empowering immigrant or refugee fathers to fulfill their roles as caregiving parents. It is important to emphasize that the extent to which Denmark's welfare system penetrates education and employment means that the public sector is in some ways more key than civil society in fostering social mobility (Beckman et al. 2015, 38).

The representation of the masculinity of Arab fathers in media and political rhetoric, as well as its lack of inclusion in integration projects, reflects what Raewyn Connell (2012) has termed a "marginalized form of masculinity." This type of masculinity is constructed and suppressed in contrast to the hegemonic, "correct," superior, and dominant masculinity (Connell 2012, 81). When Arab men and fathers are portrayed as "backward," it works to construct the "Danish man" as "modern" and possessing the correct "Danish values." Connell emphasizes how race relations can play an integral part in such dynamics where, in white-supremacist contexts, "black masculinities" play symbolic roles for white gender constructions (Connell 2012, 80–81). Drawing from Connell, we see how Arab fathers' physical appearances may be constructed as "signs for suspicion," which points to the importance of discussing processes of racialization in the Danish context.

The marginalization of Arab masculinity on the macro scale could influence Arab fathers' being in the world. Alim, the father from the opening vignette, explained it this way: "I also think that [refugee fathers] have the feeling that they are not being taken seriously enough, and that they are seen as kind of evil people, right? That they are people who oppress their wives. . . . There is a perception that the father should be left out, because otherwise it could be harmful for the child. . . . There has been greater sympathy for the mother and no sympathy for the father, and this has resulted in the father being left out for many, many years."

Alim is a former educational leader in a youth club, where he took the initiative to involve fathers in the club's activities. His remarks characterize the sentiments and feelings captured by the concept of mistrusted masculinity (Jørgensen 2017).

"I AM A GOOD MAN—I'M A GARDENER!"

I have suggested that on a Danish macro level, Arab masculinity could be seen as what Connell (2012) terms a marginalized masculinity. I now aim to move from the macro to the micro level by presenting the Arab fathers' stories. Inspired by Inhorn's concept of "emergent" masculinities and fatherhood (Inhorn 2012; Inhorn, Chavkin, and Navarro 2015), I hope to challenge the concept of mistrusted masculinity that Arab men in Denmark both experience and articulate.

I met Omar, a forty-seven-year-old man originally from Morocco, in the fathers' group in Skovlunden, a disadvantaged neighborhood struggling with its crime-ridden public image. It turned out that not all the fathers present lived in Skovlunden. Some, including Omar, were fiery souls who came in as "resource-strong" fathers to help other less resourceful fathers in the area. During my time with this group, the fathers repeatedly wanted to challenge or change my views on the disadvantaged neighborhood and on them as "Arab fathers."

Omar had worked as a gardener for eighteen years. He had five children, and he told me with pride that they had all received, or were studying to receive, good educations. His eldest daughter had acquired the highest grades and was a midwife, which in Denmark is one of the most difficult professions to enter. Omar underlined how important it was that "everyone was free to have their own opinions" but that he would still switch television channels when someone from the Danish People's Party talked badly about Muslims or "foreigners" on television. He did not want his children to feel that Danish people were racists, he said. He was constantly worried they would lose self-esteem and feel unwanted.

In my interview with Omar, the theme of mistrust came up when he told me about his meeting with a *pædagog* at his one-and-a half-year-old daughter's nursery institution:

> My daughter, when she started in the nursery, I said to the pædagog that her Danish is not so good. . . . One day she bit one of the other children, and she did it again, and then eventually the pædagoger from the nursery called us [Omar and his wife] in for a meeting.[6] So the pædagoger thought: "There must be violence in that home. . . . Why does she bite the other children? There must be something wrong with that home!" See how they are thinking about us!

Omar was irritated as he continued explaining to me that there can be many different reasons why a child bites, such as pain when teeth are coming in. "I have told them that I am not a sick person, I am a good man, I am a gardener! I think that if the pædagoger are stressed out, and they [the other children] just take her toys away from her, and she doesn't know the language, she can't speak the language."

For Omar, the biting was his daughter's way of communicating, and in his view the pædagoger did not do enough to help her with her language problems: "They have to get more education, to be more open toward other cultures. Because it is just so important for us—I mean, us in Denmark." After some time, Omar's daughter stopped biting the other children. Omar thought it was because the other children stopped taking her toys away from her. For Omar, this was his proof that he was a good father after all—the biting was not because of him. Yet he felt the pædagoger were still keeping an eye on him. "They think I am violent," he repeated.

I was unsure of how directly the pædagoger had accused Omar of being violent or whether he had felt he was being accused because of language difficulties. Following Jonas Frykman and Nils Gilje (2003), this is not a crucial point because the story itself is a navigation toward explaining to me the mistrust Omar perceived toward his Arab masculinity. It is the current navigation per se rather than the concrete narrative that is central—not how the story is, but how it is used in a practical sense, or how the narrative creates meaning and coherence in a specific context (Frykman and Gilje 2003, 40). Accordingly, Omar is using his experience to tell me how it is to feel mistrusted. His references to "us immigrants" implied that he was somehow also speaking for Arab men in general. I argue that Omar's story is an example of how mistrust toward Omar's Arab masculinity became a central line of becoming in his encounters with professionals in everyday life in Denmark. These encounters indicate the existence of a negative controlling image (Collins 2000) of Arab masculinity as patriarchal, aggressive, oppressive, and violent (also see Jørgensen 2017).

What complicated the situation, Omar continued, was how teenagers in Skovlunden could become involved in reproducing this negative controlling image of the Arab father. If the police caught a teenager for a small crime, and the teenager blamed the parents, then the police or social authority would most likely listen to the teenager. "They don't even have to prove anything," Omar said. To clarify his point, he continued. "If the police come, the teenager will say, 'My dad hits me'—they are actually threatening their fathers . . . and from then on, the fathers cannot do anything anymore." The father now knew that there was a case on him (he was now under observation), and from now on he had to let his son do whatever he wanted, in the worst case spending time on the streets until late at night and risking getting into trouble. Families in Skovlunden knew of cases of intervention in families (in the worst case, the forced removal of a child), and the rumors spread. "It is just like a small village," Omar said. Some families in this disadvantaged neighborhood had difficulty understanding the motivation behind these interventions mainly because of limited resources in education and Danish-language skills, and they became anxious that this kind of intervention might happen to them (also see Johansen 2013). Following Omar, this fear of state intervention in the family could lead to a more laissez-faire upbringing than the fathers in Skovlunden felt was appropriate.

CORPORAL PUNISHMENT

According to Omar, teenagers exploited the issue of corporal punishment, resulting in accusations of violence against many fathers. Corporal punishment is legal in Arab countries (UNICEF 2014), and among Arab families living in Arab countries, it is sometimes considered an acceptable practice in child-rearing. Alim thought corporal punishment had been used in child-rearing among newly arrived immigrant or refugee families, but that it was no longer a common practice in child-rearing because families had integrated Danish norms. Omar hinted, without saying it directly, that physical punishment might occur in some homes, but he emphasized that this was with love. According to Omar, drawing clear boundaries between right and wrong is an important part of caring for your child and your child's future rather than taking a laissez-faire approach to child-rearing. For Omar, slapping your children on occasion to clarify boundaries, as acceptable. The laissez-faire approach was especially disliked in the disadvantaged neighborhood of Skov-lunden, where parents worried about the "dangers" of teenage boys getting into drug sales and the like (also see Beckman et al. 2015, 28). Thus, some parents felt that corporal punishment as a form of discipline helped teenage sons stay on the right track. It was rarely parents' first choice to live in disad-vantaged neighborhoods with a high crime rate, but some families were not able to move because they were on special rent allowances (with the state supporting their rent) and could not afford other types of housing (Beckman et al. 2015, 14).

In Denmark, corporal punishment was outlawed in 1985, and the law was further strengthened in 1997. Today the public discourse in Denmark does not tolerate the use of corporal punishment. Nevertheless, a 2011 survey showed that 20 percent of asked children in eighth grade classes in Denmark have expe-rienced corporal punishment (Oldrup et al. 2011).[7] This relatively high number came as a surprise to many. A 2017 survey looking specifically at the child-rearing of "ethnically Danish youngsters" compared with "ethnic-minority youngsters" concluded that although 5 percent of boys and 6 percent of girls of Danish eighteen-year-olds surveyed answered that they had experienced cor-poral punishment from their parents, the number for "ethnic-minority young-sters" was 9 percent for boys and 8 for girls (Liversage and Christensen 2017, 77).[8] Although the "ethnic-minority youngsters" category does not tell us the num-ber of solely Arab families, children of parents with Arab origin are included in this category. The report attributed this 2 or 4 percent increase among "ethnic-minority youngsters" to their lower social class and to the so-called cultural heri-tage of countries where corporal punishment might be considered a conventional part of child-rearing (Liversage and Christensen 2017, 77) The issue of corporal punishment is blurred and complex, but it may be argued that the generally high mistrust of Arab masculinity far exceeds the marginally higher incidence of 3 percent. In Omar's stories, the accusations of corporal punishment eventually seemed to escalate into comments like, "They think I'm violent." Due to the taboo on corporal punishment and the underlying mistrust, these accusations seem to have grown out of proportion.

According to Omar, the teenagers had learned from the pædagoger and schoolteachers that it was not their parents who were in charge at home. In cases of problems or disagreements, the teenagers knew they would receive the sup-port of teachers, social workers, or welfare workers, who would say, according to Omar, "Don't worry. We will help you; it is not your dad who decides at home [i.e., we do]." Religious studies scholar Rannveig Haga has found similar reports among her Muslim interlocutors in Sweden. Somali mothers have expressed that school officials assume that they do not know what is best for their own children. According to Danish mores, children should be "free" (Haga 2015, 40). In the Swedish context, as in Denmark, the concept of freedom is closely related to secularism and individualism (see also Bach 2017). Because Muslim child-rearing is perceived as traditional, authoritative, and nondemocratic, these parents felt that the pædagoger did not view them as resources in child-rearing. Haga concludes that parents wanted their children to be reflective and independent thinkers but also resisted their own and their children's disempowerment (Haga 2015, 52).

Omar's story highlights another essential point. His daughter's negative behavior in the nursery was being explained by problems within his family. In her study of "ethnic-minority pupils" in a Danish state school, Gilliam (2017) found how a class teacher often interpreted the behavior of "ethnic-minority pupils" in the school context in terms of her ideas about the "culture" at home. For example, she would declare that the unsatisfactory behavior of "the wild ethnic-minority boys" was due to the fact that the boys' parents were unable to restrict even their own behavior, or to a lack of positive attention at home, or to the idea that their parents were hitting them (Gilliam 2017), even though the teachers knew very little about these ethnic-minority pupils' homes. In Omar's story, too, the daughter's problematic behavior in the institution was explained by issues in the home. This sharply contrasts with my finding that my interlocutors perceived the family unit as the most important social sphere, and my observation of the fathers' strong identification as fathers in the fathers' groups (see also Inhorn 2012; Naguib 2015). Nabil's story further reinforces this phenomenon.

THE RULES OF THE GAME

Nabil was forty-eight years old and had grown up as a Palestinian refugee in Beirut, where he had experienced the "war of the camps," when the Shi'a Amal militia besieged the Palestinian refugee camps of Beirut during the 1984–1990 phase of the Lebanese civil war. The refugee camp in which Nabil and his family lived had been bombed while they were imprisoned there. In 1985, he lost his seventeen-year-old brother—he had simply disappeared, and no one knew what had happened to him—and half a year later, his father also died in the war. The terror Nabil had experienced still impacted him, and it was also the first thing he chose to tell me. I had prepared questions about school-home cooperation, but Nabil opened his story with recollections of the war. This became his way of framing his life story and thus also his way of making clear that it had affected all the other things we were to talk about. Struggling with

post-traumatic stress syndrome, Nabil was eventually awarded early retirement benefit (*førtidspension*) in Denmark, a stable but low income for the rest of his life.

After fleeing to Denmark, Nabil married Dora, also Palestinian, and they had three children together. Today, Marwan is twenty-two, Yasmin is nineteen, and Amin is fourteen. Amin has special needs and attends a special school. Later, Nabil and Dora were divorced, and since then Nabil has been trying to see his children as much as possible, which has been extremely difficult after a particular life-changing episode.

When Yasmin was thirteen, she attended a sports event, after which she was supposed to move into Nabil's home for the weekend (at this time, she was living in Nabil's home every other weekend). Late in the afternoon, Yasmin sent Nabil a text message saying she would not be home at 6:00 p.m. as agreed, but maybe she could make it at 10:30 p.m. Nabil texted her back, but Yasmin did not reply. Nabil then phoned the mother of Yasmin's good friend, who had also attended the event. The mother said that Yasmin was on her way to Nabil's place, but she did not arrive, and Nabil got very worried. It turned out that Yasmin had gone home with her girlfriend and intended to sleep at her house. Nabil got very upset, and at some point his son Marwan went to find Yasmin. Marwan made a big fuss in front of the friend's mother, and in the end the police showed up and told him to leave. The friend's mother started to speak badly about Nabil and tried to convince Yasmin not to return to him. Dora then decided that she wanted full custody over Yasmin and took the case to court. Nabil was convinced that he would lose all custody rights. Moreover, at the time Yasmin preferred to stay with Dora, according to Nabil, because Dora set very few restrictions on her behavior. In Nabil's view, Dora's approach to their children's upbringing was too laissez-faire. Convinced he would lose custody, Nabil still insisted on taking the case to court because he did not want his daughter to think, when she grew up, that her father wanted to relinquish their relationship. As expected, Nabil lost all custody. From that point, he had to give in to Dora's preferences.

Sometimes she would ask him, at just a few hours' notice, to host the children at his place for the weekend. Nabil was always prepared for this; he did not want to say no to his children, and he was afraid that if he did say no, Dora would not ask him next time. According to Nabil, there was nothing he could do. These were the rules of the game.

Gradually, Dora became less reliable. On one occasion the school contacted Nabil because they were worried about his son Amin. Sometimes he did not come to school, and he seemed not to be cared for properly. Nabil had to tell the school that there was nothing he could do because he had no custody rights

over Amin, but he suggested the school write a report (*underretning*), which it did a few times.

Gradually, Dora asked Nabil to take the children more and more often, and Yasmin and Amin ended up mostly living at Nabil's house. Sometimes all three children ended up staying with him for the whole week. It was challenging for him to provide for all three children on his early retirement pension, and he was already paying monthly child support to Dora. Nabil's son Marwan almost became a street child, Nabil explained, because Dora could not control him, and Nabil had no authority to contain his behavior because Marwan's legal address was his mother's home. Marwan would leave whenever Nabil tried to control his behavior.

Today, things have changed. As Dora became less stable, Nabil managed to regain custody over Amin, who now lives permanently with Nabil. Yasmin often lived with him while she was in high school, but her legal address was still her mother's home. The new situation required many meetings with the social worker and a lot of paperwork. Nabil proudly told me about a report in Amin's case files stating that Amin was always ready and prepared on the mornings when the school taxi came to collect him from Nabil's place, which was not always the case when he was staying at his mother's house.[9]

Nabil's story reflects existing structures in the Danish welfare system. No one attempted to include Nabil in child-rearing or to empower him in his role as father until the conditions at Dora's place became unacceptable. This argument is supported by Seidenfaden's (2010) study, which shows how migrant fathers were overlooked in integration projects. In a study of similar cases with migrant fathers in the United Kingdom, Bridget Featherstone (2003) found that few specific initiatives have been developed for fathers, particularly addressing their role and identity as fathers. Featherstone also argues that initiatives to develop better visiting arrangements, or other initiatives directed at fathers, may arouse hostility from mothers and may be perceived as discriminatory, and that this needs to be understood and worked on by social workers and school pædagoger, who are often women (see also Gupta and Featherstone 2015).

During our talk, it was clear that Nabil was embarrassed by his son's behavior on that crucial night. I asked him if the incident resulted in any kind of charge or penalty for him or for Marwan. "No, no," he said. "Nothing happened. Of course, I got really angry . . . but I do not hit. No." This highlights another point made by Featherstone. In-depth investigations of criminal records of poor migrant fathers living in the United Kingdom show that the matters on record were sometimes not "real cases," and that therefore it had been wrong to prevent the specific father from seeing their children. According to Featherstone

(2003), assumptions about a certain kind of "untrustworthy" masculinity were in play in these cases. It may be argued that Nabil's case also escalated and that from a legal point of view, the incident led to too radical an outcome.

Moreover, it was Nabil's son, not Nabil, who acted out that evening, which points back to another important factor: perceptions of the father's character can be distorted by his children. As Omar's daughter's biting was explained by Omar's assumed violent behaviors, Marwan's aggressive behaviors were perceived as reflecting the conditions in Nabil's home and as an extension of Nabil's violent, uncontrollable masculinity. Nabil also mentioned that Yasmin and Marwan fought a lot as teenagers, which may also have been a factor in the dramatic event. In conclusion, the "uncontrollable" children might, in their actions, have been uncontrollable meaning-carriers of their father's personality and masculinity, and the teenager's own agendas seems to have been overlooked.

"MY WIFE WAS HEARTBROKEN, AND I SAID, 'I'LL GO DIRECTLY TO THE TEACHER'"

The third father, Kadin, was forty-four and born in Morocco. Kadin's story highlights his efforts to disturb the lines of becoming that lay in wait for him and his daughter by incorporating his own knowledge about the Danish educational system. The story exemplifies how lines of becoming are in motion, how they can be pushed a bit, and how they can change direction.

Kadin and his wife, Amira, who was also Moroccan in origin, had two children. Nadia, the youngest, was thirteen and was a student in one of the classes where I carried out my five-month participant observation. I got to know her well. She was open, talkative, and popular with her teachers. Kadin was working as a teacher at a language school, teaching Danish language to refugees and immigrants.

When I asked Kadin if he had had any negative experiences with the school, he answered, "Well, there is this single episode," and began his story. Kadin explained to me how in the grade 0 class, Nadia had had a language test and performed very badly.[10] According to Kadin, Nadia was having a bad day. The result was so poor that the teacher thought Nadia had serious problems—not only academic but also social. The teacher abruptly and severely told Nadia's mother, Amira, that there were serious problems with Nadia. Both Kadin and his wife were surprised because they had heard a quite different story from the day care center. Amira's limited command of Danish at the time made it difficult for her to react to the teacher's severe approach, and she felt "run over" by the teacher and saddened that she sounded as if she had given up on Nadia. Kadin went back to the teacher a few days later and explained that Amira would like a proper meeting about Nadia's future and would also like a representative from the school's educational administration to participate in the meeting. During the meeting, Kadin and his wife argued for a less dramatic reaction to the test, and the meeting went well. The teacher and Kadin agreed to wait and see whether Nadia needed special assistance. I told Kadin I thought he reacted properly and that many parents would not feel the same power to intervene. Kadin agreed: "Yes, exactly, that is what often happens. . . . I saw how my wife was heartbroken, and I said, 'I'll go directly to the teacher.' I told her, 'You have talked with my wife, and it was not a good conversation, so we need to talk together again.'"

Being bilingual is not perceived as beneficial in the Danish state school, and it has been argued that this category is loaded with additional meanings over and beyond language abilities (Gilliam 2009; Gitz-Johansen 2006). I argue that Nadia's father—because of his knowledge of the school system and his possession of the "correct" cultural and educational capital—managed to pull Nadia back from being placed into the category of "problematic bilingual child with special needs." By arguing "the right way," he challenged the category in which the teacher was about to place Nadia and her family. Since this incident, Kadin said, he has had no bad experiences with the school. Today, his daughter is one of the best performing in the class.

When I asked Kadin if he was a different father from his own father, he quickly agreed while laughing a bit. His father had been a builder in Morocco, and according to Kadin, "He was so different in many ways." He was a good father but was unable to help Kadin with his homework, and Kadin did not remember their having such a close relationship that he felt he had with his own children today. Kadin felt that the most important thing was for his children to get a good education and for Nadia to be happy in school. Kadin often helped his children with their homework; he and his son would discuss physics for hours, Nadia declared in an interview, in a rather "I don't get the fuss" tone.

Having a closer emotional relationship with one's child than one had with one's own father was a recurrent theme among my interlocutors. Some scholars term this generational shift "the new role of the father" (Jørgensen 2017, 3–4). This new role seems mainly to encompass having a more emotional relationship with one's children. There still seem to be gender-divided practical child-rearing tasks, such as preparing the lunch box (Bach 2017; Pless 2000). In the Danish context, this new role of the father has been studied only among native Danish middle-class fathers, but I experienced the same tendency among my interlocutors (Jørgensen 2017).

Kadin's story shows how the lines of becoming can be changed, if the Arab father has the correct capital and asserts it correctly. In our encounters and conversations and while observing the parent-teacher conferences between Nadia's teacher and her parents, I sometimes felt that Kadin had to neglect his "Arabness" in order to navigate successfully away from the mistrusted masculinity ascribed to him as an Arab father.

CONCLUSION

In this chapter, I examined how Arab fathers are influenced by intersubjective encounters with childcare and education professionals, especially in the Danish school system. Because these encounters are influenced by multiply entangled lines of becoming, I focus on the phenomenon of mistrust. This mistrust operates on different scales and becomes entangled in Arab fathers' encounters with school professionals in different ways. The fathers in this chapter strategically navigated in between and pushed these lines of becoming in their struggles to fulfill their roles as fathers and to achieve recognition thereof from significant others (Biehl and Locke 2017, 9). I then argue that the line of a mistrusted masculinity was constantly becoming entangled in the fathers' lives and forcing them to navigate it in various ways. This reveals important insight into the culture of Danish childcare institutions, and into society more broadly, where trust appears as a pivotal point for social interaction (Jørgensen 2019). In addition, that some Arab fathers were, from the very beginning, forced to earn the trust of childcare professionals points to a central inequality concerning the migrant fathers of this chapter: they had to regain trust from the outset.

Each encounter is different and may lead to a different outcome: whereas Kadin was able to change the directions of the lines that lay in wait for him and Nadia, Nabil did not have the resources to do the same. Among other factors, Nabil's poor Danish, an uncontrollable son, his PTSD, and his divorce made his "hand of cards" weaker than Kadin's. Nevertheless, he managed to regain custody of Amin.

It is notable that both Omar and Nabil described feeling "held back" from setting limits on their teenagers' behavior. By contrast, many fathers' groups founded by housing estates have a crime-reduction agenda, encouraging fathers to form "walking groups" to patrol the neighborhood in the evening to keep an eye on the "wild boys." A police officer affiliated with the fathers' group in Bøgelunden told me that the fathers "had to learn to take responsibility, as these young kids are simply running around in the neighborhood getting into crime." This is a well-known view among social workers, but the data in this study paradoxically suggest that some fathers feel prevented from setting boundaries in their child-rearing. I believe this finding deserves further investigation in social projects addressing these issues.

This study also shows how the children of the Arab fathers could be a kind of floating signifier. In navigating toward their own goals, the children could affect how their fathers were perceived. The teenagers described in this chapter were pragmatic individuals situated in their own lifeworlds. They created goals and were strategic about how to reach them, because people are, so to speak, always motivated by something and acting "in order to" (Schultz and Luckmann 1974, 74–75). These goals can be achieved by using the tools that the surroundings offer, and these tools can be signs and meanings (Schultz and Luckmann 1974, 74–75) Which tool was carefully selected according to the teenagers' knowledge and experience? It may be argued that the mistrusted masculinity of the Arab father was a powerful tool: as the teenagers navigated for more freedom, the perception of a controlling, patriarchal Arab father became a tool that was ready to use to undermine the fathers' authority. The Danish value of democratic individualism as a key component in the idea of the civilizing process in Danish child-rearing—that is, the philosophy that children should grow into strong, self-regulated, and independent individuals—further reinforces these teenagers' behavior.

Mistrusted masculinity was not always a central line in the intersubjective encounters. Peter, an experienced teacher at Rosendal School, thought the Arab fathers were doing the best they could, but he knew they were often up against long working hours and physically constraining jobs that made it hard for them to attend school events (Jørgensen 2017). In other words, mistrusted masculinity did not always have to be an important line of becoming in an encounter because the professionals differed and had different experiences. Nevertheless, when the subject of mistrust came up in my interviews, most Arab fathers had endured at least one episode of being mistrusted. Such experiences can leave their mark and color fathers' general perceptions of others' perceptions of them. Returning to the theory of intersubjectivity, these assumptions about the others' experience of my experience are central. In other words, what I think you think means something.

NOTES

1. *Pædagoger*, or "pedagogues," are specially trained educators mainly working with children in nurseries, kindergartens, and afterschool clubs.
2. This sentiment of mistrust also existed among immigrant and refugee fathers from other Middle Eastern and South Asian countries, who shared some

of the same characteristics (certain racialized characteristics, being Muslim, difficulties speaking Danish, etc.) as the Arab fathers in this study.

3. "Western countries" include all twenty-eight European Union countries, in addition to Andorra, Iceland, Liechtenstein, Monaco, Norway, San Marino, Switzerland, Vatican City, Canada, the United States, Australia, and New Zealand. "Non-Western countries" include "all the other countries" (Danmarks Statistik 2017).

4. This is a division of tasks found in many native Danish families (e.g., Bach 2017).

5. With the increased focus on fathers in recent years, the Danish government founded the project Baba in 2014. This project, the first of its kind, focuses on the individual and psychological development and empowerment of immigrant and refugee fathers.

6. The language has been slightly changed because Omar's (and Nabil's) Danish was a bit broken.

7. The survey found that 20 percent of the young people were exposed to physical violence from their parents within the last twelve months. Nearly 12 percent were exposed to violence more than once within the last twelve months.

8. The two surveys define "corporal punishment" slightly differently, which explains the differences in frequency.

9. Because Amin had special needs, he was picked up by a special school taxi every morning.

10. Students in the Danish grade 0 are generally six years old. The class takes place in school, and the students learn, among other things, the alphabet and basic math. It is equivalent to first grade in many countries.

BIBLIOGRAPHY

American Anthropological Association. 2012. *Statement on Ethics: Principles of Professional Responsibilities*. Arlington, VA: American Anthropological Association.

Andersen, Hans Thor, Anne Winther Beckman, Vigdis Blach, and Rikke Skovgaard Nielsen. 2014. "Governance Arrangements and Initiatives in Copenhagen." In *Governing Urban Diversity: Creating Social Cohesion, Social Mobility and Economic Performance in Today's Hyper-diversified Cities*. Copenhagen: SBi.

Andreasen, Rikke. 2007. *Der er et Yndigt Land* [There is a lovely country]. Aarhus: Tiderne Skifter.

Bach, Dil. 2017. "The Civilized Family Life: Childrearing in Affluent Families." In *Children of the Welfare State: Civilizing Practices in Schools, Childcare and Families*, edited by Laura Gilliam and Eva Gulløv, 138–164. London: Pluto.

Beckman, Anne Winther, Vigdis Blach, Rikke Skovgaard Nielsen, and Hans
    Thor Andersen. 2015. "Fieldwork Inhabitants, Copenhagen (Denmark)." In
    *Governing Urban Diversity: Creating Social Cohesion, Social Mobility and Economic
    Performance in Today's Hyper-diversified Cities*. Report 2e. Copenhagen: SBi.

Biehl, João, and Peter Locke. 2017. "Introduction: Ethnographic Sensorium." In
    Unfinished: The Anthropology of Becoming, edited by João Biehl and Peter Locke,
    1–38. Durham, NC: Duke University Press.

Christensen, Ann-Dorte, Jeppe Fuglsang Larsen, and Sune Qvotrup Jensen. 2017.
    "Marginalized Adult Ethnic Minority Men in Denmark The Case of Aalborg
    East." In *Marginalized Masculinities: Contexts, Continuities and Change*, edited by
    Chris Haywood and Thomas Johansson, 170–187. New York: Routledge.

Collins, Patricia Hill. 2000. *Black Feminist Thought: Knowledge, Consciousness, and
    the Politics of Empowerment*. New York: Routledge.

Connell, Raewyn W. 2012. *Masculinities*. Cambridge: Polity.

Dalgaard, Nina T. 2016. "The Impact of Islam and the Public and Political
    Portrayals of Islam on Child-Rearing Practices: Discursive Analyses of Parental
    Accounts among Muslims Living in Denmark." *Culture and Psychology* 22, no. 1:
    65–79.

Danmarks Statistik. 2017. *Indvandrere i Danmark* [Immigrants in Denmark].
    Copenhagen: Danmarks Statistik.

Dindler, Svend, and Asta Olsen. 1988. *Islam og Muslimer i de Danske Medier* [Islam
    and Muslims in the Danish media]. Aarhus: Aarhus Universitetsforlag.

Ewing, Katherine Pratt. 2008. *Stolen Honor: Stigmatizing Muslim Men in Berlin*.
    Stanford, CA: Stanford University Press.

Featherstone, Bridget. 2003. "Taking Fathers Seriously." *British Journal of Social
    Work* 33, no. 2: 239–254.

Frykman, Jonas, and Nils Gilje. 2003. "Being There: An Introduction." *Being There:
    New Perspectives on Phenomenology and the Analysis of Culture*, edited by Jonas
    Frykman and Nils Gilje, 7–52. Lund: Nordic Academic Press.

Gilliam, Laura. 2009. *De Umulige Børn og det Ordentlige Menneske* [The impossible
    children and the decent human being]. Aarhus: Aarhus Universitetsforlag.

———. 2017. "The Impossible Bilingual Boys: Civilizing Efforts and Oppositional
    Forms in a Multi-Ethnic Class." *Children of the Welfare State: Civilizing Practices
    in Schools, Childcare and Families*, edited by Laura Gilliam and Eva Gulløv,
    138–164. London: Pluto.

———. 2018. *Minoritetsdanske Drenge i Skolen: Modvilje og Forskelsbehandling*
    [Minority Danish boys in school: Recentment and discrimination]. Aarhus:
    Aarhus Universitetsforlag.

Gitz-Johansen, Thomas. 2006. *Den Multikulturelle Skole—Integration og Sortering*
    [The multicultural school—integration and classification]. Roskilde: Roskilde
    Universitetsforlag.

Gupta, Anna, and Brid Featherstone. 2015. "What about My Dad? Black Fathers and the Child Protection System." *Critical and Radical Social Work* 4, no. 1: 77–91.

Haga, Rannveig. 2015. "Freedom Has Destroyed the Somali Family: Somali Parents' Experiences of Epistemic Injustice and Its Influence on Their Raising of Swedish Muslims." In *Making European Muslims: Religious Socialization among Young Muslims in Scandinavia and Western Europe*, edited by Mark Sedgwick, 39–55. New York: Routledge.

Hervik, Peter 2015. "Race, 'Race,' Racialisering, Racisme og Nyracisme [Race, 'race,' racialization, racism and new racism]." *Dansk Sociologi* 1, no. 26: 29–50.

Ingold, Tim. 2012. "Looking for Lines in Nature." *EarthLines Magazine* 3:48–51.

———. 2015. *The Life of Lines*. New York: Routledge.

Inhorn, Marcia C. 2012. *The New Arab Man: Emergent Masculinities, Technologies, and Islam in the Middle East*. Princeton, NJ: Princeton University Press.

Inhorn, Marcia C., Wendy Chavkin, and José-Alberto Navarro. 2015. *Globalized Fatherhood*. New York: Berghahn Books.

Jackson, Michael. 1996: *Things as They Are: New Directions on Phenomenological Anthropology*. Indianapolis: Indiana University Press.

———. 2013. *Lifeworlds: Essays in Existential Anthropology*. Chicago: University of Chicago Press.

Jensen, Sune Qvotrup. 2010. "Masculinity at the Margins: Othering, Marginality and Resistance among Young Marginalized Ethnic Minority Men." *Nordic Journal for Masculinity Studies* 5, no. 1: 6–26.

Johansen, Mette-Louise E. 2013. *In the Borderland: Palestinian Parents Navigating Danish Welfare State Interventions*. PhD dissertation. Copenhagen: Aarhus University and DIGNITY.

Jørgensen, Anne Hovgaard. 2017. "Overcoming Mistrusted Masculinity: Contesting Ethnic Minority Fathers' Involvement in Home-School Cooperation in Denmark." *Gender and Education* 31, no. 3: 377–393.

———. 2019. *Becomings of School-Fathers: An Ethnographic Exploration of Migrant Fathers' Experiences and Navigation of Home-School Cooperation Practices*. PhD diss., Danish School of Education, Aarhus University.

Liversage, Anika. 2016. "Minority Ethnic Men and Fatherhood in a Danish Context." In *Fatherhood in the Nordic Welfare States: Comparing Care, Policies and Practice*, edited by Godný Björk Eydal and Tine Rostgaard, 209–230. Bristol: Policy.

Liversage, Anika, and Christiane Præstgaard Christensen. 2017. *Etniske minoritetsunge i Danmark* [Ethnic minority youth in Denmark]. Copenhagen: SFI.

Naguib, Nefissa, 2015: *Nurturing Masculinities: Men, Food, and Family in Contemporary Egypt*. Austin: University of Texas Press.

Oldrup, Helene, Sara Korzen, Maia Lindstrøm, and Mogens Christoffersen. 2011. *Vold mod børn og unge* [Violence against children and adolescents]. Copenhagen: SFI.

Pedersen, Lars, and Bodil Selmer. 1991. *Muslimsk indvandrerungdom* [Muslim immigrant youth]. Rønde: Aarhus Universitetsforlag.

Pedersen, Marianne Holm, and Mikkel Rytter. 2011. *Islam og Muslimer i Danmark: Religion, Identitet og Sikkerhed efter 11. September 2001* [Islam and Muslims in Denmark: Religion, identity, and security after September 11, 2001]. Copenhagen: Museum Tusculanum.

Pless, Trees. 2000. "Muslim Families from Morocco in the Netherlands: Gender Dynamics and Fathers' Roles in a Context of Change." *Current Sociology* 48, no. 4: 75–93.

Rasmussen, Jon Dag. 2017. *En Upåagtet Verden af Bevægelse* [An unheeded world of movement]. PhD diss., Aalborg University.

Said, Edward 1986. "Orientalism Reconsidered." *Cultural Critique* 1 (Fall): 89–107.

Schultz, Alfred, and Thomas Luckmann. 1974. *The Structure of the Life-World.* London: Heineman Educational.

Seidenfaden, Line. 2010. *Den Uhåndterbare Målgruppe—Mænd med Etnisk Minoritetsbaggrund i Krydsfeltet Mellem Integration og Ligestillingspolitik* [The unmanageable target group: Men with ethnic minority backgrounds in the intersection of integration and equality policies]. MA thesis, Copenhagen University.

UNICEF. 2014. *Hidden at Plain Sight: A Statistical Analysis of Violence against Children.* New York: UNICEF Division of Data, Research and Policy, Data and Analytics Section.

ANNE HOVGAARD JØRGENSEN is Assistant Professor at University College Copenhagen in Denmark.

SIX

—ᴍᴠ—

DOING GENDER IN SHATILA REFUGEE CAMP

Palestinian Lads, Their Pigeons, and an Ethnographer

GUSTAVO BARBOSA

INTRODUCTION: "OH, THESE EUROPEANS!"

"I hate having to do it, Gustavo!" exclaimed my friend Jihad, complaining about yet another workshop on gender he had had to facilitate. Jihad, twenty-eight years old, was a social worker at a local nongovernmental organization (NGO) in the Shatila Palestinian refugee camp in the southern outskirts of Beirut, Lebanon. In cooperation with its European counterpart, the NGO was hosting a series of lectures on reproductive health for young Shatila residents, both boys and girls. The European partner financing the exercise had provided the social workers with supporting material, a DVD, and a guidebook, both in Arabic and English, that established the procedures for the workshop. Jihad thought it better to carry out some adaptations to the general guidelines to render them more culturally appropriate. "I tell the participants that one of Prophet Mohammed's wives was his boss and that it's not a problem to have women in leading positions. The local director at our center in Shatila is a woman. But it's true that it's taken even me forever to understand what 'gender' is."

It should come as no surprise, then, that his and his organization's commitment to the initiative was half-hearted. The boss, a Shatila resident, once expressed frustration with the topic to him: "Oh, these Europeans! They should give us their lives so that we can implement their agenda. We lead lives very different from theirs!"

For the workshop, Jihad also used another stratagem to help participants grasp the elusive concept of gender. On a whiteboard, he wrote the word *gender*, Arabicizing it by placing the article "al" (equivalent to "the") in front:

137

"al-gender." He invited participants to share with others what they understood by the concept: "People come up with the most unbelievable definitions. During one workshop, a participant said that gender is a terminal disease." I regretted not having participated in Jihad's activity, and it seemed I had missed yet another golden opportunity. Therefore, I did what any ethnographer would do: I invited myself to the next workshop on gender that Jihad was to facilitate in a couple of weeks.

This chapter is written based on the supposition that the participant in Jihad's workshop who defined gender as a terminal disease may have had a point, even if the remark was probably unintentional.[1] I want to advance the hypothesis that as a concept, gender does not necessarily work in all settings and at all times. Arguably, all over the "NGO world" and in much of academia, it has indeed been the case that gender has tended to be defined in terms of relations of power and subordination. As such, gender requires men and women with different access to power. In the case of the Arab East, such a perspective has contributed to strengthening Orientalizing views of brutal, all-powerful, and misogynist men, with their veiled women requiring outside assistance to portray their fates and express their voices. Such a definition of gender fails to capture the experiences of those with very limited access to power, like the Shatila *shabāb*, the lads from the camp. This chapter does not depict the shabāb as emasculated or as terrorists in the making, living a crisis of masculinity due to the specific political-economic constraints placed on them and the ensuing incapacity to perform a gender. Rather, it takes issue with the concept of gender as understood by certain NGOs and puts forth the case that defining gender in terms of power relations alone is restrictive.

This chapter relies on data gleaned from the workshop conducted by Jihad, the one I finally attended, that illustrates the highly stereotyped and moralizing views international NGOs have of gender systems in settings deemed to be conservative, like Shatila. I rely on ethnographic evidence from the workshop to claim that if understood solely as relations of power and subordination, gender does not "travel" well. Indeed, the undue transposition to other ethnographic settings of how the notion has come to be understood in light of important but geographically circumscribed power struggles in Euro-America has serious heuristic and analytical shortcomings. Once freed from such a limiting framework, shabāb's lives appear as ethnographically much richer than those of supposedly brutalizing and brutalized Arab men. One can even empathize with some of their struggles—to start independent households, to find brides, to start families—and understand that not all fights are about cock (Geertz [1973] 2000).

I then present an arena of sociality where, until recently, the Shatila shabāb displayed sex-roles: raising and hunting pigeons. The shabāb will be observed in these practices of care toward their "non-cocks"—the pigeons, and ultimately the ethnographer. I explore the differences between this "non-cockfight" and the Balinese cockfights of Clifford Geertz's ([1973] 2000) famous text. Understanding what was entailed by shabāb's practices of care and love has invited my repositioning in the field, forcing me to realize that there may be more and less to gender than simply power struggles.

This chapter is based on two years of participant observation in Lebanon, including one during which I lived in Shatila. Fieldwork, conducted mainly in Arabic, sometimes with translations into English and commentaries provided by my research assistants, consisted of informal interactions, workshops dedicated to discussing 1970s and 1980s nationalistic songs and present-day rap with older and younger refugees, and interviews with pairs of fathers and sons.[2] The chapter starts with entrapments, such as the political-economic restrictions endured by Shatila shabāb on one side and the epistemological constraints impinging on NGO practitioners and gender theorists on the other. But toward the end, it flirts with freedom, because love—this many-splendored and liberating thing—enables unexpected kinds of empowerments.

POWER ENTRAPMENTS: A BRIEF HISTORY OF SHATILA

"As the Arab saying goes, 'only his pocket shames a man' (al-rijjāl mā bi'ībū illā jībū)," thirty-one-year-old Ahmad told me, commenting on his difficulties to earn a decent living. We were sitting in the well-kept sitting-room of his tiny dwelling in Shatila with his sixty-six-year-old mother and his twenty-three-year-old wife, who had just put their eight-month-old daughter to bed. An unexpected item of decoration hung from one of the walls: Ahmad's diploma in accounting from one of the local institutes. Realizing my surprise, Ahmad explained, "I've never managed to get a job as an accountant. So I framed my diploma and hung it there." Ahmad's troubles finding a position commensurate with his level of education reflect Palestinian refugees' burdened access to the labor market in Lebanon. A law dating back to 1962 and tightened in 1982 forbade seventy-two professions and trades to them (Natour and Yassine 2007). The law was replaced by a new one in 2010 but with little effect in practice: unemployment levels remain very high among Palestinians in Lebanon. It is shabāb like Ahmad who pay a particularly high price.

Ahmad's family lives on the ground floor apartment just below his mother, Um Ahmad, who owns both dwellings. "That is, my mother owns the walls, not the ground," Ahmad clarified. "For we as Palestinians aren't allowed to own property in Lebanon," he added, giving lived evidence to the effects of Law 296/2001, which in practice forbade Palestinian refugees to acquire property in the country (Natour and Yassine 2007).

These days Ahmad makes his living in the cramped entrance room of his house by giving private classes to high school students. He makes an insufficient US$300 per month, tutoring some thirty students from 9:00 a.m. to 9:00 p.m. The summer months witness a sharp decline in his income due to school holidays. One summer, he earned some money by making deliveries, but he thinks of himself as too old and overqualified for that kind of work.

Ahmad's biography intimately reflects Palestinians' fate after 1982. It was during that year that Israel invaded Lebanon; the Palestine Liberation Organization and its guerrillas, the *fidā'iyyīn*, were forced to evacuate the country (Peteet 1991, 2005; Sayigh 1979, 1993), and the infamous Sabra and Shatila massacres took place, killing some three thousand residents of the camp and surroundings (Nuwayhed Al-Hout 2004). Actually, 1982 marks the demise of the *'ayyām al-thawra* (1967–1982), or the "days of the revolution," the heyday of the Palestinian Resistance Movement in its military form, and the iconic male figure associated with them, the fidā'iyyīn, in Lebanon and other diasporas (Kanafani 2005, 2008).

On expulsion from Jordan in 1970, the Palestinian leadership and guerrillas relocated to Lebanon, which became the main focus for Palestinian political and military activity until 1982. Through the 1969 Cairo agreements, Palestinians gained virtual autonomy for the administration of the camps and official permission to launch attacks against Israel from Lebanese territory. With funds flowing in from the Arab oil states, the Palestinian leadership erected the military and bureaucratic apparatus for its functioning in the camps, which went through a period of nationalist fervor. Shatila became then a cradle for the fidā'iyyīn. It is with certain nostalgia that Ahmad remembers growing up during the 'ayyām al-thawra: "The fidā'iyyīn were like Conan, walking in the alleys of the camp, all-powerful, with their guns attached to their waists. We so much wanted to be like them." His life, however, could not be further apart from that of a *fidā'ī*.

Shatila's bare two square kilometers have actually been the stage for several of the episodes marking the scarred history of Lebanese-Palestinian relations. Lebanon is a country of some four million inhabitants belonging to eighteen different religious communities.[3] The country, located at the intersection of various regional and international interests, has historically been prone to conflict. To safeguard their sectarian interests, the different Lebanese confessions search for the support of powerful foreign allies. Since 1948, on their expulsion from Palestine, Palestinians have also played a role in Lebanese sectarian politics.

The Lebanese Civil War (1975–1990) was the result of historic divisions within the country, but Palestinians did lend it a helping hand, serving as catalyzers for its explosion (Picard 1996; Traboulsi 2007). When it ended, legislation depriving Palestinians of civil, social, and economic rights began to be reinforced more consistently. The 1989 Taef Agreement signaled the official end to the war and sanctioned the exclusion and scapegoating of Palestinians. Some Lebanese justify the denial of rights to Palestinians, the majority of whom are Sunni, in the interest of protecting Lebanon's so-called fragile confessional equilibrium. As of recently, the Palestinian community in the country has become dependent on financial and emergency aid provided by the United Nations Relief and Works Agency for Palestine Refugees in the Near East (UNRWA) and increasingly by international NGOs. Today, Shatila is a sprawling and increasingly vertical shantytown, home to an estimated population of thirteen thousand,[4] who face a dearth of social services. When reflecting on his fate, Ahmad talks about his dreams, and even they look bleak.

> To tell you the truth, without the help of my mother, I wouldn't have completed my education. My mother's work wasn't nice, because she was serving people. But it was honest work. We don't like to put women in that situation. We like women to stay in the house and be the lovely lady. That's how we think as Arabs. But these days we need the support of our ladies. . . . I have a dream: I want to sleep one night, one night only, not having to worry with the next day, not having to worry with what will happen if the milk is over, if my daughter or my mother gets sick. What if I can't even pay for my mother's medication; then what did she raise me for?

EPISTEMOLOGICAL ENTRAPMENTS:
A BRIEF HISTORY OF GENDER

On an oppressively hot summer evening in 2007, I was attending English classes for adults in the Mar Elias Palestinian camp in Beirut. The students had varying levels of command of English, so the teacher spoke mainly in Arabic. For a moment, she switched into English to say "gender equity."

It served as a prompt for me to provoke her: "You don't have a word for *gender* in Arabic."

She replied: "Of course we do; it's *jins*."

I gave no solace: "But *jins* is actually *sex*, no? It is not *gender*."

She didn't give up either: "*Jins* is *sex*; *jins* is also *gender*. There isn't a problem here, all right?"

Late twentieth-century gender theorists disagreed and maintained that there was a problem there. They argued that as the cultural elaboration of the supposedly natural differences between men and women, gender could not be subsumed into sex. Since the inception of this debate in the 1970s, gender tended (often within academia and particularly beyond, among NGO practitioners) to obliterate sex because it enabled political mobilization and calls for change. Psychologists, philosophers, sociologists, and anthropologists joined forces to show that masculinity and femininity were constructed attainments that, because they were often at the base of inequalities, had to be politically denaturalized. Within such a framework, the differences between masculinity and femininity meant an inequality (Leacock 1983), which scaffolded a hierarchy of different access to power by men and women (Ortner 1974; Rosaldo and Lamphere 1974; Strathern 1988). Men were hastily associated with power and women with the lack thereof. Liberal ideology took as its task to dismantle this power imbalance, drafting scholars for the implementation of this political agenda.

It is helpful here to redeploy J. Halberstam's (1998, 2002) analysis of female masculinity concerning masculinities without maleness. Reflecting queer studies and new gender politics, Halberstam argues that masculinity studies have consistently ignored female forms of masculinity. Accordingly, he explores enactments of masculinity even in the absence of male embodiment. If, following Halberstam, there can be masculinity without male embodiment, then I propose that there can also be male embodiment without hegemonic masculinity.

Venus Boyz, a 2002 movie directed by Gabriel Baur, seems inspired by Halberstam's studies. It proposes a journey through the universe of the female masculinity of drag kings in London and New York. In a particular scene, one of the characters says, "Every time I put on a suit jacket, I feel a little bit more powerful." But what of people like the Shatila shabāb, who cannot or have no reason to put on a suit jacket or military gear? On the ground, ideals of masculinity may have a complex relation to practice, varying from place to place and time to time. Unable to replicate the heroic personas of their forebears, the fidā'iyyīn, the shabāb from Shatila, with considerably less access to power, quietly try to live their lives, engaging in the relatively mundane routines of building houses, getting married, or hunting pigeons.

DOING GENDER: A WORKSHOP IN SHATILA

Unlike the previous occasion, no dramatic definitions were offered when Jihad wrote "al-gender" on the whiteboard during the workshop I attended. The guidebook prepared by the European NGO did anticipate that participants may not be acquainted enough with the concept and reported that in pilot sessions, some suggested that gender was a mobile brand, a name, a law, a provocation, and a competition—though again, in the latter three cases, I suspect that the participants might have had a point.

Some twenty boys and girls participated in the workshop, ranging in ages from fifteen to twenty-four. The boys clustered at the two edges of the table, with the girls in between. A female facilitator, Rola, worked together with Jihad to direct the discussions. When Jihad wrote "al-gender" on the whiteboard, only one of the boys volunteered that al-gender was about roles (*al-'adwār*). The others were somewhat more candid, stating that they simply did not know what it was, that it was the first time they were hearing the term, or that al-gender was sex (*al-jins*).

Following the manual, Jihad divided the whiteboard into two columns, identified with the headers male (*dhakar*) and female (*untha*), and challenged participants to enumerate characteristics for each. The participants suggested for male the following qualities: facial hair, huge muscles, Adam's apple, fertilizing capacity, hard work, going out of the house, masturbation (*al-'āda al-sirriyya*; literally, "the secret habit"), not shy, and harshness. Under female, they ascribed the following: the headscarf, breasts, work, pregnancy, the ability to give birth (*al-qudra 'alā al-'injāb*), cleaning the house, not leaving the house, child-rearing, menstruation (*al-dawra al-shahriyya*; literally, "the monthly cycle"), the womb, shyness, and softness. Using markers of different colors, Jihad differentiated between the features that were bodily traits (*al-ṣifāt al-jasadiyya*) and thus sex (*al-jins*), and those that were roles (*al-'adwār*) or social types (*al-naw' al-'ijtimā'ī*), thus, gender (*al-jindir*). He continued: "Gender changes from society to society." One of the young men thought it relevant to remark, "Yes, one needs to take religion into consideration."

The next activity of the workshop, also prescribed by the manual and slightly adapted by Jihad, aimed at consolidating participants' understanding of gender as different from sex. The whiteboard was again divided into two halves, identified by a girl's name and a boy's name, Hala and Jad. Jihad invited the participants to list what they would give as presents to Hala and Jad on their fourth, tenth, and eighteenth birthdays. For their fourth birthdays, Hala would receive a Barbie, pink pajamas, and earrings, and Jad would receive a bicycle, a Spider-Man toy, and a football. Hala's tenth-birthday gifts would be a dress and a golden necklace, whereas Jad's would be a scooter and, yet again, a football. Hala would receive another golden necklace, makeup, a car, a book, and a computer for her eighteenth birthday; Jad, for his turn, would receive a motorcycle, a car, a book, a computer, a PlayStation, and a silver bracelet. Jihad remarked that the lists contained both common and different items, because some objects were considered appropriate for a girl and others for a boy. Somewhat theatrically, he asked his audience, "What is gender?" The participants completely understood his point; nevertheless, one of the girls reacted, "Boys always want more things than us," which triggered a wave of laughter.

The third activity of the workshop was particularly revealing. Jihad and Rola distributed green and blue cards to the participants, irrespective of sex. He explained, "Those with the blue cards can't do anything, apart from remaining seated. Those with the green cards can do whatever they feel like." A green card holder turned on some loud music on his mobile; some others rushed out of the building to stretch their legs and smoke much-needed cigarettes. Another male green card holder opted to tease the unlucky girl holding a blue card. "Now, you'll swap your cards," Rola instructed. It was the girl's turn to take her revenge.

Once the activity was over, Jihad prompted the participants to share with others the way they felt when in possession of the differently colored cards. Faithfully observing the manual's guidelines, Jihad divided the whiteboard once more into two columns, labeled "no power" (*da'īf*; literally: weak) and "power" (*quwwa*). While in the "quwwa" position, participants stated that they felt special (*mumayyazīn*), gained their rights, and were able to express themselves. Under the respective column, they suggested the inclusion of the words *freedom, mobility,* and *safety.* The content under the heading "no power" was more dramatic. When holding the blue cards, the Shatila boys and girls reported that they experienced boredom, humiliation, restrictions, emotional stress (*al-'infi'āl*), rage, and being blocked and forced into silence. Ultimately, Jihad and Rola conducted the activity very well, and the European NGO's objective was attained. Indeed, the manual reads, "Make the point that gender relations are power relations, and that subordination (power-over) should be replaced by cooperation (power-with) and empowerment (power-to)."

On my way out of the center, in the alleys of Shatila I bumped into another friend of mine, Omar, a twenty-eight-year-old greengrocer. He grew up hearing about workshops similar to Jihad's and asked where I had spent the whole morning.

> Gustavo: I've attended a workshop at an NGO.
> Omar: Oh, what was the workshop about?
> Gustavo: Al-gender.
> Omar: And what's that?

Still under the influence of Jihad's workshop, I replied with an expression that sounds even more bizarre in Arabic than in English: "It's the 'social sex' (*al-jins al-'ijtimā'ī*)."

"Ah, that's bullshit," Omar reacted in English.[5]

Difference does not necessarily lead to the establishment of a hierarchy—and even when it does, the ranking of superiority may contradict the outsider's expectations and change through time and context. Shatilans do not require a workshop to teach what is tautological to them: that men and women are different, both physically and socially, whether or not they have a word for the latter. Rather, it may be the case that some of us need a workshop to understand how Shatilans conceptualize and practice that difference.

During a previous meeting at Jihad's NGO, a group of Norwegian photography students came to make a first acquaintance with camp residents before going around Shatila taking photographs for an exhibition back home. After making us wait for a couple of hours, the students, some fifteen boys and girls, finally arrived. To general bewilderment and almost embarrassment, all the Norwegian girls were veiled, whereas barely half of their Palestinian hosts were dressed the same way. At a certain point, a female organizer discreetly encouraged one of the Norwegian girls to remove her hijab. All the others followed, to reveal a fiesta of different haircuts and colors—including pink—much to the amusement of Shatilans.

The workshop on gender described earlier is indicative of the expectations international NGOs have of sex/gender systems in certain settings, particularly in the Global South. First, it was part of a series on reproductive health, medicalizing sexuality in a place considered conservative like Shatila. Second, all the activities of the workshop followed a strict dichotomizing logic—sex/gender, Jad/Hala, power/no power—as if difference necessarily entails an opposition and, in the case of the last pair, the creation of a hierarchy. Last, the utilization of the colored cards introduced the idea of gender as a disparity in terms of access to power. This is a hasty transposition of a notion of gender informed by certain NGOs' agendas, as well as by important but nonetheless geographically circumscribed political struggles in Euro-America. The automatic transplantation of the notion into settings like Shatila, where both women and men today have very limited access to power, raises serious issues.

The dissonance between NGOs' understandings of gender and local renderings of the complex is not simply a problem of translation. Talal Asad (1986) reminds us that languages are unequal when it comes to power relations among them. When NGOs are deploying and promoting their understanding of the English word *gender*, they expect it is their interpretation of this term that will impact and influence local renderings of the complex, such as those suggested by the Arabic jins.[6] Roger Keesing (1968, 84) argues that social statuses should always be defined contextually rather than categorically, so as to bridge "the

Figure 6.1: Pigeons over Shatila. © Gustavo Barbosa

gap between our descriptive models and the complexities of social relations on the ground." Similarly, I advance the case for a mandatory contextual definition of concepts such as gender. That the mandatory contextual definition of concepts should always be the case in ethnography, so as to reflect social practice from close, may be less tautologically obvious than expected. Sometimes even ethnographers opt for blinkers imperiling their views. Geertz (1980, 121) gets the point when he writes in the *Negara* that "impressed with command, we see little else." Yet somewhere else, Geertz has let himself be mesmerized by command and power in spite of perhaps there being much more to see and deeper plays demanding thicker descriptions. As a matter of fact, in Shatila at least, but maybe also beyond, not all fights are about cock.

NON-COCKFIGHTS: FREEDOM IS A MANY-SPLENDORED THING

This image is not infrequent in Shatila today. Every warm afternoon, the sky over the camp is swarmed with flocks of pigeons. However that the breeders of the birds are Shatila shabāb is unusual. The practice of raising pigeons was common among the shabāb until some fifteen years ago; since then, it has largely been discontinued. Ahmad reflected on the tragic end of his years as a pigeon-raiser: "I was really sad and angry when the guy of the Security Committee of the camp, together with my brother, killed Hanun. Hanun was my favorite pigeon, with his red feathers. He hatched at our place here in Shatila and was the leader of my bunch. He used to come to me whenever I called, sit on my knees, and eat right from my hand. Hanun was just like a dog."

Ahmad's father did not anticipate the annoyance to himself and to his neighbors when he brought his teenage son a female pigeon. After a while, Ahmad remarked to his father that he was worried the pigeon was feeling too lonely and might die if not provided with a partner. His father was always willing to comply with his studious son's demands. Thus, he bought Ahmad a male pigeon. A talented handyman, Ahmad's father also constructed a coop on the roof of the house to accommodate the new couple. It should not have come as a surprise to Ahmad when, a few weeks later, he opened the coop gate and found newly laid eggs. He celebrated his pet's fertility: "The female was like a machine, man. She was very fat; she couldn't even fly. But every three months, she laid two eggs."

After a while, Ahmad had six pigeons, and the flock was further enlarged by yet another two, given to him by a friend who lost interest in his pets due to being saddened by the death of one of them. Very soon, Ahmad was raising, mating, buying, and selling pigeons. He developed his own expertise in the activity and was delighted to try to initiate me into the art of differentiating the various kinds of pigeons: Chefar, named after the word *Chevrolet*, for being big; Buaz, after the name given to a brand of falcons, because they are very tall; and the Yahudiat (Jews), because, Ahmad clarified, "those pigeons come from Palestine." In a year, the coop was running the risk of overpopulation. It housed thirty-seven birds, which ate away in corn, wheat, and penicillin when needed, part of the family's limited budget. "All very loyal to me," Ahmad rejoiced. "They never ran away." By then, he began to fly his pigeons.

And the problems started. "It's just like in life," Ahmad told me, exploding in laughter. "The male always goes after the female." He was explaining how to fly the pigeons. First, the birds are set free. Always following a leading male, they take off. But they tend to return too quickly, so the raiser, to keep them airborne, throws stones at them and whistles. That generated protests from Ahmad's neighbors. Once it is time to get the band down, the raiser waves the female of the leading male to attract him back. The flock comes down in circles, and once on the ground, the birds hum.

What attracted the Shatila shabāb to the practice was not only flying the birds. While in the sky, pigeons from different flocks eventually mix. And then there's the hunt (*al-ṣayd*). If one's birds get into someone else's flock, the former will try to attract the birds of the latter the next time the respective bands are simultaneously in the sky. This soon led to all kinds of problems and accusations of theft among the shabāb.

To avoid escalating tensions, one of the pigeon-raisers, a married man, came up with a timetable, setting different times for the various breeders to fly their bands. For quite some time—a year, perhaps—the system worked wonderfully. The source of the new difficulties was precisely Ahmad's household.

Ahmad's younger brother kept flying the birds outside of his allotted time slot. The other owners became very angry and sent a menacing message: "We're in hunt," which effectively meant that they would not restrict themselves to the timetable and would try to catch Ahmad's birds. As a good *'ibn al-mukhayyam* (son of the camp) and Shatila *shāb*, Ahmad would not back down to the threat: "A war started among us. We were all flying our pigeons at the same time and trying to get each other's birds. But my pigeons were very loyal to me, and normally I was the one who caught other owners' birds. . . . I caught three birds of one of my neighbors. They promised revenge, but I was young and stubborn, and retreat was simply not an option."

The settling of scores among the contenders happened soon after. One day, Ahmad went up to the roof and found the coop gate wide open, with one pigeon killed and ten missing. Suspicion rested with Ahmad's neighbors. Originally restricted to the skies, the dispute soon enough landed, leading to a direct confrontation among the shabāb. When Ahmad's older brother asked him how he would react, he replied, "I'll do what needs to be done." The brother accompanied him to the neighbor's house. The neighbor was challenged to go outside. A fierce fight followed, leaving the neighbor with a broken leg.

By then, the security committee of the camp concluded that the situation was unacceptable and decided to intervene. However, because the security committee knew how attached people were to their birds, they devised a lie, Ahmad explained. They concocted a story about an accident that supposedly almost happened at the nearby International Airport of Beirut. As the story goes, a pigeon was sucked into the propeller of a jet and almost took down the plane. According to the security committee, Ahmad reported, the Lebanese government decided to imprison everyone who insisted on continuing to raise pigeons. Therefore breeders had to stop flying their birds, exterminating them altogether or at least clipping their wing feathers to preclude any flight. This was not enough to make people revise their old habits. Guards of the security committee started visiting homes and killing the birds they found. Ahmad's household was not an exception. A guard came by, in the company of Ahmad's older brother. To set an exemplary model for the neighbors, he selected three pigeons to be sacrificed, and Hanun was one of them. With sadness, Ahmad recalled, "I was so angry, so completely out of control that, after, I cut the throats of all the remaining pigeons. And I yelled at my brother, saying that we weren't siblings anymore. My mother cleaned the pigeons, and for a month, they took almost all of our refrigerator. . . . But, after a month, she had to throw the pigeons away because none of us would take a bite."

Ahmad also told me Saqr's story. Saqr, about fifteen years older than Ahmad, was taken to prison because of the pigeons—in Germany. He had been among the biggest breeders in Shatila. At some point, he was presented with the opportunity to migrate, a dream cherished by several of the shabāb. Once in Germany, Saqr was perplexed to find out that pigeons do not belong to anyone in Europe. He gathered a bunch from the street and took them to his house. After a while, he was flying them, unencumbered by competition. His German neighbors, however, were even less understanding of the needs of a shāb than the ones back home. In reaction to the stone-throwing and constant whistling necessary to flying a flock, they called the police. For a short while, Saqr was behind bars.

About five years after his departure from Lebanon, already with German nationality, and married with children, Saqr paid a visit to Shatila. Unsurprisingly—and in a poignant commentary on al-ghurba, that is, longing for a place left behind—one of his first actions in the camp was to climb to his family's household roof and fly some pigeons, at a safe distance from the apparently more treacherous German skies.

Paraphrasing Geertz ([1973] 2000), the identification of the Shatila shabāb with their "non-cocks" is unmistakable—and the double entendre here is perhaps more intentional than the Balinese of Geertz's classic text. Actually, it suggests that, as it happens with the English cock, the word for pigeon in Arabic (ḥamāma) also has a sexual connotation in Lebanese colloquial. Its meaning, though, is closer to what Anglophones would describe as a "willy."

As a dramatization of local anxieties about social prestige, Geertz's Balinese cockfights are an affaire d'honneur. "Joining pride to selfhood, selfhood to cocks, and cocks to destruction," Geertz ([1973] 2000, 444) writes, Balinese men fight aggressively through their birds, striving to protect their esteem, honor, and dignity—essentially, their social standing. In Bali, only those entitled to prestige and honor can participate in serious cockfighting. It is not an activity for social outcasts: women, subordinates, youth. The situation cannot be further from Shatila. My informants are all young, poor refugees. In Shatila, non-cockfighting is not a privilege of those with prestige. It is for other reasons that the Shatila shabāb also insist on keeping their flocks airborne. After all, they have their pride to protect, too: when asked by his brother how he would react to the stealing of his pigeons, Ahmad clearly indicates his disposition to do "what a man has gotta do."

There may indeed be a tension between the "asociality" of the shabāb in their efforts at self-expression through bird-hunting and the disciplinary measures of a state-like institution like the security committee, which asserted itself violently in the episode of the pigeons. Yet it is only up to a certain extent that the security committee can be characterized as consolidating a "state-like" environment in Shatila. Shatilans have actually learned how to live without relying on state-like institutions. Here, it is the shabāb themselves, and a married one among them, who tried to organize pigeon-flying in a way to avoid disputes. On marriage, a man is considered to have come of age and to have finally achieved ʿaql, the eminent social faculty of judiciousness and prudence (Altorki 1986).

In one aspect at least, Balinese cockfighting and Shatila non-cockfighting are opposites. In Bali, an umpire is called on to ensure that the "civic certainty of the law" is strictly observed throughout, in spite of the passions aroused by the fight. Cockfighting in Bali is ultimately a state affair, a matter of men with political prestige: "When there were no bureaucrats around to improve popular morality, the staging of a cockfight was an explicitly societal matter. Bringing a cock to an important fight was, for an adult male, a compulsory duty of citizenship; taxation of fights, which were usually held on market day, was a major source of public revenue; patronage of the art was a stated responsibility of princes; and the cock ring, or *wantilan*, stood in the center of the village near those monuments of Balinese civility—the council house, the origin temple, the market place, the signal tower, the banyan tree" (Geertz [1973] 2000, 424–425).

In Shatila, where some NGOs house bureaucrats to align local morality with "modernizing" discourses on gender, the umpire, the council house, and all other state-like figures are either obsolete or simply nonexistent.

In the end, it is revealing that Shatila shabāb chose pigeon-raising as a pastime and that they selected birds, among all animals, as objects of their affection. The Shatila shabāb are immersed in the social immobility dictated by utter poverty; lack the means to travel, despite constantly lining up in embassies in Beirut only to have their visa applications rejected; and have the capacity to dream of a future overshadowed by the political-economic complexities of the refugees' situation in Lebanon. It is not difficult to understand why they appreciate pigeons, with their unencumbered freedom to fly.

A PRISONER OF LOVE

"I'm going to say it very slowly, so that you can repeat after me: *Lā ilāha illā Allāh, wa Muḥammad rasūl Allāh* [There is no god but God, and Mohammad is his messenger]." This was Shaykh Habib talking to me on the staircase leading to his apartment in Shatila. He was encouraging me to repeat the *shahāda* (profession of faith), a single but sincere enunciation of which is considered by several schools as sufficient for conversion to Islam.

It was my friend Fawaz, a militiaman in his early twenties, who took me to Shaykh Habib's house. When our friendship started to deepen, Fawaz became increasingly troubled by the fact that I was not Muslim. On that afternoon, after checking whether I had five minutes to spare, he put me on the back of his scooter and took me to Shaykh Habib's home. The shaykh was not in. As we waited a little while on the staircase, I was completely unaware of whom we were there to see and what was to follow. When we were about to leave, the shaykh arrived.

A few months before our meeting with the shaykh, on a very early morning when I was leaving the camp, Fawaz stopped me. We had already chitchatted on a few occasions. At that time of the day, Shatila alleys are still very empty, and I worried when Fawaz, who was on duty and holding his machine gun, told me, "We need to talk." My worry almost approached panic levels when he asked, "Are you Christian?" His reaction to my positive answer finally allowed me to relax. "You should consider converting and come to pray with us," he said. I agreed and never gave it a second thought until the day he asked me if I had a few minutes to spare and put me on the back seat of his scooter.

For quite some time, I thought that Shatilans' efforts at converting and "Palestinianizing" me were attempts at exerting power over me. They knew I was there doing research; by turning me into one of "them," they might be trying to ensure that I would publicize sympathetic images of the camp. It took me quite some time to realize that the endeavors at making me belong were not only about power: those most troubled by the fact that I was not Muslim and most entrepreneurial in making me fit were those Shatilans who cared about me. One of my closest friends, Anis, once observed, "Gustavo, I want to go on thinking that my God is just. And you're a nice chap. But you won't be saved, because you're Christian. I once even talked to the shaykh about it: can't a Christian be saved, if he's a nice person? The shaykh said no and that that was the will of God." The easiest way out of Anis's dilemma seemed to be my conversion.

My university training in London heightened my sensitivity to relationships of power. For that reason, and for quite a while, I insisted on framing remarks such as Anis's and Fawaz's as resulting from their desire to wield power over me. Nonetheless, I finally came to appreciate that there might possibly be other reasons informing Anis's and Fawaz's attitudes. Consequently, not only did I reposition myself in the field, but the very object of my research, gender, came to be reconceptualized beyond certain NGOs' obsession with power relations. Indeed, some NGOs' understandings of gender are deeply informed by political power struggles relating more with the politics of Euro-America than with the place where I conducted my fieldwork.

In this chapter, I have established a tense dialogue between the ways NGOs, through their workshops, and Shatila shabāb, through pigeon raising and hunting, do gender. This allows for an undoing of the former by the latter, enabling a timely critique of NGOs' almost naturalized grasp on gender—a critique, I believe, also needed in other ethnographic settings.

At the beginning of my time in Shatila, some people named me Mustapha. The g like in the English word *garden* and the v are nonexistent phonemes in Levantine Arabic, and Shatilans of an older generation, with less exposure to formal schooling and mass media, found my name, Gustavo, particularly difficult to pronounce. Some of them started calling me Gestapo (with the ge as in the French *je*). As I reacted against that, they renamed me Mustapha. When I descended from Shaykh Habib's staircase that afternoon, I had officially become Mustapha.

NOTES

1. This chapter draws on several sections of my book (Barbosa 2021).

2. Throughout my fieldwork, I tried to remain attentive to what it meant to be a man conducting research mainly with men. Despite all the differences of class and culture, I was also, in a certain sense and as will become increasingly clearer to the reader toward the end of this chapter, doing fieldwork "at home." The methodological and heuristic implications of doing research at home also from the perspective of the ethnographer's and participants' gender belonging, especially among men, certainly deserve more analytical attention than allowed by the limits of the present chapter.

3. This data reflects the time prior to the current influx of refugees from Syria, due to the civil war ravaging that country.

4. These numbers reflect a time prior to the influx of refugees from Syria.

5. If the Palestinian camp seems to remain impermeable to much of the content of NGOs' workshops, the question as to why those workshops go on

attracting participants or being held at all—beyond the fact that funding for them is available—is perfectly valid. I wonder to which extent a certain dose of what Allen (2013) has named "cynicism" is often part of NGOs' "will to improve" (Li 2007), characterizing several of their projects and interventions in the Global South.

6. For a discussion about the distance between the Arabic *jins*, with its emphasis on what members of the same category have in common, and "gender" with its emphasis on opposition and eventually the hierarchy between members of different categories, see Barbosa (2021).

BIBLIOGRAPHY

Allen, Lori. 2013. *The Rise and Fall of Human Rights: Cynicism and Politics in Occupied Palestine*. Stanford, CA: Stanford University Press.

Altorki, Soraya. 1986. *Women in Saudi Arabia: Ideology and Behavior among the Elite*. New York: Columbia University Press.

Asad, Talal. 1986. "The Concept of Cultural Translation in British Social Anthropology." In *Writing Culture: The Poetics and Politics of Ethnography*, edited by James Clifford and George Marcus, 141–164. Berkeley: University of California Press.

Barbosa, Gustavo. 2021. *The Best of Hard Times: Palestinian Refugee Masculinities in Lebanon*. Syracuse, NY: Syracuse University Press.

Geertz, Clifford. (1973) 2000. "Deep Play: Notes on the Balinese Cockfight." In *The Interpretation of Cultures: Selected Essays*, edited by Clifford Geertz. New York: Basic Books.

———. 1980. *Negara: The Theatre State in Nineteenth-Century Bali*. Princeton, NJ: Princeton University Press.

Halberstam, J. 1998. *Female Masculinity*. Durham, NC: Duke University Press.

———. 2002. "An Introduction to Female Masculinity: Masculinity without Men." In *The Masculinity Studies Reader*, edited by Rachel Adams and David Savran, 355–374. Oxford: Blackwell.

Kanafani, Samar. 2005. "When We Were Men: *Fidā'iyyn* Re-Collecting." MA diss., American University of Beirut.

———. 2008. "Leaving Mother-land: The Anti-Feminine in *Fida'i* Narratives." *Identities* 15, no. 3: 297–316.

Keesing, Roger. 1968. "Nonunilineal Descent and Contextual Definition of Status: The Kwaio Evidence." *American Anthropologist* 70, no. 1: 82–84.

Leacock, Eleanor. 1983. "Interpreting the Origins of Gender Inequality: Conceptual and Historical Problems." *Dialectical Anthropology* 7, no. 4: 263–284.

Li, Tania. 2007. *The Will to Improve: Governmentality, Development, and the Practice of Politics*. Durham, NC: Duke University Press.

Natour, Suheil, and Dalal Yassine. 2007. *The Legal Status of the Palestine Refugees in Lebanon and the Demands of Adjustment*. Beirut: Human Development Center.

Nuwayhed Al-Hout, Bayan. 2004. *Sabra and Shatila: September 1982*. London: Pluto.

Ortner, Sherry. 1974. "Is Female to Male as Nature Is to Culture?" In *Woman, Culture and Society*, edited by Michelle Rosaldo and Louise Lamphere, 68–87. Stanford, CA: Stanford University Press.

Peteet, Julie. 1991. *Gender in Crisis: Women and the Palestinian Resistance Movement*. New York: Columbia University Press.

———. 2005. *Landscape of Hope and Despair: Palestinian Refugee Camps*. Philadelphia: University of Pennsylvania Press.

Picard, Elizabeth. 1996. *Lebanon, a Shattered Country: Myths and Realities of the Wars in Lebanon*. New York: Holmes and Meier.

Rosaldo, Michelle, and Louise Lamphere, eds. 1974. *Woman, Culture, and Society*. Stanford, CA: Stanford University Press.

Sayigh, Rosemary. 1979. *Palestinians: From Peasants to Revolutionaries; A People's History*. London: Zed.

———. 1993. *Too Many Enemies: The Palestinian Experience in Lebanon*. London: Zed.

Strathern, Marilyn. 1988. *The Gender of the Gift: Problems with Women and Problems with Society in Melanesia*. Berkeley: University of California Press.

Traboulsi, Fawwaz. 2007. *A History of Modern Lebanon*. London: Pluto.

GUSTAVO BARBOSA is Associate Researcher at the Center for Middle Eastern Studies at the Fluminense Federal University in Brazil.

WELCOMING BAN KI-MOON

From Warrior-Nomads to Sahrawi Refugee-Statesmen in North Africa

KONSTANTINA ISIDOROS

INTRODUCTION

With a surprisingly tiny entourage of advisors and blue-capped soldiers in military camouflage, on March 5, 2016, Ban Ki-moon stepped out of a white Jeep marked with the blue United Nations logo and wearing the equally ubiquitous UN blue baseball cap representing the UN Mission for the Referendum in Western Sahara (MINURSO). Their shoes crunched over ancient *reg*, a geological desert pavement of rough gravel created over millennia, against the backdrop of the Sahara Desert's vast azure-blue sky emitting a sharp white light and a noiseless breath of air carrying the fine aerosol powder of Saharan sand. The United Nations secretary general walked forward to meet the United Nations representative for the Frente Polisario, part of the political leadership of the government of the Sahrawi Arab Democratic Republic (SADR). As Ban approached, Ahmed Boukhari stepped out of a traditional nomadic tent, handwoven with brown and black camel and goat hair, with an outstretched hand beneath a lightly fluttering Sahrawi flag. He wore a suit ostensibly identical to Ban's but overlain with a white *dara'a* that fittingly billowed out in its own time-honored tradition to the light breeze. Boukhari welcomed Ban, and their smiles and hands were caught in a shake by a brief flurry of clicking cameras from a few invited photojournalists before Boukhari invited Ban to join him back inside the low, flat tent to meet schoolchildren and youth representatives, look at their drawings, and drink a glass of *e-tay*, the customary sweet tea.

This quiet, unassuming encounter struck me as embodying a series of thresholds that these men were physically and ritualistically crossing. First, for the Sahrawi, this was not just a visit of human beings to a set of refugee camps but a reception for the sacrosanct spirit of a "thing": international law. It was an event that played out amid their very shy location of an ancient desert, but also that of their modest, nascent nation and state formation: the meeting captures an official state reception welcoming the principle of international law. But both the Sahrawi state and international law itself are correspondingly ethereal phenomena, "floating" like mirages, their essence dependent on how, when, and by whom they are considered legitimate and official. The encounter—in its discrete minimalism, vast desert landscape, background shades of blue and white, and quiet desert breeze—personifies a codependent moment of making a mutual legitimacy. Or perhaps I could better describe it as the moment of law itself in atmospheric suspension, undergoing rapid quivering between legitimacy and illegitimacy, like a camera lens quietly whirring to zoom in and out, trying to capture the correct static legal moment.

Second, the Sahrawi chose the first moment of Ban's welcome to comprise the crossing of a threshold of a customary tent—ordinarily and primarily a private place for human biological reproduction—between two representatives of the United Nations who otherwise met in the internal private political corridors of the UN headquarters in New York, comparable as a site of legal biology in its reproduction of human laws.

Yet third, what was missing (and unnoticed) in this rare assignation was Boukhari's *el-them* (pl. *litham*), the customary Saharan male veil. Surrounding these two figureheads were other Sahrawi officials, most with their litham either loosely unapparent around their heads or resting on their shoulders, looking more like self-evidently practical scarves to protect against the desert. Later that day, Ban was officially received by senior Polisario and SADR leaders, most of whom were the young warrior-nomads in the early formation of the Polisario in the late 1960s and early 1970s. Most of them wore their black litham discreetly around their shoulders.

This day carried immense geopolitical meaning to the Sahrawi. During my ten years studying among the Sahrawi, the el-them has been quietly ever present as the "fixtures and fittings" of usual daily life. Why would it melt into the background when so many other traditional markers such as tents, dara'a, and nomadic principles of hospitality were being displayed and enacted to receive Ban Ki-moon? This modest length of fabric—seemingly black but made of un-fast indigo (dark blue)—quietly went unnoticed as an understated part of Sahrawi and desert life when so many other "modern" markers were more explicitly on display that day, denoted, for example, by children for education, flags for nationalism, state architecture, and human military infrastructure,

Figure 7.1: Sahrawi women inside a traditional camel
and goat hair tent. © Konstantina Isidoros

all oscillating in the paradoxical simultaneity of refugeehood and citizenship.
So too does the scene appear as just men meeting men engaged in politics, war
and structural rules, leaving no room for the ancient fabric of life.

Much scholarship in Middle East feminism and popular/media attention
has focused on female veiling, but little attention has been paid to the practice
of Sahrawi male veiling. This masculine practice is equally negligible across
the wider comparative setting of the Middle East and North Africa, limited
primarily to French ethnologies on the Tuareg.[1] The first aim of this chapter is
to offer insights to how Sahrawi masculinity and their ancient practices of male
veiling and matrifocused principles of social organization have become woven into new ideas about what it means to be a "modern" man, caught between
nomadism, sedentarizing refugeehood, and military occupation, and as citizens of a nascent nation-state in exile. The second aim is to reposition veiling
in terms of men and masculinities in counterdistinction to the corpus of
scholarship on female veiling as sex segregation and female seclusion. This
does not suggest an opposite pole of male segregation and seclusion but instead
moves into the customary relationship between both men and women, not

all of whom are human. This relates to an underlying encounter of a "spirit of things," in what is usually embodied by a customary fabric and its alternative veils of orality. I have chosen to juxtapose all this with a simultaneous moment of the presence of Ban Ki-moon, an individual entirely out of place in this environment, representing matters that have fallen out of place, all of which need to be put back into place.

MEN AT WAR

The Sahrawi have been nomadic pastoralists commanding the Western Sahara Desert trade routes for at least three millennia. Feared by medieval travelers as "savage" natives and ungovernable "tribes," they have been long distinguished by European historians as warrior-theologians and enlisted as fierce warrior-nomads into Spain's colonial elite camel corps, *Tropas Nómadas*.

Ban Ki-moon's visit to the Tindouf camps was only the second visit by a secretary general in eighteen years since Kofi Annan in 1998. After having flown into Algeria's strategic military town of Tindouf, close to its southwestern desert border with Morocco, two MINURSO helicopters took Ban to the northern outskirt of Smara camp, and then a convoy of white UN and dark blue Polisario Jeeps drove him slowly down the central tarmac road into the center of the camp, where Boukhari and the tent were waiting to officially receive him. Lining the tarmac was the Sahrawi display of its modern armed soldiers. On approaching the center of Smara, Ban's small convoy was thronged by men, women, children, and the elderly, all chanting political slogans for self-determination. Some said the crowds were angry; others understood the display of deep fervor for international law. Everywhere, the el-them was in use, either covering faces, on shoulders, or being waved in the air. But another fabric of life was soundfully in action (and also always ignored analytically)—Sahrawi women were emitting their piercing ululations, casting a deafening wave, a shrill curtain, through the desert air.

The only time this has been captured textually is in John Mercer's scarce account of another political moment—a precursor to this visit that Ban will not have known about—and in which women are audibly veiling. Two days before Spain formally relinquished Spanish Sahara to Morocco and Mauritania in its secret tripartite Madrid Accords, Mercer (1976, 248) recalls the Polisario inviting approximately forty journalists in Algiers to fly south in a chartered plane to an unspecified event. In the late afternoon of February 26, 1976, the plane landed at Tindouf, and the journalists were shown the makeshift camps and hospital in their earliest stages. They were driven that night into the desert to a large camp near Bir Lehlou, where hundreds of women and children formed a wide circle around a flagpole. A guerrilla unit lined up at the foot of the pole and saluted the new Sahrawi flag, and everyone sang the new Sahrawi national anthem. At midnight, in the dramatic setting of the convoy's headlights, M'Hamid Ould Ziou, president of the provisional Sahrawi Council (which had all forty of its members present), and Mahfoud Ali Beiba Laroussi, deputy general secretary of the Frente Polisario, moved to the center of the circle. There, Ould Ziou read out SADR's first declaration of independence in Arabic, each sentence being translated into Spanish and French for the benefit of the visitors. Rockets and guns were fired, the women emitted the traditional ululations, and the Westerners applauded.

The men surrounding Ban may have lowered their veils, but another veil had been cast by women's shrill evocations, meaningfully enveloping Ban without his realizing. He then went to Rabuni camp to the Presidential Building to meet with the Polisario secretary-general Mohamed Abdelaziz and other senior Polisario and SADR leaders. Ban was among warrior-statesmen—many of whom had been there in Mercer's encounter—and the modest photographs taken to capture Ban seated with the Sahrawi statesmen also capture their black litham now formally placed around their shoulders. The litham had been lowered in the tent but began to raise in Western state infrastructural type buildings. It is interesting to note that later that day, the helicopters took Ban to Bir Lehlou, which poignantly became the headquarters of the MINURSO forces located in the Western Sahara "Free Zone" (or "Liberated Territories"), before returning to Algiers to spend the next official day's visit with the Algerian government.

In one of Ban's press speeches during this regional visit, he used the term *occupation* to describe Morocco's presence on the other side of the world's longest berm, built by Morocco. This inflamed Moroccan sensibilities into a political sulk, which briefly expelled MINURSO from Morocco's side of the berm, epitomizing the underlying tensions in this sentient warzone between the Sahrawi, Morocco, and Algeria. Between French decolonization of Morocco and failed Spanish decolonization of the Western Sahara (then Spanish Sahara), Morocco laid its territorial claims to a "Greater Morocco," incorporating all the Western Sahara and parts of Algeria, Mauritania, and Mali. In 1974, the International Court of Justice set out its legal opinion affirming Sahrawi rights to territorial sovereignty. Shortly afterward, Morocco coordinated the "Green March" as a column of Moroccan civilians advancing into the Western Sahara, ahead of Moroccan militarized troops.[2]

This triggered a long war with the Sahrawi nomadic guerrillas who had formed their liberation movement, the Polisario Front (Popular Front for the

Liberation of Saguia el-Hamra and Río de Oro), which lasted until a UN-led ceasefire in 1991. Morocco's actions are perceived by the Sahrawi and some circles of international jurors and political scientists as a military invasion and, into the present day, a breach of international law on territorial sovereignty and explicit military occupation of approximately two-thirds of Western Sahara (San Martín 2010; Zunes and Mundy 2010). Since the 1991 ceasefire, the Sahrawi have continued constructing their nation-state in exile, located inside the Algerian desert border and pursuing international legal routes for self-determination (Arts and Pinto Liete 2007; Liceras 2014). Today, those Sahrawi who support the Polisario's nationalist self-determination thesis are mostly located either side of Morocco's berm—either as an army in waiting in the Polisario's Tindouf headquarters or as civilian human rights activists living under Moroccan occupation.

Ban Ki-moon crossed various thresholds of Sahrawi masculinity that day. This chapter draws out three analytical aspects from the vignette: legitimacy, the "domestic" of social and biological reproduction, and veiling as central characteristics in customary Sahrawi principles of organization, which relate considerably to gendered interrelationships. These three aspects become layered lenses through which to examine Sahrawi notions and norms during their social transformation from nomadic pastoralism into the "new world" (a continuum we have all experienced) since the colonial period. Part of this transformation for men has been the "modernizing" transition from warrior-nomads to refugee-statesmen, reflected in the shift from conventional desert warfare to new diplomatic battlefields requiring strategic circumnavigation through the corridors of the United Nations.

I have summarized the complex issue of international legal legitimacy, but for the Sahrawi, legitimacy has customarily correlated to biological kinship—a key part of determining on-the-ground territoriality (i.e., nomadic "zones of influence"). The UN's first efforts in the 1990s to initiate voter registration toward self-determination failed because of intense contestations between Sahrawi and Moroccan determinations of "blood" rights to territory, relying primarily on patrilineal determinations (Isidoros 2017; Jensen 2005). These patrilines failed to incorporate women, who are usually property-holders of the customary tents, and therefore obscure the role of Sahrawi women-at-war. These patrilines also assumed patriarchy, which fails to capture what can be very powerful female kin-coalitions and therefore the underlying interwoven nature of gendered relations.

Female kin groups are as equally widely dispersed across this vast western territory of the Sahara as are men's, and they have been written into the cultural and biological landscape since antiquity. "Calculating men" in demographical determinations presents only half of a picture, so that Ban's meeting of Boukhari is not just the meeting of two senior "military" men. Imperceptibly behind Boukhari are Sahrawi women. Since the 1980s, in the refugee camps the Sahrawi have long used UNHCR canvas tents and the handwoven camel and goat hair tents that would have taken women years to make (and are contingent on camel numbers in familial herds). Today, they are made and used sparingly, mostly for cultural-political festivals and anniversaries, displayed as cultural heritage. The handwoven tent used to receive Ban was an act of biological hospitality, where trust in Ban was high enough to lead him symbolically across one of the most important thresholds in Sahrawi life. This threshold also represents one of territorial and cultural authenticity, evocative for the Sahrawi as Ban's (inadvertent) itinerary having to move from the camps' location in exile on Algerian soil into the Liberated Territory to visit his MINURSO troops at Bir Lehlou.

Also striking is how Ban arrived in the Sahrawi midst: their dark blue Polisario Jeeps provided the real protective infrastructure around Ban, not his UN troops who, in the middle of a desert, would have been largely unable to protect him. This reminds me of a much earlier counterpart of Ban's: General Francisco Bens (1904–1925), one of the first Spanish colonizers, also replayed in Mercer's rare account above. When Bens first arrived, he wrote of the little colony as "a warehouse and a flag, far from Madrid," but as a master diplomat Bens built bridges of trust with some of the Sahrawi tribes. Studying Bens's memoirs, San Martín charts his changing personal perception from a negative image linked to existing precolonial conceptions of uncivilized inland tribes with a lust for blood to his learning of Hassaniya and his journeys into the interior guided by and under the protection of the tribes (Isidoros 2015). Part of the descriptive quietness in the opening vignette relates to the continuing quiet admiration that the Sahrawi receive worldwide. The Sahrawi as warrior-nomads and now as refugee-statesmen have a long history of turning political foes into biologically legal kin. Ben's memoirs have little account of women, but they are always there, even if appearing on the outer periphery of Western eyes, in the interplay between the male litham and female ululations.

Receiving Ban in this most recent encounter by the Polisario and SADR leadership signifies his entering a sentient warzone and crossing over a "modern" threshold of nation and state, which are Western structures of patriarchy. Receiving Ban, first by Boukhari and in the tent, reflects traditional crossings of tent thresholds, which require skilled biological navigation between genders, through the midst of potential female coalitions and into the deepest heart of

Figure 7.2: Traditional tent with the Sahrawi national
flag. This is very similar to the tent Ban Ki-moon
entered on his visit, surrounded by throngs of Sahrawi
cheering his arrival. © Konstantina Isidoros

"family," where children are present. It also reflects the shift in battlefields, into
the United Nations as new forms of relatedness between UN officials playing the
Kiplingesque Great Game. On the basis of international law, the Sahrawi right to
self-determination and territorial sovereignty is legitimate, and Morocco's annexa-
tion of Western Sahara is a contravention. In other words, everyone knows that the
Sahrawi have law on their side, but it is biological authenticity that is at the heart
of the stalled self-determination attempted by the United Nations in the 1990s.

Although these analytical suggestions unfold a series of customary thresholds that the parties in the vignette were crossing, the rest of this chapter
focuses on the practice of male veiling. On the surface, the tent encounter
was a public encounter between men, yet the Sahrawi el-them, a sign of warrior masculinity, was muted to the sound of women's receiving ululations.
The thresholds enveloping the encounter between Ban and Boukhari come
down to customary ontologies, best explained through an examination of contextual history, where we catch the glimpse of the Sahrawi
el-them.

AL-MULATHTHAMUN: THE VEILED OR MUFFLED ONES

Historical references to the Moors and male veiling first appear in accounts of
early Arab travelers, historians, and biographers, with regard to the Almoravid
empire stretching over the western Maghreb and Al-Andalus. Almoravid

comes from the Arabic *al-murabitun* (pl. *al-murabit*), which denotes "one who is tying," or figuratively, "one who is ready for battle at a fortress," and is related to *ribat*, a frontier monastery-fortress (*rabat*: to tie to unite, to encamp). These Arab scholars refer to them as *al-mulaththamun*, "the veiled/muffled ones" (from litham in Arabic), with some suggestions it was a custom adapted from southern Sanhaja Berbers (Hart 1962; Norris 1982).

Richard Smith (2003, 490–492) locates al-Yaʻqubi as the first Arab author to describe the Saharan Berbers "a people called Anbiya of the Sanhaja, who have no permanent dwellings. It is their custom to veil their faces with their turbans." Ibn Khaldun's fourteenth-century account speaks of a "veiled Sinhaja [*sic*] who live in the desert of the Maghreb on the fringe of the sandy deserts which lie between the Berbers and the Sudanese Negroes." Subsequent Arab scholars correlate the litham to the Sanhaja such as al-Bakri: "They do not remove these veils under any circumstances. A man does not distinguish his relative or friend unless he is wearing the veil. Thus if one of them is killed in a battle and his veil is removed, nobody can recognize him until the covering is put back." Interestingly, this last quote contrasts with Western fear of veiling (mainly women) as rendering a person indistinguishable.

As the descendants of this antiquity, this veiled legacy is a cultural transmission into the contemporary practice of Sahrawi male veiling and linguistically into Hassaniya as a noun *el-them* and a verb *mutalaththimi*. Whether it emerged for practical reasons in a desert ecology by earlier inhabitants and passed on to the emerging Arab empires, or it was brought into North Africa with the arrival of Islam, the Sahrawi el-them has played an important practical, political, and symbolic feature in the fabric of life in the Western Sahara Desert for at least three millennia.

Of the two major sociolinguistic groups in the Sahara Desert, the Tamashek speakers in the central-eastern desert became epitomized by the French as the Tuareg and "les hommes bleus." A niche group of Saharan studies historians and anthropologists, such as Dominique Casajus, Jeremy Keenan, Susan Rasmussen, Robert Murphy, and Johannes Nicolaisen, have focused considerably on the Tuareg. The Sahrawi on the western side of the Sahara have only recently received anthropological attention, previously appearing anomalously under the conflated French term *Maure* (the Moors in English). In historical European literature, they are often indistinguishable from the Tuareg unless principally identified as Hassaniya speakers in Mauritania, but when they do appear, they are equally distinguished as legendary warrior-nomads and warrior-theologians commanding the Saharan trading and raiding system in the western and Atlantic desert territories. One striking phenomenon that both sociolinguistic groups share is the practice of male veiling.

The Tuareg are fabled for their distinctive and visually striking male veiling practices. Their *tagelmust* seems to express greater significance to outsiders and scholars, whereas the Sahrawi el-them bears a minimalist quality in display of status, identity, and wealth and has not been historically captured as romantically and prolifically as the Tuareg tagelmust in photographs and film. In this sense, the tagelmust seems to more strongly communicate Pierre Bourdieu's (1990, 53) "conscious aim [to] express mastery." Its intricate folds provide something structurally concrete for the analyst to grasp, something ceremonially "fancy" as a starting point in contacts between scholars and interlocutors. Austrian anthropologist Ines Kohl (2009) explores how young Tuareg males express their masculinity and beauty by increasing the elaborateness of their traditional dress. For some reason, unlike the Tuareg, the Sahrawi have a markedly different, plainly unelaborate *technique du corps* (Mauss 1935). However, elaboration is relative. The visually striking and more noticeable tagelmust attracts greater attention and seems to communicate a great deal to the (analytical) eye, but the Sahrawi el-them can be better understood as expressing a mastery in understatement—in its lesser embellishment and amplification.

Classical anthropological attention to male veiling practices focuses on the Tuareg. These predominant hypotheses overlap and generally correlate male veiling with social conduct and expression, "veiled" by ritual, symbolism, and identity. Casajus (1985, 1987) and Keenan (1977) first discovered veiling as a way to prevent evil spirits from entering the body. Rasmussen (1991) focuses on rules and displays of formality and ceremony, moral values (*takarakit*, translated variously as reserve/respect, honor, shame, and embarrassment), and Islamic doctrinal prescriptions for modesty in relation to access to property. Similar connections have been made with class and age-sets. Keenan (1977) found the tagelmust related to the higher sociopolitical status of men over women, whereas Nicolaisen (1961) found it rooted in interactions toward women. Murphy (1965) saw male veiling as an idiom of male privacy creating symbolic social distance, whereas Claudot-Hawad (1992) uniquely points to men's dangerous encounter with the "wild" of the Sahara—a counterpoint to Sherry Ortner's (1974) nature:culture thesis.

THE FABRIC OF MASCULINE LIFE

Fieldwork observations and interlocutors' explanations find these interpretations applicable to Sahrawi veiling. The Spanish colonial period and war years prior to the 1991 ceasefire produced the very first few visual images and ciné film of the Sahrawi by Spanish soldiers and administrators. Men are consistently captured wearing the el-them, whereas women usually have their faces and arms uncovered. Despite not capturing moments when women might have veiled, neither did they produce essentialized/exaggerated references to male veiling, even though these images clearly indicate a romantic capture of the exotic native Other.

These colonial records clearly portray Sahrawi men wearing the el-them and dara'a and women wearing *e-taglidi*, a scarf wrapped over the upper torso, and *el-zar*, a white skirt gathered around the waist, or just e-taglidi as a full-length single body scarf. The e-taglidi passed high above the head over long hair plaited (sometimes right across the forehead hairline) into a high bun to the front of the head in which small valuables were hidden (referred to me as "like the *makhzan*" [treasury]). Although it could be raised to hide or protect the face in the same way as the el-them, hiding the face does not seem to carry a prescription for women in the same way as the el-them does for men. The e-taglidi was crafted from the same fabric as the el-them, positioned or used differently, and nuanced around differentiations not of gender but of roles and tasks requiring different habitus, bodily knowhow, and tools.

Contemporary Sahrawi men, not women, are still the principal and customary wearers of the head covering, el-them, where it closely represents the conventional Euro-American interpretation of the Arab-Muslim veil as substantially covering the head and face. Although men may use different folding and wrapping techniques, they tend to follow a fairly similar structure. Unlike the section of e-taglidi covering women's heads, in its maximal usage, el-them leaves a thin slit for the eyes, making it difficult for an onlooker to distinguish them. Attention is not paid to any overt displays of complex folds or design of the Tuareg tagelmust.

In its most basic but primary functionality in an arid-zone climate (sand and powder storms, cold winter, summer heat), men tightly cover their heads. Adjustments can loosen or tighten it, and its simplicity means it can also be efficiently dismantled in such a manner that it appears to fall apart into the hand (unlike the complex winding and unwinding of the *tagelmust*). In agreeable weather or informal social settings, it is more loosely wrapped around the head or shoulders, with the entire face and neck open and visible.

The Sahrawi say they feel the cold easily and discern the smallest changes in temperature. The el-them helps maintain balanced body heat, creating a thermosphere against the outside temperature. This works to the same scientific principles as wearing warmer clothes to build up layers of heat or staying cool (diminishing core body heat) by drinking hot tea. Notably, the primary black

color of the el-them bears high heat absorption and retention qualities, a preference also found in the traditional handmade tent made with darker camel hair.
The el-them is used as much in the August temperatures reaching at least fifty
degrees Celsius as during January's zero to subzero temperatures. The same is
ascribed to women's black e-taglidi and the traditional camel and goat hair tent.

Of all these fabric signifiers, the black e-taglidi and white el-zar have disappeared except at cultural heritage festivals, and they have been replaced by the
contemporary *melhfa* (pl. *lemlaḥef*), worn by women since the early 1980s. The
melhfa now features bright colors and patterns and is worn as a single length
wrapped around the whole body and without hair tied high so that the fabric
falls flat over the head. The customary color of black in el-them, e-taglidi, and
tents is crucial. Although the camel hair is technically more of a dark brownish
color and makes up most of this fabric, from even a short distance it not only
looks black but is also culturally understood to be black. Interlocutors ascribe
these "black" fabrics as their historical symbolic marker of the Hassaniya-
speaking sociolinguistic group, distinguishing against the "blue" of the Tuareg.

These references to the black and white fabrics refer to a customary cloth
nilé, which is a thin, translucent, gauzy muslin, preferably with a heightened
metallic sheen, of either unfast indigo or white dye (Balfour-Paul 1997). The
unfast indigo easily rubs off onto the skin and carries great significance
attached to extreme beauty. Traditional songs referring to a man or woman
whose skin is "black" stained by the indigo is an implicitly coded reference to
immense beauty. The dye is also perceived to provide protection from the sun
and sand and to wipe the body down from dust/sweat. There is reluctance to
wash nilé fabric, and not just because of the unfast dye. What we would perceive
as accumulated dirt is an increase in the special ethnobotanical properties of
nilé to protect against dirt.[3] White nilé is customarily worn in el-them form
by elderly men of significance, such as shaykhs or renowned poets, musi-
cians, artists, or clerics, likely an influence of Islam reaching the Sahara in the
late seventh century.

A host grandmother elaborated on one particular historical purpose of the
el-them, namely to mask/protect individual male identities on battlefields and
during raids on encampments. She described rules of war relating to what could
not be plundered: females, children, or the elderly, and the smaller subsistence
herds kept nearby, inside encampments. So too were the interiors of women's
tents (again, concepts of makhzan) intended to be untransgressable—a place
in which valuable assets (children, livestock, the elderly) are sacrosanct. Com-
pensation out of raiding plunder was customarily allocated to the enemy for

loss of warrior-males on the battlefield and contraventions of what should not have been raided.

Male interlocutors offered a distinct range of explanations of el-them: privacy, concealment/shyness, and anonymity; handsomeness, beauty, and being a man; completing and making elegant a man's presentation of himself to others; social reserve, gentility, self-composure, and modesty (*sahwa*, remarkably similar to Tuareg takarakit as both cultural signifier and personal behavior); and religious reserve, modesty (*haya*), and piety as much for men as women in one's relationship with god. Women likewise gave a range of explanations for e-taglidi, but clearly with different degrees of covering and behaviors for composures and tasks.

Black litham reflect the black tent embodied through the fabric of gendered symbolic divisions of labor: the el-them becomes men's mobile tent, which men put up and take down as a moving makhzan, whereas the tent as women's property is women's "veil," which they put up and take down. In Ban's visit, the female tent was raised and the men's veils were lowered. Biological kinship was offered as customary hospitality, signaling that certain death (in war) was diminished.

REFASHIONING SAHRAWI MASCULINITY

Increasingly since the 1991 UN-led ceasefire, the Sahrawi have appeared in photographs, films, books, journalistic articles, online blogs, and social media, in relation to the rise in year-round humanitarians, campaigners, and commentators visiting the war zone and the refugee camps. The el-them is accidentally captured by this external audience by virtue of its quiet presence rather than for aesthetic beauty or overt meanings. The Sahrawi are not headlined as "men of the black veil"; their modern political problem takes prime position (as "the last colony of Africa" and "the forgotten conflict"). Yet the el-them is a popular gift and souvenir enthusiastically donned by visitors conveying a "got the T-shirt" form of authenticity.

The el-them remains a functional item, not succumbing to the modernizing, "civilizing," and nationalizing narrative. It retains deep historical association to the Sahrawi as ancient desert warriors on camelback in a long lineage back to *al-mulaththamun* in antiquity, as a uniform of authenticity in their recruitment into the Spanish *Tropas Nómadas,* and as Cuba-influenced guerrilla fighters during the 1960–1970s war years wearing modern camouflage uniforms with the el-them. It has evaded overt transformation, remaining a politically serene symbol of cultural heritage and authenticity. The underlying semiotic of the el-them remains embedded in internalized ontologies of masculine warriorship. In the other kind of undisturbed quietness, that of a quiet admiration from international jurists and campaigners, the Sahrawi have transformed from leg-endary warrior-nomads into skilled refugee-statesmen building their nascent nation-state. This perception floats ethereally in international legal terms above their headquarters of the Tindouf refugee camps. And they are seen as soldier-diplomats, dexterously navigating through international law and human rights and through the corridors of the United Nations, the European Union, and the African Union. Lowering the el-them communicates the idea of not being at war with the onlooker; it signifies a moment of intended negotiation for peace and of alliances (political and economic) through a new vehicle of biological reproduction, that of international law.

The khaki colored el-them appeared in the 1960s as part of the early anti-colonial Sahrawi military uniform of camouflage. The light blue one has Mau-ritanian connections to the matching blue dara'a, most usually given as gifts to foreign visitors to the refugee camps (perhaps in foreign conflation of all Moors famed for the blue veil). Both white and light blue fabric continues to be widely used as matching dara'a robes for men dressing up for occasions such as at weddings or ʿId celebrations. In everyday use, the cheaper cotton el-them in black, blue, white, and khaki is worn with Western male attire—trousers, shirts, sweaters, and jackets. This overall appearance remains shabby, vastly different from the intricateness of the tagelmust. The black-indigo nilé version remains the most meaningful to an internal audience.

Although Sahrawi soldiers wear khaki camouflage military uniforms, in a contemporary setting, all men of fighting age wearing their ordinary, everyday clothes and el-them constitute a fighting force of warrior-nomads in waiting. On the other side of the berm, Sahrawi youth living under Moroccan occu-pation wear the black el-them, and women wear very colorful lemlaḥef as a crystal-clear identity signal to the armed forces of resistance to occupation, much like the secret spraying of resistance graffiti and the banned Sahrawi flag. The latter two are highly charged and politically provocative acts that can trigger the wrath (i.e., torture and disappearance) of Moroccan security forces.

The el-them remains a masculine and semiotic fabric of life, whereas its match-ing female e-taglidi is lost in its past everyday-ness. Since the 1991 ceasefire, the growing external audience of international legal, political, and humanitarian visitors share a quality of being "in solidarity" with their hosts, a phenomenon that has transformed politico-heritage meanings to other items. E-tay (tea) and e-taglidi are performed—Bourdieu's (1990, 53) "expressed mastery" again—in the heritage narrative about the Sahrawi configuring a nation-state and the struggle for self-determination. To illustrate, e-tay is reconstructed into a story about failed decolonization, whereby each glass narrates a journey from bitter political entanglement to sweet freedom. The change from e-taglidi to melhfa has been figuratively woven into the fabric of social reform as women's equality, literacy, and strength of character. The el-them and dara'a epitomize Sahrawi masculinity as both traditional and modern, but all four have gained momentum and prominence as cultural symbols of traditional and authentic identity during a modern period of transition to nationalism. Visitors proudly learn how to wear el-them and melhfa and make e-tay; the fabrics and colorful teapots are frequently given as cultural gifts to departing foreign visitors.

Similarly, the el-them has become quietly synonymous to the Sahrawi for those in the geopolitical theater of the United Nations and diplomatic battlefields of international law. Yet the el-them has remained a tacit Sahrawi "internal" object, practice, and bodily vocabulary. By internal, I mean private and undisclosed; it has not yet been "externalized" for consumption by foreign observers. Unlike for the Tuareg, it has not yet been ascribed major significance; it remains meaningless to the external vocabulary, and it is precisely that underplay that I think is fascinating. This explains why so many litham sat quietly on shoulders and seemed to melt into the background on such a rare day as Ban Ki-moon's visit. These litham were actually everywhere, among the Sahrawi men and women who formed the huge throngs outside the tent and the Parliamentary buildings.

So why were the principal Sahrawi leaders not fully veiled? Because this event was akin to a council of war, a meeting of enemies, a moment of alliance making, and an opportunity for peace negotiation. The male veil must come down as an act of equalizing submission between the dangerously powerful. The rules are complex because in everyday life when men approach and cross a tent threshold, there are customary regulations centered around the performance and actions of masculinity that structure when one must be fully veiled and when one loosens the veil.

CONCLUSION

There is an element of playfulness in this unfolding analysis of male veiling during a brief ethnographic moment. The way these veils are worn and moved in everyday life, their practical and metaphorical communications, are themselves very playful—in a serious manner, of course—as much as anthropology is a playful art of capturing brief practices of meaning over a series of analytical thresholds. Afsaneh Najmabadi (2005, 132–155) has argued that veiling is more than a performance of cultural authenticity; it is rather a marker of the homosocial affectionate world of men and women. Radhika Chopra (2006, 154) discusses gendering the veil, "invisible" men, and men's domestic labors: "Veiling must expand beyond the primary focus on clothing and must be viewed as a system that frames bodily styles, speech forms, and the language of gestures."

The el-them elucidates the minutiae of its "bodily knowing" in a series of embodied practices to protect the authenticity of Sahrawi masculinity and to serve as a metaphor for power, where an international theater is briefly played out in a desert setting. These are embodied strategies of struggle (presenting the underlying suffering) and self-determination (presenting the goal). The subtleties of this fabric kick into play as a range of communicative adjustments of correction, composure, and (in)conspicuousness that oscillate between marking and distancing in- and out-group identities. They also incorporate those out-groups—drawing the metaphorical veil around Ban Ki-moon in a heightened and historic moment of importance. In Bourdieu's sense, this is an underlying feedback loop of a logic of practice. Likewise, in Rasmussen's (1991) sense of "veiled self, transparent meanings," the male el-them continues its ancient meaning and contemporary use, but as more than just culture, to move "betwixt and between" (Turner 1967) a new wilderness in international law. The failure of international law to assert Sahrawi independence of the postcolonial Western Saharan nation-state is a failure of Western masculinity, creating legal-biological pollution through which Sahrawi men must now operate—in the betwixt spaces of diplomatic war and international law. Julie Peteet (2000) finds similar rituals of resistance as rites of passage for political consciousness, whereby the symbolic creates a dialogic of power and transformation.

Men are "moving" these fabrics, drawing them open and closed in similar forms of spatial hermeneutics found in the beautiful symbolism of Bourdieu's (1970) early theoretical work on the Kabyle House.[4] This range of interpretations brings nuanced analysis of masculinity to counter "harem theory" (Abu-Lughod 1989; Alloula 1986), which holds that harems have long been stereotyped as full of sexualized women hidden by men. I previously counterargued for the "circulation of men" (Isidoros 2018). Challenging the old Oriental stereotypes, men also seek the feminine domestic space for privacy, safety, and confidentiality. These nomadic tents are places too where women actively protect and defend their menfolk. This chapter catches the brief ethnographic moment of men hiding men: the Sahrawi screening Ban Ki-moon as one of the most important allies, inside the symbolic traditional tent, and in a dangerous location—a sentient warzone. The use of the tent as female property is shared as a male harem (or anti-harem to harem theory)—men using and needing the domestic interior to conduct their intensely serious and life-threatening political engagements. In many ways, the best place to plan life-death "battle strategies" is "in the kitchen," or in the tent.

Ban Ki-moon entered a Sahrawi "world reversed" (Bourdieu 1970, 753) of customary Sahrawi male movement between and across female tents, and of failed international law in the movements between traditional warrior battlefields and contemporary diplomatic statesmanship. The desert is akin to Turner's (1967) "forest of symbols." The el-them is a mobile tent in its own right. Both sit on the beige desert horizon like little black hats, each containing an equally agile *harim* inside them.[5] Opening and lowering both—inviting entry and a full gaze—creates a threshold that must be crossed to enter and gaze on (and to leave and look out from). Both are a means of (re)ordering matters that are out of place. In another of Bourdieu's (1990) senses, in one day's visit, Ban moved through the Sahrawi sociocultural universe, which contained not binary oppositions of abstract disembodied rules but a phenomemology of "other words," mutually enforcing oppositions in and of "other worlds" in order to create a conjunction of collective understanding and practice. Ban's visit denoted sets of values being inverted. Entering the female tent and the lowering of male (*and* female) veils illuminate a customary Sahrawi threshold as a site of passage to encounter and resolve socially marked trajectories, and in a rite of passage along alliance, separation, and inversion of what have otherwise been previously opposing principles such as East/West, masculine/feminine, dominant/dominated, and contemporaneously law and its failure (Bourdieu 1980, 158). The fabric of the tent and of the el-them carry the metaphors of the logic of meaning and practice.

Perhaps most extraordinary for Sahrawi masculinity is the contradistinction to the Tuareg who have become denigrated as "terrorists" and "insurgents" in their own independence movement, Azawad. The same veil operates in two independence movements and two male identities—one internationally legally confirmed, the other not. Ban's visit to the Sahrawi evoked a series of unspoken "middles of nowhere" caught in tacit "betwixts and betweens" of war and peace. That two cultural masculinities came together, face-to-face in this vast and ancient desert, literally "out of the blue." One was embodied symbolically by the black-indigo nilé fabric of the el-them and the other by the official UN shade of blue (Pantone 279), and the other was embodied by the same light blue as the el-them and dara'a, all alongside the intermingling of the Sahrawi white dara'a and white UN Jeeps.

NOTES

1. The Tuareg are a large Berber ethnic confederation inhabiting the central-eastern side of the Sahara (eastern Algerian desert to southwestern Libya, Mali, Niger, Burkina Faso, and farther south in northern Nigeria).

2. See Spadola (2013) for a fascinating anthropological insight.

3. Henna possesses similarly treasured properties—of healing, cleaning, beauty, and protection against dirt. Washing also makes it fade.

4. For example, light/dark, political/sacred, birth/death.

5. Harim, also known as *zenana* in the Indian subcontinent, properly refers to domestic spaces that are reserved for the women of the house in a Muslim family.

BIBLIOGRAPHY

Abu-Lughod, Lila. 1989. "Zones of Theory in the Anthropology of the Arab World." *Annual Review of Anthropology* 18:267–306.

Alloula, Malek. 1986. *The Colonial Harem*. Minneapolis: University of Minnesota Press.

Arts, Karin, and Pedro Pinto Liete, eds. 2007. *International Law and the Question of Western Sahara*. Leiden: International Platform of Jurists for East Timor (IPJET).

Balfour-Paul, Jenny. 1997. *Indigo in the Arab World*. London: Routledge.

Bourdieu, Pierre. 1970. "La Maison Kabyle ou le Monde Renversé" [The Kabyle House or the world reversed]. In *Échanges et communications: mélanges offerts à Claude Lévi-Strauss à l'occasion de son 60e anniversaire*, edited by Jean Puillon and Pierre Maranda, 739–758. Paris: Mouton.

———. 1980. *The Logic of Practice*. Stanford, CA: Stanford University Press.

———. 1990. *In Other Words: Essays towards a Reflexive Sociology*. Cambridge: Polity.

Casajus, Dominique. 1985. "Why Do the Tuareg Veil Their Faces?" In *Contexts and Levels*, edited by Robert H. Barnes, Daniel de Coppet, and Robert J. Parkin, 68–77. *Journal of the Anthropological Society of Oxford, Occasional Papers* 4.

———. 1987. *La Tente Dans la Solitude: La Société et les Morts chez les Touaregs Kel Ferwan* [The tent in solitude: Society and the dead with the Kel Ferwan Tuareg]. Cambridge: Cambridge University Press.

Chopra, Radhika. 2006. "Invisible Men: Masculinity, Sexuality, and Male Domestic Labor." *Men and Masculinities* 9, no. 2: 152–167.

Claudot-Hawad, Hélène. 2009. "'Woman the Shelter' and 'Man the Traveller': The Representation of Gender among the Tuaregs." Paper delivered at second World Congress on Matriarchal Studies, San Marcos and Austin, Texas.

Hart, David M. 1962. "The Social Structure of the Rgibat Bedouins of the Western Sahara." *Middle East Journal* 16, no. 4: 515–527.

Isidoros, Konstantina. 2015. "The Silencing of Unifying Tribes: The Colonial Construction of Tribe and Its 'Extraordinary Leap' to Nascent Nation-State Formation in Western Sahara." *Journal of the Anthropological Society of Oxford* 7, no. 2: 168–190.

———. 2017. "Unveiling the Colonial Gaze: Sahrawi Women in Nascent Nation-State Formation in the Western Sahara." *Interventions: International Journal of Postcolonial Studies* 19, no. 4: 487–506.

———. 2018. *Nomads and Nation-Building in the Western Sahara: Gender, Politics and the Sahrawi*. London: I. B. Tauris.

Jensen, Eric. 2005. *Western Sahara: Anatomy of a Stalemate*. London: Lynne Rienner.

Keenan, Jeremy. 1977. "The Tuareg Veil." *Middle Eastern Studies* 13, no. 1: 3–13.

Kohl, Ines. 2009. *Beautiful Modern Nomads: Bordercrossing Tuareg between Niger, Algeria and Libya*. Berlin: Reimer.

Liceras, Juan S. 2014. *International Law and the Western Sahara Conflict*. Oisterwijk, Neth.: Wolf Legal Publishers.

Mauss, Marcel. 1935. "Les techniques du corps" [Body techniques]. *Journal de Psychologie* 32, no. 3–4.

Mercer, John. 1976. *Spanish Sahara*. London: Allen and Unwin.

Murphy, Robert F. 1965. "Social Distance and the Veil." *American Anthropologist* 66, no. 6: 1257–1274.

Najmabadi, Afsaneh. 2005. *Women with Mustaches and Men without Beards: Gender and Sexual Anxieties of Iranian Modernity*. Berkeley: University of California Press.

Nicolaisen, Johannes. 1961. "Esai sur la Religion et la Magie Touregues" [Essay on Tuareg religion and magic]. *Folk* 3:113–162.

Norris, Harry T. 1982. *The Berbers in Arabic Literature*. London: Longman.

Ortner Sherry. 1974. "Is Female to Male as Nature Is to Culture?" In *Women, Culture and Society*, edited by Michelle Z. Rosaldo and Louise Lamphere, 67–88. Stanford, CA: Stanford University Press.

Peteet, Julie. 2000. "Male Gender and Rituals of Resistance in the Palestinian Intifada: A Cultural Politics of Violence." In *Imagined Masculinities: Male Identities and Culture in the Modern Middle East*, edited by Mai Ghoussoub and Emma Sinclair-Webb, 103–126. London: Saqi Books.

Rasmussen, Susan J. 1991. "Veiled Self, Transparent Meanings: Tuareg Headdress as Social Expression." *Ethnology* 30, no. 2: 101–117.

San Martín, Pablo. 2010. *Western Sahara: The Refugee Nation*. Cardiff: University of Wales Press.

Smith, Richard L. 2003. "What Happened to the Ancient Libyans? Chasing Sources Across the Sahara from Herodotus to Ibn Khaldun." *Journal of World History* 14, no. 4: 459–500.

Spadola, Emilio. 2013. "'Our Master's Call': Mass Media and 'the People' in Morocco's 1975 Green March." In *Anthropology of the Middle East and North Africa: Into the New Millennium*, edited by Susan Slyomovics and Sherine Hafez, 260–284. Bloomington: Indiana University Press.

Turner, Victor W. 1967. *The Forest of Symbols: Aspects of Ndembu Ritual*. Ithaca, NY: Cornell University Press.

Zunes, Stephen, and Jacob Mundy. 2010. *Western Sahara: War, Nationalism, and Conflict Irresolution*. Syracuse, NY: Syracuse University Press.

KONSTANTINA ISIDOROS is Lecturer in Anthropology at St Catherine's College and Research Affiliate of the Institute of Social and Cultural Anthropology at the University of Oxford. She is author of *Nomads and Nation-Building in the Western Sahara: Gender, Politics and the Sahrawi*.

PART III

MASCULINITY AND FAMILIAL FUTURES: SEX, MARRIAGE, AND FATHERHOOD UNDER THREAT

EIGHT

—ɯɯ—

DESIRING THE NATION

Masculinity, Marriage, and Futurity in Lebanon

SABIHA ALLOUCHE

INTRODUCTION

The fictive and imprecise category of the "Arab man" has been documented as effeminate (Najmabadi 2005), violent (Accad 1992; Aghacy 2009; Ghannam 2013; Ghoussoub and Sinclair-Webb 2000), and emotionally inferior (Allouche 2015; Massad 2008). Recent scholarship on Arab masculinities has sought to examine them beyond the lens of security, Islam, and negative representations in Western media by bringing forth novel conceptualizations focused on Arab men's emotional investment in family life and by drawing our attention to further underresearched masculinities.

Conversely, this chapter goes beyond ethnographic delineations, bridging the gap between anthropological writing and political analysis in order to show how invocations of masculine ideals, illustrated by my interlocutors' narratives about masculinity and marriage, are constantly shifting. These perceptions emerge at the intersection of perceptions about the nation's Others—namely, Syrian refugees—and ongoing economic precarity. To this end, the chapter introduces the concept of the m'attar, understood as the "lesser man," in the context of contemporary Lebanon in order to showcase the enmeshment of nationalistic ideologies with gendered affects.

The discourse surrounding the m'attar is almost entirely absent from the literature on masculinity or on gender in the Middle East. This omission reveals how certain knowledges are deemed more important and are therefore more likely to be exported than others. Moreover, and by virtue of its very ontology, the m'attar directly challenges the globally produced and consumed stereotype of the Arab man as inherently violent.

The m'attar is often contrasted with and constructed in opposition to the *shāṭer* (pl. *shāṭara*). The shāṭer is astute inasmuch as he is cunning, ingenious, sharp, and streetwise. Contrariwise, the m'attar is pitiful and piteous and, generally speaking, far from poignancy and power of presence. The production of polarized attributes in relation to hegemonic and subordinate masculinities is not new. Nonetheless, this chapter shows how the nation reproduces itself through the concomitance of affective attachments with gender. Precisely, it illustrates how the relocation of the m'attar to the realm of the Syrian Other works toward reinforcing Lebanese-ness, understood as sophistication, reciprocity, and empathy, as ideal masculine attributes.

The data related in this chapter pertain largely to my female interlocutors. This fact ought not to be seen as outside the aim or scope of this edited work, which places masculinity at its forefront, center, and margins. As John Scott (1986, 1074) reminded us, to think about gender analytically is "to treat the opposition between male and female as problematic rather than known, as something contextually defined, repeatedly constructed." A similar view can be found two decades later in Afsaneh Najmabadi (2005, 1) to whom an analytical use of gender means that "sources about men are also sources about women" and vice versa.

Based on fieldwork I conducted over ten months between 2015 and 2016, I discern a shift in the discourse of marriage in Lebanon from "becoming parents" to "becoming partners." Similar findings have been documented in contemporary Jordan (Adely 2016), Turkey (Hart 2007), or Iran (Afary 2009). More emphasis is placed on partnership and empathy than on fulfilling one's marital duties, to name husbands as "breadwinners" and wives as "good wives/mothers." This shift challenges traditional household dynamics and could easily be misconstrued as gender equality. Whereas traditional expectations associated with marriage still exist, emotional investment and joint decision-making is equally important. At the same time, my fieldwork informed me that the ideal Lebanese husband is constructed along highly nationalistic lines defined in opposition to the Syrian Other. Such findings are troubling given the long history of kin alliances and transnational links between Lebanese and Syrians citizens, which pushes me to conceive of hope as a highly gendered trope that reproduces gender inequality. I thus argue that current articulations of masculine ideals produce marriage as an illusionary space of equality between husband and wife since the shift toward "becoming partners" still reproduces preexisting masculine societal privileges, albeit in an increasingly precarious economy and anti-Syrian context. Furthermore, and under an increasingly virulent neoliberal economy, the elevation of the Lebanese man "above all other men" emerges from the broader realization that traditional gendered household responsibilities—husbands as "breadwinners" and wives as "good wives/mothers"—have become unattainable. Throughout the chapter, I draw directly on my interlocutors' narratives and the major themes that saturated my fieldwork in support of my argument.

This chapter first reflects on the fieldwork that informed my work. It then draws on my data in order to showcase the relocation of the m'attar to the Syrian Other. The chapter concludes by pondering the conflation of hope with nationalistic attachments in order to conceive of hope as a gendered affect that works toward the production of the nation through exclusionary processes.

NOTES ON FIELDWORK

The fieldwork took place between January and September 2015 and further shorter periods in 2016. It was conducted in the cities of Beirut (Lebanon's capital) and Tripoli (Lebanon's second largest city). It was my wish to do a thorough fieldwork in Tripoli, but the events during 2014 and 2015 meant that the city was regularly shut down and mobility was reduced. Further shorter periods of follow-up work took place throughout 2016.

Tripoli, unlike Beirut, is hardly the site for ethnographic work conducted in Lebanon. A cosmopolitan city, Beirut is the geographical site of the highly centralized Lebanese state, which results in the proliferation of both local and global businesses, including Lebanon's largest universities and publishing houses. Tripoli's population is almost exclusively Sunni Muslim. However, despite this gap, both cities housed similar narratives on romantic love and spouse selection.

For this research, I interviewed twenty cis heterosexual couples preparing for imminent marriage both jointly and separately. I conducted the interviews in Arabic before transcribing them and eventually translating them into English. My interlocutors ranged between twenty and thirty-five years old, and most had pursued some level of education on graduating from high school. Also, most hailed from what could be categorized as middle-to-low-income backgrounds. In this chapter, a middle-to-low income refers to a life that, albeit escaping prevalent definitions of poverty, is nevertheless lived in uncertainty. For instance, most of my interlocutors' parents were or had been indebted over a prolonged period as a result of acquiring the necessary tuition fees for their children's schooling and further education. Another example is that of Lina, whose family was "living it to a minimum" at the time of my fieldwork because all their savings went to covering her mother's medical bills following her diagnosis with breast cancer.[1]

On another note, Lebanon is understood in this work as the locus of myriad collectives that endure precarity simultaneously but separately and distinctively. These collectives include but are not limited to ordinary Lebanese citizens who increasingly find themselves unable to cope with a deteriorating economy, forcibly displaced Syrian citizens who lack the means to rent property, the Palestinian population who has been confined to its camps since the 1950s, and migrant foreign workers who endure colorism and further discriminatory processes on a daily basis. Their everyday befits what Asef Bayat (2013, 15) terms "quiet encroachment," or the "discreet and prolonged ways in which the poor struggle to survive and to better their lives by quietly impinging on the propertied and powerful, and on society at large." Although each group encounters and displays a distinct type of precarity, what most interests me is the nationalistic logic that ensues, whereby the Lebanese national self is defined in relation to the lesser Syrian Other. Here, the Syrian Other is best understood as a distilled rhetoric that encapsulates foreignness.

My data hereafter demonstrate the roles of both language and practice in relocating the m'attar to the realm of the Syrian Other. I argue this relocation is necessary for the professing of Lebanese-ness as a quintessential masculine ideal in addition to reflecting how nationalist sentiments are produced in tandem with gendered attachments. In other words, hegemonic masculinity increasingly emerges at the intersection of perceptions of the nation's Other—namely Syrian refugees and a life of precarity.

THE M'ATTAR AS THE SYRIAN OTHER

M'attar, in the Lebanese context, is understood as he who lags behind. Primarily, the m'attar is overall content. He is highly impressionable and rarely challenges the situation in which he finds himself. The m'attar is a mostly gendered construct, because he who is deemed m'attar is usually understood as occupying a subordinate position vis-à-vis his wife. On one occasion, I joined Suha and her female friends for a coffee and a chat at her house.[2] Suha informed us that her fiancé, Qassem, had his loan application rejected by a multitude of banks: "How pitiful of you, Qassem! You don't succeed at anything!"

One of her friends replied, "Qassem is too ādami [the local equivalent of gentlemanly], perhaps too much."

When surrounded by his wife and daughters, the m'attar is easily eclipsed because he leaves most of the talking and the decision-making to them. His daughters, if unmarried, are likely to wear revealing attire in addition to carrying themselves in a flirtatious manner, which is often interpreted as a clear shortcoming of the m'attar's authority as head of the household. The m'attar, then, is a mostly docile figure and is primarily positioned in opposition to a wife who is deemed "strong," *awiyyeh*, or *shallūf* in Lebanese dialect.

The m'attar is also constructed in relation to further masculinities. A man who succeeds in businesses in particular or in life more generally is deemed shāṭer, a positive connotation for what could be otherwise perceived as a con man. A shāṭer's "victims" are described as *m'attareen*, the plural of m'attar. Despite implying some level of cunning and dishonesty, shāṭara also embraces desired and positive connotations such as high intelligence and an exceptionally adaptive nature, which allows one to overcome tricky situations, notably Lebanon's labyrinthian bureaucracy. A man who is shāṭer successfully navigates the bureaucratic, logistical, and sociopolitical dilemmas in which he finds himself. For example, Karim, in order to avoid standing in the long line at the Ministry of Education, offered 15,000 Lebanese pounds (approximately ten US dollars) to the person at the head of the line if he would switch places. Opinions about Karim's actions ranged from "unethical" to "clever," as seen by the array of reactions observed; he did, nevertheless, "get the job done."[3] In the same vein, women who succeed in finding wealthy husbands are qualified as *shettār*. Seen uncomfortably through a feminist lens, shāṭara portrays women as "manipulative" (Constable 2003, 2014) beings who capitalize on their "erotic power" (Hakim 2010) and whose sexual prowess ought to be regulated for the sake of social order (Mernissi 1987).

Conversely, when the m'attar finds himself in precarious situations, he is understood to have brought it on himself because of his own lack of scrutiny. Working-class men who rely on side jobs in order to maximize their income often find themselves "cheated" or "abused." Equally, men from the urban bourgeoisie could well fall under the designation of m'attar. Often, they hold onto their permanently allocated civil servant jobs and show little interest in climbing the social order. In this sense, the m'attar could or does inhabit a hegemonic space at least financially and politically speaking.

The m'attar must not be confused with the ādami, or the gentleman. The ādami is someone who "does not throw others under the bus" in their pursuit of upper social mobility, something that the shāṭer often does. The ādami carries a pious meaning too, seeing that the ādami is someone who upholds moralistic values typically found in religious rhetoric, notably kindness and fairness. In popular discourse, the ādami is nostalgically expressed, often in contrast to the insatiable appetite of Lebanon's elite and its class of business oligarchs. It is no wonder, then, that Suha's friend remarked that perhaps Qassem is "too ādami."

Te'tir, the substantive form of m'attar, or the state of being m'attar, is also reiterated in everyday vernacular geopolitical debates. Lebanon is reproduced as m'attar, given its lack of sovereignty and the fact that its domestic politics are dictated by neighboring hegemonic powers, including Saudi Arabia, Iran, and, more recently, Turkey. At the social level, however, te'tir is expressed in relation to the Syrian refugee; in this case, its meaning can be stretched to absolute wretchedness and desolation, in addition to reflecting simple-mindedness and a lack of sophistication in matters typically related to taste and consumerism. In what follows, I show how the racialization of the m'attar, exemplified by the intersection of a precarious economy and nationalism, produces affective, hegemonizing, and often imaginary narratives surrounding Lebanese masculinity.

For Farah, work is simply a temporary occupation. She shows no sign of professional progress and would rather text her fiancé all day on WhatsApp than work on the interminable case files piling up on her desk, a decades-old and heavily chipped piece of furniture occupying a dimly lit corner in a bleak-looking office within an unassuming building in the *Burj ḥammūd* neighborhood. When I asked Farah what work meant to her, she replied, "Pfff. I couldn't care less about my work! So what? Life does not depend on my work! It's not like I am solving the crisis of the Middle East!"[4]

Farah's views on her career echo the work of Lamia Shehadeh (1999, 67–68), who remarks that work constitutes a "means of financial support" for women in Lebanon rather than "an avenue for self-expression and stimulation" and is discarded once economic stability is achieved, either through marriage or inheritance. Farah continued: "I want to contribute to the household. The salary is important. But it doesn't mean that I want to become a manager of the sort. Who can afford not to work nowadays? All I have to do is retrieve whatever folder my boss is looking for. I don't want to get involved a tiny bit more, and I couldn't care less."[5]

Whereas Farah showed little enthusiasm toward her career, Layal exhibited a highly positive attitude vis-à-vis work: "My mother is bored all the time. I feel rather sorry for her. She is a housewife. She never worked a day in her life. Sometimes she assists my father with his shop, but apart from that, her life is quite empty."

For Layal, as was the case for many of my interlocutors, both male and female, the traditional view that holds that adulthood emerges alongside marriage is increasingly seen as "ludicrous." "What a *maskhara* [mockery]. I've been working for six years now, and I contribute to the finances of the household. I am paying for my own car, and I help with my grandmother's medical bills. No one is going to treat me like a child anymore! Whether I am married or not!"

When I asked Layal if she would consider leaving work once she gets married, she categorically rejected such a prospect. On the contrary, she remarked that "marriage leads to misery," a point that Mahmood, her fiancé, agreed on. "Look at all the married women! They give birth, and that's it. I do not intend to quit life. I want to enjoy life with Mahmood and our children."

This novel rapprochement between wife and husband deviates from widespread depictions of the Arab woman as zealously confined to her household. At the same time, we should resist viewing it from a "celebratory" stance exclusively. After all, most of my interlocutors had at least one relative living and working abroad, which could influence what might be thought of as their progressive perspectives. My female interlocutors in particular often stressed the financial difficulties in which their male counterparts find themselves. As Jana remarked, "The other day [my brother and I] saw a Filipina [referring to a migrant female domestic worker from the Philippines] walking a dog. My brother envied the dog so much. My brother hasn't had a job for two years now. The jobs he comes across are too demeaning, and he is undoubtedly better off without them."[6]

Although Jana is oblivious to the racist and sexist rhetoric that she evokes, her narrative reflects how work and societal understandings of masculinity are mutually constitutive: a man does not exist outside of his work, and the nature of one's work—regardless of his level of expertise—directly contributes to him being placed along the echelon of a particular masculinity. At the same time, Jana's own admission that her brother "is better off" without a job than with a "demeaning" one indicates how both men and women contribute to the consolidation of systems of masculinities and femininities. Whereas a disdain for manual labor characterizes the view of the majority of the young Lebanese men with whom I spoke, most of these men aspired to occupy jobs with the title of mudīr, or manager. For many Lebanese men, the title of mudīr distinguishes them from lesser masculinities that verge on the definition of the m'attar. Still, this title is a mere performance: it does not necessarily imply a managerial position, with all the qualifications it entails. If anything, the mudīr, despite the title, often finds himself performing manual work and administrative tasks: organizing shelves as a supermarket manager, attending customers as a café manager, or minding the petrol transfer pumps as a petrol station manager.

Jeena, like many of my female interlocutors, reproduces Lebanese men as sophisticated when juxtaposed against further Arab men:

Jeena: I'm not going to marry a Palestinian man, let alone a Syrian one, am I now?

Me: Why not?

Jeena: Come on now! Unbelievable. Look around! Whom do you see? There are only Syrians and God-knows-what in this country.

Me: But surely not all Syrian and Palestinian men are "bad" . . . .

Jeena: Come on! Our men are special. They are educated, clean, and they've seen the world![7]

Jeena contributes to the hegemonizing of certain masculinities at the expense of others. Although Jeena puts little weight on wealth, she nonetheless insists on the importance of a Lebanese man who is not m'attar. By elevating the Lebanese man, she reiterates the patriarchal and gendered patterns of connectivity and relationality in Lebanon (Joseph 2001), which elevates the men and the elders at the expense of women and children. Consequently, she inadvertently reproduces Lebanon's "control/care paradigm" (Joseph 2001), in which men simultaneously control and care for women. Ultimately, Jeena perceives marriage as a space of shared affectivities and long-term partnership. Her narrative is mostly absent from the literature on marriage and kin relations in the Middle East, seeing how both are usually depicted as a "fact of life" in addition to being examined through a lens that reinforces the role of the state and the relevance of the personal status code. Similar views emphasizing Lebanese-ness were raised by Sam, a fortysomething single man and owner of a female fashion store in Tripoli: "Where are the good men? They have all gone. This country is being ruled by ze'rān [thugs] . . . te'tir! Utter te'tir! Thugs and m'attareen, who else do you find when you look around?"[8]

When I asked Sam if he would consider moving abroad, he answered, "I am almost fifty. I am single. This store is all I have. You think one can simply pack and go? And for what? To live in the Gulf?"[9]

Undoubtedly, economic hardship pushes a large number of Lebanese citizens, notably men, to seek work opportunities elsewhere. Those who "fall behind" or are not employed remain in a least desired situation. Following Sam's logic, if the "good men" are gone, then the particular femininities that coproduce "good men" must be gone, too. Femininities and masculinities do not emerge independently of each other; to the contrary, they are mutually constitutive. It is also important to remind ourselves that one community's "good men" (and women) are distinct from another's. Patriarchally informed connectivity in Lebanon dictates particular patterns for forging relationships with others, and despite my interlocutors' romanticization of the "Lebanese man," it is imperative that we remember that the "Lebanese man" is always situated within one's sect. Clearly, not only are affectivities gendered, but they also succumb to further societal constructs, including sect.

A GENDERED FUTURITY

In this chapter, the excess of the appropriation of the slogan of "Lebanon is for the Lebanese" is best captured in my female interlocutors' understandings of Lebanese masculinity through and in opposition to the Syrian Other and further racializes others. Desire contributes to the gendering of each of the nation-state, love, marriage, and the nuclear family. Desire reflects how a nation imagines itself through the desiring of certain bodies over other bodies. This translates in the erection of barriers around bodies deemed "too honorable" or "too precious" to access, evident in the ways in which my interlocutors celebrate and articulate love while injecting it with a highly nationalistic lexicon.

Catherine Lutz and Lila Abu-Lughod (1990) critique the culturally revitalizing, often essentializing, and psychology- and learning-theory-driven existing works on emotions. They include a variety of contexts to support their overall view of emotions as a valid source of knowledge and as socioculturally constructed. In the context of the United States, Lauren Berlant (1999, 54) conceives "national sentimentality" in order to describe how those emotions that resonate with the "national" justify the excesses of the state: the "nation is peopled by suffering citizens and noncitizens whose structural exclusion from the [utopian American] dreamscape exposes the state's claim of legitimacy and virtue to an acid wash of truth telling that makes hegemonic disavowal virtually impossible, at certain points of political intensity."

Lebanese-ness as an attribute of ideal masculinity encompasses both immaterial and tangible concepts. How an affect emerges has to do with material underpinnings that shape it in the first place. Every day, we are faced with objects and places that are engulfed with particular affects, which allow them to evoke specific feelings in us. Following my interlocutors, marriage is seen as a space of mutual care and synchronicity. This "make-believe," I argue, is the result of an increasingly neoliberal climate where the present is lived in anticipation and is imagined along gendered tropes and masculine lines.

Mary Zournazi (2002) introduces her edited anthology on hope by stating that "hope can be what sustains life in the face of despair" (14–15). Like most critical affect scholars, she maintains the link between hope and the lived reality. Following Zournazi, hope cannot be disassociated from happiness or optimism; at the same time, she argues that the visions of happiness one might experience are but an "imagined reality" that works toward attenuating one's sense of "instability"—an argument that echoes the concept of "ontological security."

To speak of hope as a universal concept is to strip it from its economical and material meanings, in addition to eliminating the "social" entirely from it. It is akin to viewing the world through a gender-neutral or colorblind lens, or to ignoring the intersection of gender or race in the production of uneven bodies. Speaking of hope, Duggan states, "When I think about *hope*, I set it alongside *happiness* and *optimism*, which I immediately associate with race and class privilege, with imperial hubris, with gender and sexual conventions, with mal-distributed forms of security both national and personal. They can operate as the affective reward for conformity, the privatized emotional bonus for the right kind of investments in the family, private property and the state" (Duggan and Muñoz 2009, 276).

Seen through a feminist lens, hope becomes increasingly difficult to summon—a state of affairs cultural theorists refer to as a "crisis of hope." Nicolas Kompridis (2006, 247) goes as far as to argue that whatever "change" we experience is but "a symptom of our powerlessness rather than . . . the product of our own agency." Indeed, the intersection of relationality with a patriarchal order results in an affective paradox in Lebanon: love becomes entangled with power. The instrumentalization of gender during the era of nation-building across the Arab world and elsewhere is well documented in the literature (e.g., Abu-Lughod 1998; Kandiyoti 1991; McClintock 1995; Yuval-Davis 1997). For the sake of the nation, women are constructed as the "symbolic bearers of the collectivity's identity and honor, both personally and collectively" (Yuval-Davis 1997, 45). Similar state-sponsored understandings of women became apparent in the aftermath of the Arab Spring, with each of Tunisia, Libya, and Egypt's newly elected governments inaugurating their rule with laws and decrees that target women specifically.

Just as the nation-state regulates citizens every day, the Lebanese-ing of the "ideal husband" contributes to the gendering of both hope and futurity. My reading of my interlocutors' narratives brings forth the work of Suha Sabbagh (1996), who argued that the Lebanese civil war resulted in the breakdown of the social order, which in turn led to the intensification of family ties. Lina Khatib (2008, 448) builds on Sabbagh's work to argue that "the increased adherence to the family can be understood in the context of a society lacking an official protector." More recently, Deniz Kandiyoti (2013) conceptualized "masculinist restoration" in an attempt to theorize the recent backlash and "alienation" (Jabiri 2018) that Arab marginalized bodies, particularly women, have been enduring since 2011. In a similar vein, I view the renewed interest in the Lebanese man as a neo control/care paradigm that reinforces the paradox of the entanglement of love with power in Lebanon. Nevertheless, this renewal occurs in an increasingly militarized climate that brings forth what Cynthia Cockburn (1999) calls an "ethics of purity": where an "ethic of purity" prevails, women and marginalized selves become a tool to distinguish a community from another. This is seen in the renewal of racial confrontations between the Lebanese population and the Syrian refugees for example, or in increasingly violent cases of domestic violence observed at the time of fieldwork (Allouche 2017). Both scenarios recall a masculinity in crisis that is struggling to come to terms with a plunging economy, increased unemployment, and a high immigration rate. Moreover, this purity is increasingly defined along anti-Syrian lines. It seems current articulations of masculine ideals are the result of Lebanon's crumbling economy and the Lebanese state's failure to foster a national home. In other words, they are the refashioning of the aesthetics of the very same patriarchal social order that has governed the lives of Lebanese men throughout history.

NOTES

1. Interview with Lina, March 2016, Beirut.
2. Breakfast gathering with Suha and her friends, May 2014, Tripoli.
3. Fieldwork notes, July 2014, Beirut.
4. Interview with Farah, May 2014, Burj Hammūd.
5. Interview with Layal, March 2014, Tripoli.
6. Interview with Jana, August 2014, Beirut.
7. Interview with Jeena, September 2015, Jbeil.
8. Interview with Sam, February 2014, Tripoli.
9. Interview with Sam, February 2014, Tripoli.

BIBLIOGRAPHY

Abu-Lughod, Lila, ed. 1998. *Remaking Women: Feminism and Modernity in the Middle East*. Princeton, NJ: Princeton University Press.

Accad, Evelyn. 1992. "War/Masculinity versus Life/Freedom." In *Sexuality and War: Literary Masks of the Middle East*, edited by Evelyn Accad, 160–164. New York: NYU Press.

Adely, Fida. 2016. "A Different Kind of Love: Compatibility (Insijam) and Marriage in Jordan." *Arab Studies Journal* 24, no. 2: 102–127.

Afary, Janet. 2009. "The Sexual Economy of the Islamic Republic." *Iranian Studies* 42, no. 1: 5–26.

Aghacy, Samira. 2009. *Masculine Identity in the Fiction of the Arab East Since 1967.* Syracuse, NY: Syracuse University Press.

Allouche, Sabiha. 2015. "Western Media as 'Technology of Affect': The Affective Making of the Angry Arab Man." *Graduate Journal of Social Science* 11, no. 1: 120–142.

———. 2017. "Dis-Intersecting Intersectionality in the Time of Queer Syrian Refugee-ness." *Kohl: A Journal of Body and Gender Research* 3, no. 1: 59–77.

Bayat, Asef. 2013. *Life as Politics: How Ordinary People Change the Middle East.* Stanford, CA: Stanford University Press.

Berlant, Lauren. 1999. "The Subject of True Feeling: Pain, Privacy and Politics." In *Cultural Pluralism, Identity Politics, and the Law,* edited by Sarat Austin and Thomas R. Kearns, 49–84. Ann Arbor: University of Michigan Press.

Cockburn, Cynthia. 1999. "Gender, Armed Conflict and Political Violence." Paper presented at the World Bank, Washington DC, June 10–11.

Constable, Nicole. 2003. *Romance on a Global Stage: Pen Pals, Virtual Ethnography, and "Mail Order" Marriages.* Berkeley: University of California Press.

———. 2014. *Born out of Place: Migrant Mothers and the Politics of International Labor.* Berkeley: University of California Press.

Duggan, Lisa, and José E. Muñoz. 2009. "Hope and Hopelessness: A Dialogue." *Women and Performance: A Journal of Feminist Theory* 19, no. 2: 275–283.

Ghannam, Farha. 2013. *Live and Die Like a Man: Gender Dynamics in Urban Egypt.* Stanford, CA: Stanford University Press.

Ghoussoub, Mai, and Emma Sinclair-Webb, eds. 2000. *Imagined Masculinities: Male Identity and Culture in the Modern Middle East.* London: Saqi Books.

Hakim, Catherine. 2010. "Erotic Capital." *European Sociological Review* 26, no. 5: 499–518.

Hart, Kimberly. 2007. "Love by Arrangement: The Ambiguity of 'Spousal Choice' in a Turkish Village." *Journal of the Royal Anthropological Institute* 13, no. 2: 345–362.

Jabiri, Afaf. 2018. "Gendering the Politics of Alienation: Arab Revolution and Women's Sentiments of Loss and Despair." *Feminist Review* 117, no. 1: 113–130.

Joseph, Suad. 2001. "Civic Myths, Citizenship, and Gender in Lebanon." In *Gender and Citizenship in the Middle East,* edited by Suad Joseph, 107–136. Syracuse, NY: Syracuse University.

Kandiyoti, Deniz. 1991. *Women, Islam, and the State.* Philadelphia: Temple University Press.

———. 2013. "Fear and Fury: Women and Post-Revolutionary Violence." openDemocracy, January 10. https://www.opendemocracy.net/en/5050 /fear-and-fury-women-and-post-revolutionary-violence/.

Khatib, Lina. 2008. "Gender, Citizenship and Political Agency in Lebanon." *British Journal of Middle Eastern Studies* 35, no. 3: 437–451.

Kompridis, Nicolas. 2006. *Critique and Disclosure.* Cambridge: MIT Press.

Lutz, Catherine A., and Lila Abu-Lughod, eds. 1990. *Language and the Politics of Emotion*. Cambridge: Cambridge University Press.

Massad, Joseph. 2008. *Desiring Arabs*. Chicago: University of Chicago Press.

McClintock, Anne. 1995. *Imperial Leather: Race, Gender, and Sexuality in the Colonial Contest*. New York: Routledge.

Mernissi, Fatima. 1987. *Beyond the Veil: Male-female Dynamics in Modern Muslim Society*. Bloomington: Indiana University Press.

Najmabadi, Afsaneh. 2005. *Women with Mustaches and Men Without Beards: Gender and Sexual Anxieties of Iranian Modernity*. Berkeley: University of California Press.

Sabbagh, Suha. 1996. *Arab Women: Between Defiance and Restraint*. New York: Olive Branch.

Scott, Joan W. 1986. "Gender: A Useful Category for Historical Analysis." *The American Historical Review* 91, no. 5: 1053–1075.

Shehadeh, Lamia. 1999. *Women and War in Lebanon*. Gainesville: University Press of Florida.

Yuval-Davis, Nira. 1997. *Gender and Nation*. London: SAGE.

Zournazi, Mary. 2002. *Hope: New Philosophies for Change*. Annandale: Pluto Australia.

SABIHA ALLOUCHE is Lecturer in Middle East Politics at the University of Exeter and serves on the advisory board of Beirut-based organization *Kohl: A Journal for Body and Gender Research*. Her work has been published in the *Journal of Middle East Women's Studies*, the *International Journal of Middle East Studies*, and *Middle East Critique*.

MASCULINITY UNDER SIEGE

The Use of Narcotic Pain Relievers to Restore Virility in Egypt

L. L. WYNN

INTRODUCTION

How is Viagra like the opioid pain reliever tramadol (Tramal)? I asked myself this question in April 2013 as I was conducting interviews about Egyptians' ideas regarding Viagra. Whenever I asked people about Viagra, without being prompted they kept mentioning tramadol even though the drugs have vastly different mechanisms of action and effects on the body. Sildenafil (the generic term for Viagra) is a vasodilator that produces erections but is not in itself mood-altering (Spindler et al. 2007). Tramadol is a moderate-strength opioid pain reliever that alters mood and can be erection-inhibiting (Hashim et al. 2020), although it may be useful for treating premature ejaculation (Abdel-Hamid et al. 2016). Sildenafil is widely available from pharmacies in Egypt without prescription, whereas tramadol is tightly regulated and can be obtained only by prescription or illegally from dealers. In short, from an objective, neuropharmacological perspective, the two drugs appear to be completely unrelated. Yet my research participants sometimes spoke about the two drugs interchangeably, as if they were vitamins that a man (or woman) might take every morning to give them "energy" to make it through a hard day's work. Other times they drew sharp distinctions between the two, yet they still spontaneously brought tramadol into the conversation as though discussing one automatically triggered discussion of the other.

And sometimes the same person would describe the two drugs as simultaneously interchangeable and radically different. I encountered this one evening in April 2013, when my Egyptian research assistant, Layla, led me through a twisting series of back alleys in the old Jewish Quarter (*Harat el-Yehud*) of the Al-Hussein neighborhood in Cairo to interview some of her acquaintances. We emerged from one alley into a hidden courtyard next to a small community mosque, shaded by a massive tree. My nine-year-old son, who was accompanying me on this field trip, started taking pictures of the colorful lights illuminating the mosque while Layla introduced me to Fouad and Hussein, two of her male acquaintances from a nearby brass workshop (*warsha* in colloquial Egyptian). "This is Professor Lisa from Australia," she told them. "She is affiliated with Al-Azhar University, and she is doing a research project on Viagra."

I shook their hands and then hung back quietly while Layla explained the details of my project. I was visiting Cairo twice a year (as I had been doing for the past five years) to document people's relationships with emerging reproductive health technologies in Egypt (see Foster and Wynn 2016; Wynn 2013, 2016; Wynn, Moustafa, and Ragab 2013). I had decided to conduct a series of formal interviews to supplement my ethnographic observations and the anecdotal accounts I was hearing about the use and sharing of sildenafil. The research was funded by the Australian Research Council and had been approved by the Human Research Ethics Committee at Macquarie University as well as by Al-Azhar University in Cairo, which provided me with a research supervisor to ensure the project's cultural and political appropriateness.

"Can she ask you some questions?" Layla asked as she concluded her explanation. "She won't ask you anything personal. She just wants to know your opinions about Viagra and about men in Egypt."

This was part of the strategic methodological approach that Layla and I had developed with advice from my Al-Azhar advisors. To avoid embarrassing my interviewees, I did not ask anyone about their sexual lives or their personal use of any drug (though many interviewees spontaneously offered such information). Instead, I asked a series of hypothetical questions: Who uses Viagra, and why? What other supplements do men take? What do these drugs and supplements do?

Through this interview strategy, I aimed to elicit accounts not of what Egyptians do but rather of what Egyptians imagine others do with these drugs. These imaginations ranged from fantastical urban legends to astute understandings of cultural patterns. Such stories narrate cultural beliefs about drugs and masculinity.

The 1998 approval in the United States of the drug sildenafil, brand name Viagra, unleashed a flurry of academic theorizing about the implications of the drug on how we conceptualize masculinity and pharmaceutical intervention. These analyses focused on the "little blue pill" as encapsulating projects of self-improvement, fixing broken masculinity through new medical technologies, contributing to the medicalization of sexuality and aging, creating new ideas around "normal" masculinity, and generating powerful cultural narratives around gender (Fishman and Mamo 2008; Loe 2004; Tiefer 2006). Meika Loe (2001), for example, evoked Emily Martin's (1987) analysis of the machinist metaphor underpinning biomedical framings of childbirth: the pharmaceutical production of firm erections was an intervention into injured masculinity that conceptually broke down the body into parts that could be repaired through new biomedical technologies.

Yet anthropological studies of the marketing and use of Viagra in contexts outside of North America show that the drug is associated with a wide range of conceptualizations of the relationship between masculinity, erections, and drugs beyond that of a makeover culture (Åsberg and Johnson 2009; Potts et al. 2004; Wentzell 2002). For example, medical anthropologist Emily Wentzell (2002) found that many working-class men in Mexico did not perceive erectile difficulties as a sign of masculine failure or "dysfunction" but rather a sign of appropriate aging and a mature masculinity, and they declined pharmaceutical treatment.

Similarly, my ethnographic research in Egypt suggested that people were using Viagra for very different projects than Loe (2004) and Tiefer (2006) had described for the United States. Instead of being seen as a revolutionary new medical technology lending itself to new projects of self-fashioning and body makeovers, in Egypt, Viagra was popularly seen as lying on a continuum with old projects and products of health restoration and mood enhancement. I found Egyptians talking about Viagra not as shameful but rather as commonplace and often recreational: celebratory excess that did not necessarily signal a lack. People shared Viagra with friends, gave the pills as gifts, and boasted gleefully of unending erections. I documented stories of sildenafil being given as an end-of-year bonus from a boss to employees and being used as a bribe in bureaucratic transactions. Viagra was a consumer fantasy, evoking the prestige of international brand names. Many Egyptians conceptualized it as a tool of virility enhancement rather than virility restoration (Wynn 2016). The Egyptian government broke patent not long after Viagra was approved, and soon there were over a dozen locally produced brands available in Egyptian pharmacies, with brand names such as Phragra, Virecta, Kemagra, and Vigoran. Most pharmacists sold it without prescription.

On that evening in April 2013, I sat down on a bench in a secluded courtyard with Fouad and Hussein (pseudonyms that they chose) to ask their opinions

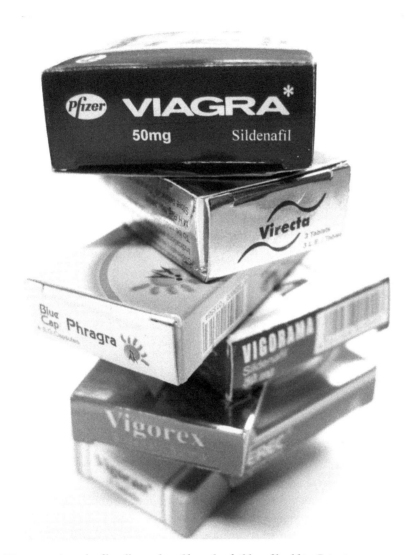

Figure 9.1: A stack of locally produced brands of sildenafil sold in Cairo in 2009, including Viagra, Virecta, Phragra, Vigorama, Vigorex, Erec, and Vigoran. © L. L. Wynn

about Viagra and masculinity. My son sat next to me and started playing games on his electronic tablet. My research assistant, having explained the project and introduced us, sat at a distance, commenting that it would be inappropriate for an unmarried woman to sit in on a conversation with men about sexuality. Her choice of seating performed distance for the sake of respectable appearances, but the space she placed between herself and our conversation was only symbolic; she was close enough to overhear our conversation and periodically interjected comments when I was struggling to convey a concept, or she would rephrase someone's response for me if he used an unfamiliar word. The interviews were conducted in Arabic, and the quotes were translated to English for this chapter.

After Fouad and Hussein consented to participate in a recorded interview, Fouad glanced at my son, playing a computer game and ignoring the conversation he could not understand. "Your son, he doesn't speak Arabic?"

"No, he can't understand anything we say."

Fouad looked relieved. It was no doubt bizarre to be asked questions about erectile dysfunction by a white, American Australian woman. Yet my son's presence lent cultural legitimacy to the encounter: he was proof that I was a married woman with enough experience to talk about sexuality, unlike Layla, my never-married research assistant who was sitting some five meters away and pretending not to be part of the conversation. At the same time, the fact that my son spoke no Arabic meant that my interviewees did not have to feel embarrassed or censor their comments about sexuality in front of a child.

"So," I reiterated, "I am not asking about people's personal experiences with Viagra. I just want to know your opinion in general. Who uses it? Young or old people?"

"Both," said Fouad. "I have used it, too. And I know some guys who have used it. If a man sleeps with his wife, he takes one pill of Viagra, or tramadol."

"Yes," I interjected, "I have heard that people do use tramadol, too."

"Viagra and Tramal are used to give him something extra. It makes him strong for fifteen, thirty minutes."

"I found that here there are fish shops who call their products 'sandwich Viagra,' so it made me wonder, do people talk about these subjects without it being shameful, embarrassing?" I asked. "Because in Australia, some people might consider it shameful to admit they use Viagra."

"Not here."

"Here, anyone can use it?"

"Yes, anyone. I use it. I have a wife and a boy, and I use it. Every time I sleep with my wife, I take one. And one tramadol, and I have no problem. There's no shame."

"I also heard," I continued, "that people gift each other Viagra."

"Sure, I have bought it for my brother, and for my friend. It's to make us happy. It's not shameful." Then he added, in an apparent non sequitur, "America destroyed us with it."

His friend Hussein joined the conversation for the first time. "Tramadol, it's not very good. They are destroying us and our youth with it. It's not good for the body. But Viagra is okay."

Fouad interjected, "The Egyptian police are the ones who introduced tramadol here."

"Why?" I asked.

"So it destroys our youth, so we don't have an army," he replied. "This is what America wants. America wants all of the youth to be addicted to it. So they wake up in the morning and take tramadol. So that in the morning, [a man] cannot get out of bed unless he takes a pill."

Intrigued by the way the men kept bringing up tramadol, I asked, "What is tramadol, exactly?"

"It's red. It's a red pill, and it has a cross [on it]."

"Where do you get it from? From the pharmacy?"

In Arabic, as in English, the phrasing "Where do you get it from?" could be interpreted as asking where people in general obtain the drug, or it could be read as a personal question. Fouad interpreted it as the latter.

"I get it from a guy here," he replied. He continued:

> It's the same people who deal cocaine. It must have some kind of powder [*boudra*, a transliteration for *powder* that means cocaine in Egyptian colloquial] in it because he has to take it in the morning so he can get out of bed and go to work and so on. Three-quarters of Egyptians are using it. It's a real shame. Three-quarters of Egyptians are using it, and some women, too. It does give energy for one or two hours, but then it's gone. So it gives you energy for a little bit, and then you go back to normal. When someone feels tired, he takes just one. Just one pill. The whole day he will be fine [*tamam*], but at night he will be tired. Then he has to take another so his body feels it.

Hussein jumped into the conversation again. "I wish they would ban tramadol, because as long as it is available here, the Egyptian youth are being damaged. But Viagra is a different issue, and it has nothing to do with tramadol. They are two different things; it's chemical, just like cocaine."

Fouad added, "Viagra is different; you can take it and eat, it's not a problem. Tramadol makes you not want to eat. But Viagra you can eat, and all countries use it."

"Tramadol only costs two and a half pounds; that's why everyone uses it. Everyone uses it—girls, boys, and everyone," Hussein stated. "Viagra is not shameful; what is shameful is tramadol. Viagra is no problem; all countries use Viagra. Mohammed Morsi also takes Viagra."

"Is that what people say?" I asked.

"Sure, swear to God, I know. Everyone wants Viagra; it's easy. I mean, every-one who is married wants to sleep with their wives. I take one pill, no problem."

"And now our youth has been completely destroyed," Fouad interjected pessimistically. "Especially after the revolution, because there is no tourism. Our rights are gone. We as people have rights, and our youth has rights, too. [The police] take the money; they love the money. American and Australia, any country, they bring these drugs to Egypt to get us addicted, so it forces the youth to steal and stuff."

DRUGS NARRATE A STORY ABOUT MASCULINITY AND POLITICAL ECONOMY

In this rambling interview, it becomes clear that Egyptian accounts of Viagra tell a bigger story about masculinity and the relationship between gendered bodies, pharmaceutical products, and recreational drugs. In this interview as in many others, my Egyptian research participants described Viagra as synonymous with vitamin supplements, the pharmaceutical narcotic tramadol, and illicit drugs such as cocaine and hashish. Informants, both male and female, described all these as drugs that enhanced virility and sexuality, that gave one energy and strength. Some people mentioned taking one Viagra pill every day in the morning (and/or one tramadol pill), like a vitamin—not as a precursor to sexual activity, but as a general supplement to enhance their health and energy levels.

Yet all these substances were also, at times, described as addictive, creat-ing dependence, and having a degenerative effect on the body. Indeed, as can be seen in my interview with Fouad and Hussein, research participants often categorized Viagra as similar to recreational drugs like cannabis, cocaine, and pharmaceutical opioids, suggesting that for many, these drugs existed within the same semantic domain despite wildly divergent mechanisms of action.

Whereas some presented Viagra as a drug of celebratory excess or something mundane gifted to friends and used to sexually satisfy one's wife, others used it as a metaphor for describing masculinity in crisis. When Fouad and Hussein recounted conspiracy theories about America, Australia, and the Egyptian police using Viagra and tramadol to weaken Egyptian men and the army, they were not just telling a story about particular drugs; they were telling stories about Egypt's economy, masculinity under siege, export geopolitics, and the relationship between bodies in pain and pharmaceutical products.

In these interviews, I would ask about Viagra, and like Fouad and Hus-sein, respondents would often make a comment about their use of tramadol, referring to it as Tramal (the brand name), "faraola" ("strawberry"), or "red Viagra" (referring to the color of the package and making explicit the connection they saw between the two drugs). Tramadol is an opioid pain reliever roughly equivalent in potency to codeine (Lee, McTavish, and Sorkin 1993). Initially, I disregarded it when I asked about Viagra and people brought up tramadol. I thought my informants were confused or misunderstanding me. I did not understand why anyone would consider tramadol as the equivalent of sildenafil. A narcotic pain reliever, I assumed, would be erection dampening, not erection enhancing, and indeed, recent Egyptian research has demonstrated this (Hashim et al. 2020).

Eventually, though, tramadol was coming up in conversation persistently enough that I realized I needed to take it seriously and explore its use. Why were these different drugs with such different neuropharmacological effects seen as equivalent? Why did mentioning one (Viagra) trigger discussions about the others (tramadol, hash, cocaine, vitamins)? Were these drugs seen as part of a semantic continuum?

I therefore followed up on the original interviews with additional interviews asking not only about Viagra but also about hashish, tramadol, vitamins, and other pills or supplements. I interviewed twenty-six men and women, young and old, in urban Cairo and Alexandria until I achieved thematic saturation. These interviews were mostly conducted in Arabic, except for some interviews with doctors who were fluent in English and preferred to speak with me in English. My field assistant, Layla, further conducted and recorded twenty-nine short interviews with men about what they thought masculinity meant, and what were the pleasures and challenges of their lives.

In this chapter, I review their responses, teasing out the beliefs they reveal, and then I explore the underlying narratives that underpin even contradictory accounts of what drugs do. What I found was a narrative about masculinity under siege, men in pain, and how what men ingest can help them to absorb the shocks and blows of an ailing economy, failing and exhausted bodies, the challenges of kinship and male responsibility, and environmental pollution.

In the next section, I analyze the formal interview responses, grouping them into themes. Interviews took place in people's places of work, in houses in Alexandria or Cairo, or in cafés, with respondents who ranged from upper-middle-class professionals to poor, working-class, and precariously employed residents of the 'ashwa'iyyat (the unplanned apartment complexes, sometimes glossed as slums) of these two cities. I provide basic information about age, gender, and profession/job in order to help contextualize people's comments. Yet while there were different ideas about drugs that partly related to respondents' educational level, many beliefs were widely shared regardless of class, gender, and age.

After reviewing the themes that emerge in interviews, I then analyze and discuss these themes with reference to Norman Zinberg's (1984) theory of drug, set, and setting, Jerome Himmelstein's (1983) and Desmond Manderson's (2005) understanding of drugs as sociopolitical theater, and Manderson's (1995, 800) analysis of drug symbolism and its deployment as emotional imagery to tell stories about morals, belonging, and the body politic.

INTERVIEW THEMES

"Everybody Uses Viagra"

When asked, "Who uses Viagra?" my interlocutors offered a range of often-contradictory responses. Many said that it was for "older men" or "men over forty." But just as many stated that it was used by young people, and some stated that women used it as well.

Syed Ali, a thirty-five-year-old barista, commented, "Viagra is meant to be used by older people, but of course those who don't have any heart problems. Younger people use it to last longer during sex with their wives." Ali, a thirty-four-year-old engineer, said that men gave Viagra and hashish to their friends as a wedding present, "so he can enjoy his wedding night." Nada, a forty-year-old housewife, commented that "old and young and everyone" use Viagra "so they can enjoy life with their wives." Farouq, a thirty-five-year-old odd-jobs man, opined that Viagra was the drug of choice for Thursdays (the end of the work week) and said, "Young and old people use it these days." Bassam, a forty-seven-year-old street vendor, stated that both young and older people used Viagra "to enjoy life."

Many respondents claimed that a majority of the population used sildenafil. Adil, a married tailor aged thirty-two, said that "it's normal" ('adi) for people of all ages to take Viagra and believed that some 70 percent of Egyptians used the drug. A married man working in the silversmith quarter of Cairo said, "Three-quarters of Egyptians are using it, and some women too. It's a real shame."

Physicians had more sophisticated understandings of the physiological causes of erectile dysfunction, but they shared laypeople's beliefs in a veritable national epidemic of erectile dysfunction, caused by social, economic, and ecological problems. One professor of obstetrics and gynecology at the University of Menoufeyya stated that 45 percent of Egyptian men suffer from erectile dysfunction and claimed that it occurred among the young and old, rich and poor. Even more dramatically, a professor of andrology at Al-Azhar University claimed that 60 percent of Egyptian men suffer from erectile dysfunction, many of whom treat the condition with Viagra. He believed that the exceptionally high rates of erectile dysfunction in the population were the result of environmental pollution and the exhaustion of men who worked long hours to make a living in Egypt's precarious economy. Yet another professor of gastroenterology at Cairo University, married and in his thirties, stated with certainty, "The majority of Egyptian men have this problem nowadays. More like 50 to 60 percent. I went to so many doctors, and they told me. And I used to see patients [with this problem]. There were many, many of them."

Viagra as Treatment for "Psychological Problems"

The professor at Menoufeyya University claimed that the widespread use of Viagra revealed not a physiological problem but rather a "psychological problem" in users, and it derived from the general attitude of depression in society. This belief was echoed by several other respondents. When asked why people take Viagra, Adil, aged thirty-two, married, and employed as a tailor, said, "For their psychological problems, of course." When I asked Abdelrahman, a married forty-year-old taxi driver, "If a man has a problem performing sexually, what would he do to solve this problem?" he responded, "Well, firstly, [he must make sure] that he has no financial or psychological problems. Sometimes things are okay financially and all, but psychologically he is not prepared from pressures and problems in the country or problems in the family."

Viagra on a Continuum with Illicit Recreational Drugs

A comparable number of respondents saw Viagra as a recreational drug, similar to hashish and opium, suggesting an intriguing duality, or perhaps complementarity, between Viagra as treatment for psychological or socioeconomic problems and Viagra as celebratory pleasure or recreational treat. The professor from the University of Menoufeyya opined that there was a link between the popularity of Viagra and hashish. "Eastern people," he claimed, traditionally used hashish and opium as sexual enhancements because of the way both drugs created a sense of pleasurable disorientation. As these drugs became less available due to government crackdowns, there was, the professor argued, a turn to pharmaceutical products to supply the same sexual enhancement, particularly as Viagra became increasingly available and less costly. He suspected that the promotion of sildenafil was a deliberate government strategy to decrease the use of illicit recreational drugs in Egypt.

Similarly, Amal, an upper-middle-class journalist in her fifties, implicitly equated Viagra with vitamin supplements and hashish, a pharmaceutical alternative for an illegal drug.

> Viagra is a problem that spread so rapidly in Egypt. The reasons for that are the political, social, and economical problems. These problems affect the subject of sex in a very big way. Even exhaustion, in order for a man to have an income, he works long hours, and it can be frustrating, so of course no man will be able to have a normal sexual relationship while he is feeling frustrated, or if he is in need of money, or if he worries about the future and how he will be able to provide. So in reality, it becomes some sort of release. So because he is unable to accomplish himself socially or economically, he feels that sex is what fulfills his manhood. So when he consumes Viagra, he feels that it will give him more strength, and longer sex. So he feels that it fulfills . . . some sort of satisfaction. . . . When the man gets old, he'll start needing vitamins, but he is basically a normal person who is physically healthy. But he takes supplements so he is not exhausted at work, to help improve his memory, because memory fades with age, so he could take supplements to improve his bones, for his brain, for his intellect, memory. So many men, when they get older, they feel that this can compensate for the loss of his sexual abilities. A while back—I don't know if you know this or not—hashish in Egypt was not forbidden; a lot of religious people did not consider hashish *haram*. So they used to consume it because they believed that it helped with sexual drive. So when it became criminalized and then Viagra was on the scene, they substituted hashish with Viagra.

Amal's equation of Viagra with other recreational drugs echoes Fouad's comments in the interview described at the beginning of this chapter, where Viagra was equated with tramadol and the pharmaceutical products were, in turn, portrayed as not only containing a substance similar to cocaine but also sold by the same people who sold illicit drugs.

Viagra Gives Strength or Energy

When I asked Umm Hassan, a fifty-five-year-old housewife living in the slums of Alexandria, for her impressions on who uses Viagra, she said, "I hear that young and old, married and unmarried. Some young guys use it to get them high, and to make them strong. And others use it for sex. The young ones to give them strength and energy for work. To increase the energy in their bodies. And those married use it for sex with their wives."

Abu Hassan, a fisherman in his seventies and Umm Hassan's husband, replied, "[A man] uses [Viagra] in three situations: for his own pleasure personally, at the same time it puts him in a good mood/gets him high [*biyita'milu dimagh*], at the same time it helps it with having sex. Meaning it is three things, because it gets him high, it makes him feel "*fresh*" [said in English], and ... it gives him strength as well as energy to perform his sexual rights."

Tramadol as Sexual Enhancement

A number of people claimed that tramadol was an aid to sexual function, suggesting one of the reasons it was often equated with Viagra. Syed Ali, a thirty-five-year-old barista, stated that people use tramadol "for sexual pleasure and entertainment." Mustafa, a forty-eight-year-old coffee shop attendant, stated that "young guys" used tramadol "for sex with women." Sayed, a twenty-eight-year-old laundry/dry cleaner employee, claimed that most young people used tramadol "for happiness and entertainment. And to enjoy sex." Eid, a forty-five-year-old driver, said that "some people use [tramadol] for sex, and others use it for physical health."

Tramadol Used for Energy, Health

Eid's comment was a common interpretation of the use of the drug; many viewed tramadol as giving people energy for sex but also for their everyday work lives (similar to many views on Viagra). Mohammed, a thirty-five-year-old silversmith, claimed that "three-quarters of Egypt's youth" used tramadol and that "some use it for energy/strength; others use it for sex." Hanafy, a thirty-two-year-old construction worker, said that people use tramadol "for energy," while "older men and young men who can't achieve erections" use Viagra, and young people use hashish "to get in a good mood" (*yerawwah dimaghu*). Hassan, a forty-year-old married mechanic, said that tramadol was used by "tradesmen and drivers" because "it gives them energy and more power." When asked whether he spoke of power and energy for work or for sexual purposes, he replied, "Both." Nada, a forty-year-old housewife, argued that young men use tramadol "to improve their mood [*mizag*] and to have energy for work and going out." Hussein, a forty-three-year-old ticket collector on trains, said that "questionable young guys" use tramadol "to give them energy when they are hanging out for fun," and Abdullah, unemployed and in his forties, and Kareem, a thirty-five-year-old construction worker, both independently stated that young people use it "to give them energy at work." Marwan, a thirty-four-year-old engineer, said, "Most tradesmen [use it] because it gives them energy and power so they can work long hours or not sleep."

Tramadol Is Like a Vitamin

A few research participants, both male and female, told personal accounts of using tramadol daily at the start of their workday, and they claimed that it was like a vitamin supplement. For example, Farouq, a thirty-five-year-old odd-jobs man, claimed, "Half of the Egyptian population [uses tramadol] so they can work. . . . It gives physical energy in general just like vitamins. We love using it like vitamins." But he also noted it created a dependency and was hard to stop using. "When it stops working, a person becomes on edge and violent," he said.

Tramadol and Viagra Are Addictive

The theme of addiction surfaced often, with people telling cautionary tales about men getting addicted to Viagra, transforming their recreational use into dependence, and rendering them unable to have sexual relations without taking some sort of drug. Abu Hassan, a fisherman in Alexandria in his midseventies, claimed,

> [Using Viagra while young] will affect him during intercourse when he gets older. Because he will be desensitized to the drug. Because after a while, he will not be able to have sex without it. This is a supplement that went through his body and will need to be used every day. Just like those who snort powder [i.e., cocaine] . . . it's an unnatural thing. It destroys the nervous system. And yes, in the beginning it will give energy, because it's *"fresh"* [he used the English word], it will make you happy, it will give you strength, but later on it will become an addiction. . . . Those who say it will not have an effect later on are wrong. I agree it will give energy and all, but it's harmful.

Abu Hassan also likened it to nicotine addiction:

> Smoking is a sickness [*marad*] in one's body. So I cannot just quit all of a sudden. So imagine with Viagra: for someone to quit, they have to get treated or go to a rehab center here, like a general hospital, to stay from a month to three months. . . . But the young people here, they abuse their brains. They will go after anything that will help them feel fresh, happy, and high. So, when he gets married, he would already be used to such things in a young age. So, if he takes it and has sex with a woman, it may affect him later. Even with having sex with his wife, if he doesn't take it, he will not be able to have sex.

Mahmood, a thirty-five-year-old carpenter, warned that tramadol "affects the kidneys and you can get addicted to it." Mohammed, a thirty-five-year-old silversmith, commented that many women used tramadol as well as men: "It starts with women using it to have enough energy to clean their houses, but the problem is that they get addicted to it. When I went to the hospital, I found that there are a lot of women with me there." He had sought addiction treatment and claimed he was still addicted but was able to manage his dependence by taking only three pills a day. When he stops taking it, he said, "I become easily irritable, and my body feels tired, and I get suicidal."

Life's Challenges

My Egyptian research assistant, Layla, asked male respondents, "What brings you joy in life? What are the challenges you face in life?" Mahmood, a thirty-five-year-old carpenter, described his challenges as "when I get overworked and have no energy to perform at work. Getting home too exhausted and getting little sleep. These are my daily struggles. But other challenges are the rising cost of living and bad traffic." Marwan, a thirty-four-year-old engineer, also independently said that the challenges of life for Egyptian men were "the cost of living and traffic." When asked whether men use drugs to enjoy life or to bear life's challenges, he replied,

> No, they use it so they can bear life's challenges. Because most users for example, I know some guys who look fine, but they use drugs to last longer at work. So they can work and be in an altered state because as soon as they are aware of their situation, they become depressed and desperate, and they say that all they do in life is work only to make ends meet. Three-quarters of the people, from the well-off to the poor, use drugs to have more energy and to alter their mood [mizag], to have a little fun and to escape life. But you know if someone's job is rewarding, they wouldn't use drugs at all.

Happiness in Life

For Syed Ali, happiness in life (farhat il-hayah) was when "my family is happy and there are no complications in life." Two themes came up repeatedly in interviews. For some, happiness was money and having enough of it to get by or to enjoy oneself. For many others, happiness was family and being able to take care of one's family. The two were often described as being intertwined. Hossam, a forty-year-old construction worker, said that for him, the best thing in his life was "when I can provide for my family, and when they do not need anything. I would be happy when I have money and can provide for my family." Mohammed said that joy in life was "when I have money and I'm comfortable. When I have money, I am able to provide for my kids and wife, and I'll be able to buy whatever I want." Abdullah, employed in unspecified work and in his forties, said that what brought him joy in life was "to be able to provide for my family and get them everything they want." Farouq said that joy in life for him was "when I can afford to buy two kilos of meat for my kids. Because meat is very expensive."

What Does It Mean to Be a Man and Be Masculine?

Finally, my research assistant asked twenty-nine Egyptian men and women in Cairo and Alexandria, "What does masculinity mean to you?" Overwhelmingly, respondents linked masculinity with an ability to care and provide for family. Hassan, a forty-year-old married mechanic, said, "Real masculinity means that you don't let your family need anything. And that he is a respectable man, has a job and is committed to it [multazim] . . . that he respects and treats [his wife] well and at the same time provides for his family and makes sure she doesn't need anything." Ramadan, a thirty-eight-year-old married driver, said, "Masculinity is that one takes care of his family and work and future." Nagdy, a sixty-seven-year-old fisherman, said, "Masculinity is about responsibility. Masculinity is the responsibility of having a wife and kids." Hossam, an unmarried mechanic in his twenties, said, "Masculinity is being able to keep people's secrets and keep his family's secrets and being able to provide for his family. And when others describe him as a real man, not when he thinks he's masculine." Mahmood, a thirty-five-year-old carpenter, said, "Masculinity is providing for one's family and protecting them." Marwan, a thirty-four-year-old engineer, said, "Masculinity is a man who protects his family and home, and is a good man, and is able to provide for his family and is responsible for them." Kareem, a thirty-five-year-old construction worker, said, "Real men get involved in their job and life and keep their promises. And he is good to others." Bassam, a forty-seven-year-old street vendor, said, "Masculinity means good manners and being able to provide for your family and taking care of your kids."

DISCUSSION

In these interviews, we see a sometimes confusing mix of ideas about what sildenafil, tramadol, vitamins, and other drugs (including cocaine and hashish) are and what they do for the body. Some people said that only old people used sildenafil; others claimed that it was mainly used by young men. Some said that both men and women use tramadol and sildenafil. Some drew careful distinctions between sildenafil and tramadol. Some collapsed sildenafil, tramadol, vitamins, and illicit drugs like hashish and cocaine into the same category, regarding all or most of them as simultaneously energy-giving, sexually stimulating, and also addictive, with the ability to sap strength over the long term.

What unites these disparate viewpoints is a shared understanding that there are substances that people ingest to give energy (at least in the short term) and enable them to work hard, enhance their sexual prowess or experience, or "set a mood."

It is useful to place these comments in the context of Egyptians' use of pharmaceutical and apothecary products. In Cairo and Alexandria, there are pharmacies on nearly every block. Egyptians refer to pharmacists as "*el-doktor*," granting them the same authority accorded to physicians. Other than narcotics, most drugs can be accessed without prescription. Pharmacies, and consultations with pharmacists, are central to the lives of urban Egyptians.

Many parts of town additionally feature apothecaries that sell arugula oil, ginger and ginseng extract, and mysterious apothecary blends with pictures of rhinoceros horns and bee stingers on the packaging, all promising to give men energy, strength, and vitality, their phallic and animal imagery adding that extra metaphorical punch. Indeed, one informant told me in all seriousness that Viagra was made from dried and ground-up sea cucumber, a piece of phallic imagery that draws our attention to the fact that Viagra is not (only) seen as a revolutionary global pharmaceutical product but rather a variation on indigenous medical treatments that were homely and familiar. Restaurants sold "Viagra soup" and "Viagra sandwiches" (containing crab and shrimp), and at the date market, the plumpest, sweetest varieties were dubbed "Viagra" by canny salesmen (Wynn 2016).

At first, when I started asking people questions about Viagra, I disregarded their references to cocaine, tramadol, and vitamins as off topic. I was doing a research project on reproductive health technologies, including medication abortion (mifepristone, misoprostol, and methotrexate), emergency contraceptive pills (levonorgestrel and ethinyl estradiol), and erectile dysfunction drugs (sildenafil citrate). Tramadol, cocaine, and hashish were recreational drugs that seemed to me to have little to do with sildenafil. Vasodilators, opioid pain relievers, coca-derived stimulants, cannabinoids, and vitamin supplements have remarkably different mechanisms of action and, according to medical science, should have very different effects on the body. Yet again and again, I found my informants equating all of these.

As Zinberg (1984) points out, the way individuals experience a drug is not simply the result of its objectively described neuropharmacological effects. A drug experience is produced through a complex interaction between the drug (its neuropharmacology), the "set" (which encompasses the psychological mindset of the person taking the drug and the expectations of what it will do), and the "setting" (the social context in which the drug is taken). Only seeing drug experiences as produced through an interaction between drug, set, and setting—the pharmacological substance, culturally shaped user expectations, and the social environment surrounding use—can explain why Egyptian men regard a narcotic pain reliever as giving them strength to work as well as producing erections, or why they might take Viagra as a daily supplement to give them energy.

Placing these accounts of drugs, what they do, and who uses them in broader social context reveals a pattern that makes it clear that my informants were not going off topic. When my Egyptian informants gave accounts of both recreational sildenafil use and the use of tramadol to enhance their sex lives, they were telling stories about the way their life struggles and drug use intersected with ideas around masculinity. Drugs are "good to think with," and they carry meaning with "metaphoric and metonymic connotations" (Whyte, van der Geest, and Hardon 2002, 346.). Egyptians' accounts of sildenafil, tramadol, and other drugs were metonymical commentaries on the struggles and joys of men's lives, on certain generational groups and classes of society, and on heterosexual and homosocial relationships. When Egyptians claimed that a majority of the population was using Viagra or other drugs to enhance virility, they were commenting on masculinity in crisis and on the country's problems.

Indeed, popular discourse around erectile dysfunction in Egypt has long blamed it on social, economic, and ecological dysfunction. Kamran Asdar Ali (2003) discusses how a 1996 film starring the famous Egyptian comedian Adel Imam, *Al Nom fi el-Asal*, revolves around a police chief's investigation into epidemic of erectile failure in Cairo, which turns out to be contagious because Imam's character is soon unable to perform in bed. The affliction is cured when Imam's character leaves the crowded, polluted city and spends the night with his wife in the desert; the wider epidemic is explained as the result of depression and hopelessness "due to people in Egypt being constantly exposed to misinformation and lies on television and in the newspaper by the political establishment" (Ali 2003, 321). Ali (2003, 330) argues that "the social and economic deprivation of the Egyptian poor and the concomitant pressure on families to curtail family size is experienced as a form of violence that socially castrated and humiliated the men with whom I spoke, in the process depriving them as well of their masculinity and manhood."

The movie was released two years before Viagra entered the market, but it is readily apparent how the Egyptians I interviewed took up similar themes of social critique in discussing the need for Viagra and other drugs. Like the Adel Imam movie, they explained the use of Viagra, tramadol, and other drugs and vitamins as responding to the effects of poverty, hard work, city pollution, and political disenfranchisement.

Drugs and drug controls are "symbolic counters in wider social conflicts" (Himmelstein 1983, 17). They tell a story about class conflict and intergenerational difference. The stories that we tell about drugs are stories we tell about the kinds of people we imagine who use them, the reasons for their use, and the impact of this use on wider society. Stories about drugs and addiction are accounts replete with symbols, scapegoats, and metaphors. "The mythology of drugs dramatizes what it supposedly looks like to lose one's identity, responsibility, and agency" (Manderson 2005, 50). Indeed, the mythology of Viagra and tramadol in Egypt dramatizes Egyptian men's fear about losing their masculinity by being unable to sustain their responsibilities toward their families.

In the interviews that I conducted, only one man spoke about addiction treatment, though a few others talked about personally experiencing addiction to various drugs, including Viagra (which, biomedically speaking, is not regarded as an addictive drug) and tramadol. It is striking that amid what is often described as a global opioid epidemic, the dominant narrative in my respondents' accounts is one of addiction managed and incorporated into productive, everyday lives. This is, in fact, characteristic of the many drug users who manage drug dependencies through social rituals and sanctions while remaining productive members of society (Zinberg, Jacobson, and Harding 1975).

Yet as described in the interview with Fouad and Hussein at the beginning of this chapter, discussions about addiction were often not personal but rather hypothetical, telling a story about addiction in individual bodies reflecting a disorder of the body politic and the specter of predatory state and international actors (such as the police and foreign governments). Stories about the state fostering addiction in order to control a population tell a metaphorical story about the ways that the state enters the body and a narrative about export geopolitics.

In recounting conspiracy theories about how the Egyptian police and the American government were supplying Egyptians with tramadol to foster weakness and dependence, a story about individual Egyptian male bodies having their strength sapped through addictive drugs becomes a metaphor for a weakness and dependence writ large across the geopolitical landscape. Just as I have described (Wynn and Trussell 2006) for emergency contraception, social debates over individuals' use of pharmaceuticals are a displaced language for talking about the body politic. Manderson (2005, 49) notes, "The demonization of drugs gives us a ready-made explanation—at once powerful and mundane— for the failure of our law and morals to effectively solve the social problems that seem to be increasingly more endemic."

The story is not unique to Egypt; anthropologist of art Kirsten Scheid (personal communication) reports that the use of tramadol in Gaza is so widespread that a Palestinian artist recently made a replica of the Dome of the Rock out of emptied capsules, as commentary on the relationship between individual drug use and the political economic context, and news outlets feature stories about tramadol seizures across the Middle East, hinting at a regional epidemic.

At the same time that these interviews tell a story about the political economy, they also tell a story about kinship and family obligation. The repetitiveness of men's responses when asked to define masculinity was striking. Multiple respondents, all interviewed separately, offered remarkably similar definitions of masculinity in terms of a man's role as economic provider and his ability to protect and care for family. To be a man meant caring for dependents. Comments about how men need drugs to work so that they can bring home food for their families evoke Nefissa Naguib's (2015) account of the responsibility that men feel to provide for their families, particularly when it comes to food; fulfilling that obligation was not only what it meant to be a man, but what brought them happiness.

In a socioeconomic context where men feel like they are constantly in the grip of pain, strength-sapping labor, and environmental threats that erode their good health, a drug that relieves pain and numbs the mind is a drug that thus restores virility. As Himmelstein (1983, 18) argues, "The dominant image of a drug may be shaped partly by the substance's role as a symbol in wider social conflict." In a context where masculinity materializes through caring and providing economically for one's family, yet where Egyptian men are fundamentally vulnerable to a precarious economy rife with inflation and job instability, a drug that relieves the pain of hard labor and thus enables men to provide is a drug that symbolically restores their masculinity; having energy to work and energy to perform sexually are coterminous.

BIBLIOGRAPHY

Abdel-Hamid, Ibrahim A., Karl-Erik Andersson, Marcel D. Waldinger, and Tarek H. Anis. 2016. "Tramadol Abuse and Sexual Function." *Sexual Medicine Reviews* 4, no. 3: 235–246.

Ali, Kamran Asdar. 2003. "Myths, Lies and Impotence: Structural Adjustment and Male Voice in Egypt." *Comparative Studies in South Asia, Africa and the Middle East* 23, no. 1: 321–334.

Åsberg, Cecilia, and Erica Johnson. 2009. "Viagra Selfhood: Pharmaceutical Advertising and the Visual Formation of Swedish Masculinity." *Healthcare Analysis* 17, no. 2: 144–157.

Fishman, Jennifer R., and Laura Mamo. 2006. "What's in a Disorder: A Cultural Analysis of Medical and Pharmaceutical Constructions of Male and Female Sexual Dysfunction." *Women and Therapy* 24, no. 1–2: 179–193.

Foster, Angel M., and L. L. Wynn. 2016. "Introduction: Sexuality, Reproductive Health, and Medical Technologies in the Middle East and North Africa." In *Abortion Pills, Test Tube Babies, and Sex Toys: Exploring Reproductive and Sexual Technologies in the Middle East and North Africa*, edited by L. L. Wynn and Angel M. Foster, 1–12. Nashville: Vanderbilt University Press.

Hashim, Mostafa Ahmed, Amany Haroun El Rasheed, Ghada Abdel Wahed Ismail, Mona Ibrahim Awaad, Mahmoud Mamduh El Habiby, Nesreen Mohammed Mohsen Ibrahim, and Mai Seifeldin Abdeen. 2020. "Sexual Dysfunction in Tramadol Hydrochloride Use Disorder Male Patients: A Case-Control Study." *International Journal of Clinical Psychopharmacology* 35, no. 1: 42–48.

Himmelstein, Jerome L. 1983. "From Killer Weed to Drop Out Drug." *Contemporary Crises* 7, no. 1: 13–38.

Lee, C. R., D. McTavish, and E. M. Sorkin. 1993. "Tramadol: A Preliminary Review of its Pharmacodynamic and Pharmacokinetic Properties, and Therapeutic Potential in Acute and Chronic Pain States." *Drugs* 46, no. 2: 313–340.

Loe, Meika. 2001. "Fixing Broken Masculinity: Viagra as a Technology for the Production of Gender and Sexuality." *Sexuality and Culture* 5, no. 3: 97–125.

———. 2004. *The Rise of Viagra: How the Little Blue Pill Changed Sex in America.* New York: NYU Press.

Manderson, Desmond. 1995. "Metamorphoses: Clashing Symbols in the Social Construction of Drugs." *Journal of Drug Issues* 25, no. 4: 799–816.

———. 2005. "Possessed." *Cultural Studies* 19, no. 1: 35–62.

Martin, Emily. 1987. *The Woman in the Body: A Cultural Analysis of Reproduction.* Boston: Beacon.

Naguib, Nefissa. 2015. *Nurturing Masculinities: Men, Food, and Family in Contemporary Egypt.* Austin: University of Texas Press.

Potts, Annie, Victoria Grace, Nicola Gavey, and Tiina Vares. 2004. "'Viagra Stories': Challenging 'Erectile Dysfunction.'" *Social Science and Medicine* 59:489–499.

Spindler, Hilary H., Susan Scheer, Sanny Y. Chen, Jeffrey D. Klausner, Mitchell H. Katz, Linda A. Valleroy, and Sandra K. Schwarcz. 2007. "Viagra, Methamphetamine, and HIV Risk: Results from a Probability Sample of MSM, San Francisco." *Sexually Transmitted Diseases* 34, no. 8: 586–591.

Tiefer, Lenore. 2006. "The Viagra Phenomenon." *Sexualities* 9, no. 3: 273–294.

Wentzell, Emily. 2002. *Maturing Masculinities: Aging, Chronic Illness, and Viagra in Mexico*. Durham, NC: Duke University Press.

Whyte, Susan Reynolds, Sjaak van der Geest, and Anita Hardon. 2002. *Social Lives of Medicines*. Cambridge: Cambridge University Press.

Wynn, L. L. 2013. "Hymenoplasty and the Relationship between Doctors and Muftis in Egypt." In *Islam in Practice*, edited by Gabriele Marranci, 34–48. New York: Routledge.

———. 2016. "'Viagra Soup': Consumer Fantasies and Masculinity in Portrayals of Erectile Dysfunction Drugs in Cairo, Egypt." In *Abortion Pills, Test Tube Babies, and Sex Toys: Exploring Reproductive and Sexual Technologies in the Middle East and North Africa*, edited by L. L. Wynn and Angel M. Foster, 159–171. Nashville: Vanderbilt University Press.

Wynn, L. L., Hosam Moustafa, and Ahmed Ragab. 2013. "Social Class and Sexual Stigma: Local Interpretations of Emergency Contraception in Egypt." In *Critical Issues in Reproductive Health*, vol. 33, edited by Andrzej Kulczycki, 85–102. New York: Springer Series on Demographic Methods and Population Analysis.

Wynn, L. L., and James Trussell. 2006. "The Social Life of Emergency Contraception in the United States: Disciplining Pharmaceutical Use, Disciplining Sexuality, and Constructing Zygotic Bodies." *Medical Anthropology Quarterly* 20, no. 3: 297–320.

Zinberg, Norman E. 1984. *Drug, Set, and Setting: The Basis for Controlled Intoxicant Use*. New Haven, CT: Yale University Press.

Zinberg, Norman E., R. C. Jacobson, and W. M. Harding. 1975. "Social Sanctions and Rituals as a Basis for Drug Abuse Prevention." *American Journal of Drug and Alcohol Abuse* 2, no. 2: 165–182.

L. L. WYNN is Associate Professor of Anthropology at Macquarie University. She is author of *Love, Sex, and Desire in Modern Egypt: Navigating the Margins of Respectability* and editor (with Angel M. Foster) of *Abortion Pills, Test Tube Babies, and Sex Toys: Emerging Sexual and Reproductive Technologies in the Middle East and North Africa*. In 2019, she was elected president of the Australian Anthropological Society.

TEN

—ᴍ—

PALESTINIAN SPERM-SMUGGLING

Fatherhood, Political Struggle, and Israeli Prisons

LAURA FERRERO

INTRODUCTION

From October 2015 to February 2016, I spent four months in Palestine, during which time I interviewed fourteen wives of prisoners.[1] They share more in common than just having their husbands in an Israeli jail; they are part of a smaller category comprised of about fifty women who became mothers during their husbands' captivity.

What sounds like a miracle, or at least an unbelievable story, is made possible by the following elements: brave Palestinian men and women, widespread social support on a sensitive issue, medical equipment, a "secret" strategy, and religious fatwas. This phenomenon can be seen through many lenses, but here, I put the intimate sphere at the core of my analysis. In so doing, I do not state that politics and conflict are not fundamental aspects of the life of every Palestinian, but I try to counterbalance a description of Palestinian men as dominated only by politics and of Palestinian masculinity as defined only by fighting and heroism. If in the last decades resistance against the Israeli military occupation opened new arenas of masculinity alongside the more "classical" view of the "real man" described as a person who is part of a family and a community (Joseph 1999), I think it is now time to reconsider how fatherhood and the devotion to family are pivotal to the construction of masculinity in Palestine. When men are in captivity—due to their active involvement in the resistance—new reproduction technologies can become strategic tools to imagine and realize the ideal of fatherhood.

The Palestinian men at the core of this chapter are political prisoners serving their detentions in Israeli jails. All of them have been condemned to long or life sentences. According to the Israel Prison Service, they fall into the category of "security prisoners," defined as "a prisoner who was convicted and sentenced for committing a crime, or who is imprisoned on suspicion of committing a crime, which due to its nature or circumstances was defined as a security offense or whose motive was nationalistic" (Baker and Matar 2011). Abeer Baker and Anat Matar (2011) noted that most of the prisoners who fall into this category are Palestinians, because this definition is vague enough to consider all Palestinians "security threats." The Israel Prison Service detains and imprisons thousands of Palestinians, putting them into a single category that becomes a means of justifying treatment characterized by brutal arrest, prohibition from meeting a lawyer, torture, and arrest without a trial (Baker and Matar 2011).

The Palestinian women I met are their wives. They are referred to in Palestinian Arabic as *fāqida*, a word originating from a verb (*faqada*) that means to be deprived of something or someone.[2] They are women who experience a *fuqdān* (loss) in their everyday lives. A fāqida is the wife, mother, or daughter of a political prisoner or of a *shahīd*, literally a martyr or someone who has been killed by the Israeli army or during a fight against the occupation. Wives of prisoners are suffering, in the words of Rita Giacaman and Penny Johnson (2013), a "triple captivity" of the Israeli colonial system, the Israeli prison, and the post-Oslo Palestinian political landscape with its isolating effects in their own communities. In such a context, they are at the same time "proud" and "lonely" (Buch Segal 2015, 34) because they experience an emotional hardship that results from "the tensions between what everyday life can be like during the absence of a detained husband and what is expected socially" (31), that is, to be proud of their husbands. An example of this ambivalence can be seen in the discourse on divorce. Formally, Islamic family law in Palestine allows a woman to ask for a divorce in the case of prolonged absence of her husband (Johnson and Hammami 2013), but the proportion of Palestinian women who ask for divorces because their husbands are in prisons is very low (Welchman 2000). The explanations can be found in the challenges encountered by divorced women in Palestinian society (Rubenberg 2001), who generally remain proud of their husbands and aware that divorce would invite social scorn.

ON SPERM SMUGGLING

The *fāqidat* I interviewed remained loyal to their husbands and are involved in the project of enlarging their families. They have been impregnated with the sperm of their partners and given birth to sons and daughters while their husbands are serving their sentences. In August 2012, Dalal Zaban gave birth to the first Palestinian child born as a result of in vitro fertilization (IVF) treatment after her husband smuggled sperm out of the Israeli jail.[3] Her baby is known as *safir al-hurriya* (ambassador of freedom), and following Dalal's example, more than fifty children have been conceived in the same way. These cases made the smuggling of sperm and the consequent pregnancies a transversal phenomenon that interested women from cities, villages, and refugee camps as well as educated, uneducated, working, and unemployed women with husbands involved in either secular or religious parties. Despite evoking initial suspicion, this practice is viewed favorably by most of the Palestinian population, thanks also to massive media coverage (Berk 2014) as well as political support.

In the West Bank, most cases have been treated at the Razan Center, a private clinic with three branches: Nablus, Ramallah, and Bethlehem.[4] This clinic is at the core of the practice because it provides free treatment to prisoners' wives.[5] When he welcomed me to the laboratory, Dr. Zyad Abu Khairazan, the nephew of Dr. Salem Abu Khairazan, who is known as the inventor of this practice, explained that they undertake an ICSI procedure when treating prisoners' wives. He was proud to show me the equipment in the laboratory that, he said, "is very modern; it is second in the world only after equipment available in Israel." ICSI is a variant of IVF designed to overcome male infertility problems: "As long as one viable spermatozoon can be retrieved from a man's body . . . this spermatozoon can be injected into an oocyte under a high-powered microscope, effectively forcing fertilization to occur" (Inhorn 2012, xvi).[6] Even if the prisoners are biologically fertile, they are affected by "political infertility" (Berk 2014). Bringing the sperm from the jail to the hospital is so difficult, dangerous, and uncertain that the seminal fluid is considered unique and precious. As a result, ICSI is preferred to IVF, which is less likely to result in a pregnancy. As soon as a sperm sample reaches the clinic, doctors—in these cases available twenty-four hours a day—examine it, and if they detect living sperms, they immediately freeze them. Due to the sperm's scarcity, doctors try to use the minimum quantity necessary to undertake the treatment, leaving the rest divided into samples in a freezer. From one dose of sperm, they can freeze up to five samples, each one a potential newborn.

This phenomenon is referred to in Palestine as *tahrīb al nuṭaf* (sperm smuggling). Palestinian prisoners are no strangers when it comes to smuggling; secret letters were traditionally passed via released prisoners or between different sections of the same prison through a system called *cabsulih* (Nashif 2008, 52–58). Due to the deep involvement of the physical bodies in the tahrīb al nuṭaf—the prisoner's body, which produces and passes the sample, and the body of the person who receives it and who has the task of passing through the control system and reaching the clinic in the West Bank—this practice is part of a larger pattern of resistance practiced by Palestinian society confronting colonization. The cabsulih, the tahrīb al nuṭaf, the beaten bodies (Peteet 1994; 1997), the sacrificed ones (Allen 2009; Pitcher 1998), the bodies of the women who undertake the treatment, and even the body of the newborn baby are "inscribing the social into the human body" (Nashif 2008, 59).

Although some women offered me unsolicited details about how the precious plastic bag was delivered to the medical center—the same details that are often reported on this issue in the news—I will not emphasize this point. I never asked any of the women how they received their samples. First, I think that this kind of sensitive question would have destroyed the women's trust in me. Second, I presume they would have never answered the question. Third, I think they give the public a plausible (but maybe nonreal) version of the facts in order to explain the event but also (more relevant) to protect it. The secrecy and the repetition offer a kind of ritual essence to this practice that takes place in a "local moral world" (Kleinman 1997, 45), which renders it acceptable. One relevant issue is the existence of a fatwa issued by Dār al-'Ifta' al-Filasṭiniyya, which proclaims that the insemination is halal if it respects some *shuruṭ* (conditions). The most important conditions, reported to me both by the hospital and by Dār al-'Ifta' in Nablus, are this existence of a valid marriage between the man and the woman, the fact that the woman should not be a virgin when she undergoes the treatment, and the presence of witnesses from both families who declare that the sperm belongs to the *'asīr* (political prisoner).

I will introduce the reader to the feelings involved in this topic through the words of Samah, and I will then analyze the public discourses and the private dimensions of the phenomenon. In both the dimensions, a gender perspective arises, so I will later concentrate on a gender analysis, turning my attention to fatherhood before drawing my conclusion.

A FAMILY FROM ASKAR CAMP

Samah is the first fāqida whom I interviewed. She lives in Askar Camp, one of the refugee camps in Nablus. She lives on the first floor of a house that belongs to her husband's family. It was easy to reach her because her husband's brother works as a taxi driver between Nablus and the camp. He was waiting for an *'ajnabiyya* (foreigner) to appear at the taxi station located on the underground floor of the central mall, and as soon as he saw me, he called to me and drove me to the entrance of the camp. From there, he spoke with a group of children who were playing in the street and told them to take me to Samah's house. She was waiting for me, and we spent a very pleasant afternoon together.

After lunch, Samah showed me a video on YouTube, a half-hour documentary on the day of her delivery, which had been previously screened at a local television station, Filastin. Pointing to different people on the screen, she explained that she was surrounded by the director of the Ministry of the Detainees, the director of the media center of the hospital, the doctors, the journalists, and her family. Samah's voice on the video expressed gratitude: "I thank God, *alhamdulillah*. I pray God, may he give to us freedom [*hurriyya*], to us, to all the Palestinian people and to all the prisoners. I thank God for this baby who came in God's will, and I thank Dr. Salem, the Razan Center, and all the staff. I thank my family and my husband's family. I thank my husband, who gave me this possibility, and I thank all Askar Camp. . . . Alhamdulillah."

Pictures on the screen were accompanied by a nationalistic song addressed to the enemy, promising resistance and victory. An anchorwoman's voice in the video narrated, "Today something blessed happened. Today, freedom [al-hurriya] is among us, and *in sha' Allah* [if God wills] Hurreya [the name of the baby] will soon be embraced by her father. In sha' Allah Samir, you will be soon with your family . . . *sumūd* [steadfastness], more sumūd to our prisoners. . . . We will fight because your cause is political and is national, and your sumūd is stronger than the pressures you are submitted to." In the video, Samah's daughter said, "I want to say to my dad . . . in sha' Allah you will be released soon, you and all the prisoners. Don't worry about us, we are okay. 'Alf mabrūk [congratulations]." The song in the background sings, "Oh enemy, oh coward, here we are and here we stay. You will suffer; in my country you will face all kind of difficulties." The video ends with pictures of the narrow street of Askar Camp and an anchorwoman narrating.

> Askar welcomes Hurreya, the baby from the prison of the occupation. Manifestations of joy filled the camp, welcoming the daughter of a man from here who has been in prison for eleven years! . . . Thank God for Hurreya and for all the ambassadors of freedom. Hurreya gave her mother joy, brought a light of hope to her father and his family, the hope that the sun of freedom will rise again in a free nation. Hurreya came from behind the bars. She is a message to confirm the strength of our people. We are *sha'b jabbārīn* [strong people].

THE PUBLIC DISCOURSE

One thing makes IVF treatments for prisoners' wives different from any other IVF in the Middle East. Infertility—and the consequent recourse to medical treatment to overcome the problem—is often perceived of as something to keep secret (Demircioğlu Göknar 2015; Inhorn 1996, 2012; Inhorn and Birenbaum-Carmeli 2008). The same often happens in Palestine when IVF or ICSI is a solution for infertility. However, when it comes to political prisoners, the treatment must be public.

The case of Amina—a thirty-three-year-old woman of Jenin—is typical in this regard. I met her at her parents' house, where she lives with her children. She married and had a daughter before her husband was arrested. While he was in prison, they divorced and remarried after some years (Ferrero 2016). At that point, they started to plan to have another child through tahrīb al nuṭaf. Amina reflected: "I was very happy. We had a new *katib al-kitāb* [signing of the marriage contract] in the court, and we had a big party. I wore a white wedding dress, I did my hair, I had a new ring, a new *mahr* [dowry] . . . everything was new. We arranged everything as if it were the first marriage, including the *'ishār* [announcement] to let everybody know that we were together again. It was important to me, because we were already thinking of having a second child through insemination."

Amina was in a very sensitive situation due to her previous divorce, but her worries about making the choice public are not unique. Women discuss the decision to become impregnated within their families and try to make the event public even before undergoing treatment, as a way of avoiding social criticism and gossip in a generally conservative society. Nadia relayed, "At the beginning, I was afraid. Every time I went out, I tried to cover my belly. . . . I was ashamed. How it could be otherwise? My husband had been in prison for seventeen years, and not everyone in the city knew I did the insemination. They were asking themselves: 'How is it possible? How did she become pregnant?' There are still people in Palestine who don't agree on this topic."

Even if the positions on the issue vary, there is widespread support for the wives of these prisoners. The media plays a significant role both in spreading the news every time a new baby is born and also in disseminating a certain discourse. Sometimes television also plays a role in the decision-making process. The wives and their families often stated that they were encouraged when they found out about a new prisoner's wife who became a mother. According to Umm Samira, the mother of a prisoner's wife, "They saw it on television. The TV broadcast everything, even the delivery! It's encouraging because you see moments of joy. You see that all the family came to assist the woman together with ministries and journalists. It is a special delivery, not a normal one. When my daughter was about to give birth, we all went to the hospital. It was like there was a party."

As in the description of Samah's video, the media presents each case as a victory against Israel and as an act of resistance. This has been happening since the first public announcements: in February 2013, four wives of political prisoners gathered at the Razan Center in Nablus to announce that they had been impregnated by their husbands via sperm smuggled out of Israeli prisons (Khalil 2013). Those cases immediately followed the birth of *safir al hurriya*, Dalal's son. The women and the doctor involved drew legitimacy from fatwas issued four years before from the then mufti Ikrima Sabri and from Hamed Bitawi, a religious leader affiliated with Hamas, in a clear response to the situation of wives of long-term Palestinian political prisoners (Johnson and Hammami 2013, 21).

As mentioned earlier, in 2013 the Dār al-'Iftā' issued a fatwa that is now considered a reference point on the topic. It is important to note that the fatwa explicitly states that the information about the treatment must be spread via local television or "by any means between the people." As Morgan Clarke (2009) showed in his analysis of fertility treatment in Lebanon, religious positions are not independent from political context. Religious-legal prescriptions generally align with fatwas issued in other Sunni countries (Inhorn and Tremayne 2012), but the political situation plays a pivotal role in applying them to prisoners and in fostering social support. The hospital decision to provide the treatment for free, for example, is seen as a political response to the denial of conjugal visits for Palestinian prisoners in the Israeli jails, even if the official explanation describes it as a "humanitarian act" (Vertommen 2017).

The conflict has historically been presented has having an important demographic character, and as a consequence, reproduction represents more than an individual event. Reproduction has been politicized and nationalized, and Rhoda Ann Kanaaneh (2002) offers many examples of how the demographic aspect of the conflict has been made central to the discourses of political leaders on both sides. Both Israeli prime minister David Ben Gurion and Palestinian leader Yasir Arafat pushed "their" women to give more sons to the nation: birthing became both a biopolitical site for colonial control and a form of biopolitical contestation or survivalism (Vertommen 2017).

As a consequence, the conflict retains a gendered aspect. Palestine is not the only context in which nationalistic propaganda discourse is gendered and in which agency is thought of as a masculine trait (Massad 1995). I use Joseph Massad's analysis as a starting point to discuss what many scholars have pointed out regarding Palestinian masculinity and femininity. In his analysis of the first documents issued by the Palestinian Liberation Organization—which functioned as a sort of constitution, defining Palestinian political goals, Palestinian rights, indeed "Palestinianness" itself—Massad stresses two main points related to gender. First, the Zionist conquest of Palestine is presented as a rape of the land (Massad 1995, 470); this metaphor equates the land to female virginity and symbolizes the loss of male virility, because in the metaphor the virile actor is the rapist/enemy. Second, the rape of the enemy changed the definition of Palestinian identity itself: whereas before the rape anyone born on the Palestinian land was Palestinian, after the rape "Palestinianness" is described as an essence transmitted from fathers to sons with the consequence that women cannot be agents of nationality (Massad 1995, 472). This gendered idea has been stressed and reinforced in subsequent documents: whereas men actively create glory, respect, and dignity, women are merely the soil in which these attributes, along with manhood, grow (Massad 1995, 474).

In general, studies of gender in Palestine are unanimous in affirming that fighting, activism, confrontation with the army, beating, and serving time in prison are part of the local idea of *rujūla* (masculinity), to the point that they can be considered part of the rituals for entering adulthood (Peteet 1994).

Kanaaneh (2002, 72) tries to understand the implications of a certain kind of masculinity for women, arguing that "nationalism conjures a gendered world in which women are principally mothers of the nation and reproducers of boys." She also stresses the effect of the "demographic war" for women, stating that women in Palestine, as well as in Israel (Yuval-Davis 1987), are considered markers of national boundaries not only symbolically but also physically throughout their duty to produce the babies for their nations.

To summarize, collective language about Palestine is built around fighting and heroism (Allen 2009; Buch Segal 2015; Kublitz 2013). At the core of this imaginary are young men who sacrifice their lives and fight against military occupation (Asad 2007; Jean-Klein 2000), whereas women are primarily represented as mothers (Kanaaneh 2002). The idea that fertility rates are linked to politics and that political factors can increase the importance of having children and raise population numbers (Fargues 2000) is the framework within which the public discourse about tahrīb al nuṭaf is formulated and explains the position of the media and of the hospital (Berk 2014; Vertommen 2017).

THE PRIVATE DISCOURSE

I approached my fieldwork looking for a political or biopolitical explanation; I expected the women to frame their and their husbands' choices as acts of resistance and was a bit disappointed when, after the first interviews, I realized that women do not describe their maternity as a threat to Israel but mainly as their right to be mothers, their husbands' right to be fathers, and the families' right to live their lives. By turning my attention to the perspectives of the families away from the media—or outside the public realm—I realized that individual choices are made according to a political framework but also within a more intimate and personal sphere that often does not emerge in collective narration. Imen, a housewife in her forties who lives close to Tulkarem, said, "The idea of doing something against Israel made my desire to have a child stronger. Israelis put Palestinians in jail, but they keep having children. . . . This drives Israel crazy! The political side is important, but for me the most relevant aspect was to build a family, to have someone to live with."

The will to have a child, enlarge the family, and keep living a "normal life" is often reported as the main reason for resorting to this practice. Rasha, an educated woman who lives by herself in Ramallah and works for an international agency, explains how the political and the private side are deeply intertwined:

> This experience has several meanings for me. I cannot say that the personal side is enough to explain it; it is not "I want a baby; that's it!" I cannot say that the political aspect is distinct from the personal side. Israelis put Palestinians in jail to forbid them from having a normal life. Not only to forbid from doing political activities, but to forbid them from having a life, a family, studying. . . . Prison makes life impossible, so having children is a message for the occupation: you cannot forbid us from living. You took my husband's body, but we are still together, we got married, we bought a house, and we had a child.

Rasha had her first, and until now only, son through this practice and explains her choice also as a way to satisfy the imperative of reproduction in a pronatalist society, as well as a way to satisfy her own desire to become a mother. She reported,

> At a certain point, I started to think: "Why don't we make a child?" I am already forty, and the probability of getting pregnant will diminish soon. Furthermore the prison is not a safe environment, so maybe my husband will get sick and his fertility will diminish[7]. . . . I don't feel like having a second child while he is in prison. Before, it was matter of having a child or remaining childless, but now I have one, so if the second comes, it will be after his father is released. He still has to serve four and a half years, the most difficult years have passed, and above all. . . . Now I have my son, and my life has changed.

Often, the decision to resort to this practice is framed as a way of avoiding the risk of divorce. According to Marwa,

> You know what can happen? The army can arrest a man. His wife is maybe thirty years old, and he is sentenced to twenty years or even ten. When he is released, she is more than forty. At the age of forty or fifty, we don't have our period anymore, so we cannot get pregnant. . . . Maybe if her husband wants a

child, he can go and marry someone else in order to have a child. Who is the victim in this case? The wife! That's why many women think: Better if I get pregnant and give my husband a child too, so when he is released, he will find his family, and he will live with me.

The hospital, framing its intervention as a "humanitarian act," also stated that the risk of divorce is part of what inspired them to "help the prisoners' wives." I often heard this version, but I was never told of a case in which it really happened. In her research in Egypt, Marcia Inhorn (1996) found the same: Orientalist views describe men as likely to divorce their wives who do not reproduce, but this rarely happens.

In my attempt to go beyond the political reading, I find myself in line with Lotte Buch Segal (2013; 2014; 2015) when she focuses on the tensions between what everyday life can be like during the absence of a detained husband and what is expected socially from the abandoned wives. The prisoners' wives about whom she wrote compel her to scrutinize aspects of human life that challenge the systems of thought normally used to understand them, like resistance, religion, or ideology, so often flagged in analysis of Palestinians. Buch Segal (2015, 39) explains, "If the feelings were actualized in public rather than in private, they would severely compromise the example detainees' wives are supposed to set (Nashif 2008). Loneliness and emptiness are thus best kept at a distance from words because they have no home in the standing language."

As the wives of political prisoners have a "public" and a "private" way of describing their husbands' absences, I argue that there is a similar double discourse on the phenomenon of having children with them. The men's captivity represents a major challenge to Palestinian families as a whole (Gokani, Bogossian, and Akesson 2015, 204), and in a situation of loneliness and uncertainty, motherhood is something that makes life enjoyable. Hadil reflected, "The whole nine months, my thoughts were addressed to the baby who was growing inside me. What would he be like? How would I live with him? Would I be able to raise him? Alḥamdulillah, when I saw him, everything changed in my life." According to Imen, "There are women whose husbands are serving life sentences. What can they do? I encourage everyone to take this step. My children filled my home, filled the gap I had inside me; they filled my life."

SON PREFERENCE

Preimplantation genetic diagnosis (PGD) allows the selection of embryos before implantation; it is often used to prevent genetic diseases, but Sunni Islamic authorities have agreed that is also allowed in case of "family balancing," when couples have children of only one sex (Inhorn 2012; Serour 2008). The Razan Center relied on a fatwa that allows gender selection when the couple has at least two children of the same sex. The media director of the center told me that until now, approximately 10 percent of the prisoners' wives used PGD, all to conceive boys. I met two women who chose to have boys and a third one who wanted to have a boy but could not for medical issues.

I asked the doctors how Islam views human interference in the natural (or divine) act of conception. They answered by citing a fatwa written by Majlis al-fatwa al-'ala (Supreme Council of Fatwa): "Who chooses is God, and the doctor is the means." As Inhorn (2012, 199) has asserted in her research in Lebanon, "science and medicine are also seen as God given," and "the physicians who employ these technologies are seen as doing God's handiwork."

Son preference is a relevant issue that emerges in a gendered discourse about tahrīb al nuṭaf, and it pushes my argument on political choices versus intimate choices a bit further. The women's explanations for this preference revolved mostly around the concept of *nasab* and security or dependence. For Fatima,

> My parents-in-law proposed it to me. They wanted male offspring, someone who could keep the family name. You know, Palestinian traditions.... What really pushed me is that I don't know if my husband will never be released. I will get older one day [and I will need help].... The second reason is that I want a *sanad* [support] for my daughters, and the third is that my husband wanted to have a son. Our society is *dhukūri* [male-oriented], loves boys. When someone gets married, the hope is always that the firstborn is a boy.

Marwa reflected, "My husband does not have a brother, and his father is dead. My husband is sentenced to life, and here in Arab society, women rely on men [*dhukūr*]. The man is who keeps taking care of his sisters and his parents . . . and he thought: 'How are they going to live?' My situation is difficult, and I wanted a son because I want someone to take care of me in the future. My daughters are also very happy to have a brother."

Fatima is from Saida, a village close to Tulkarem, but she lives in an apartment in Tulkarem with her sons and her daughter. She wears the *niqāb* (a veil that covers the whole face) as a way to satisfy her husband's desire. She explained her family's preference for a son as part of "Palestinian tradition." Marwa, who describes her husband's family as religious and conservative (*muḥāfaza*), instead mentioned the category of "Arabs," whereas the media director of the hospital talked about "Orientals." As in Kanaaneh's (2002, 237) research, however, son preference is explained more as a necessity than as an ideological act. In a context of uncertainty and statelessness, the role of the family as the security and welfare provider increases, leaving more space for the recovery of "traditional practices" such as endogamous marriages (Taraki 2006) and son preference.

The preservation of the paternal lineage remains in general relevant throughout the Muslim world (Inhorn and Tremayne 2012), and in a period of tremendous change and uncertainty, the symbolic meaning and values of patriarchy became even more important (Muhanna 2013, 154). The persistence of what Diane King and Linda Stone (2010) called "lineal masculinity," or a perceived ontological essence that flows to and through men over generations, is due to a strong link with the idea of manhood itself. By giving birth to a boy, women feel that they accomplished a familial obligation (Inhorn 2012, 88) and contributed to their own security.

When questioned about the choices behind tahrīb al nuṭaf, as well as about son preference, women do not explain them as political acts. Again, the political situation and its consequences in terms of the economic, social, and welfare situation is a fundamental part of the discourse, but the framework remains far from the everyday experience if it is not filled with the intimate hopes and fears these women reported.

THE COEXISTENCE OF POLITICAL
STRUGGLE AND FATHERHOOD

Children bring hope to their parents' lives. Although these words may be implicitly political, my interlocutors never framed their situations as such. One reason for this is the way political activism and participation changed after the second intifada. These changes are visible through the near absence of women and civil society, which affected the gender roles within Palestinian society at large (Muhanna 2013) and the role of women in particular (Johnson and Kuttab 2001).

The metaphor of the rape of Palestine equates the land to female virginity and also symbolizes the loss of male virility, because in the metaphor the virile actor is the rapist/enemy. One possible path through which to regain virility then is to struggle against the enemy. This struggle can have a twofold effect on manhood: it reaffirms the masculinity of the political activists, but it can also lead to the experience of detention, which can limit procreation. This experience can put fatherhood at stake, representing a "reproductive disruption" (Inhorn 2012, 4). The dominant discourses and conventional approaches to manhood in Palestine have always stressed the role of activism, resistance, and fighting to build "real Palestinian men," but Palestinian men's identities

and conceptions of masculinity are "closely intertwined with virility and paternity, and with paternity's attendant sacrifices" (Peteet 2000, 203). The experience of the men who became fathers thanks to tahrīb al nuṭaf must also be
viewed through the lens of the necessity of those men to become fathers and
enlarge their families. The desire to have children and the social imperative
of reproduction is normally thought of as something connected to women.
But, as Inhorn (2012, 70) shows, a "masculine reproductive imperative" also
exists within the Middle East.[8] We cannot think about tahrīb al nuṭaf without
acknowledging that it allows for the persistence and the coexistence of two
"experiences of manhood": being incarcerated for political activism and being
a father. Imen spoke about her husband in prison: "Life in the prison is also
better now. The newborn gave him hope. He has been in jail for thirteen years
and still has ten to serve. Now he has hope again; he knows that his family is
waiting for him. His personality has changed, and he still doesn't believe that
it is true! When he hears their voices from the phone, he is touched." Similarly,
Fatima reported, "Our relationship also improved. He realized what I did for
him. The babies came when he had been in prison for twelve years. He is now
serving the thirteenth year. The first twelve years were something.... This year
is something different. There is finally something nice to think about."

Changes in the political atmosphere altered both the kind of activism in
which men can engage and the role of men within the family. Whereas in the
first intifada, the participation in the national resistance used to be public, from
the second intifada onward, it became invisible—if not secret (Muhanna 2013).
Participation also became more violent, resulting in deaths and injuries related
to a crisis of masculinity (Johnson and Kuttab 2001, 33). In addition, the post-
Oslo landscape and the economic, social, and humiliating effects of occupation
marginalized some groups of men as providers and breadwinners and destabi-
lized male roles as heads of household (Gokani, Bogossian, and Akesson 2015;
Johnson and Kuttab 2001; Muhanna 2013; Sa'ar and Yahia-Younis 2008; Taraki
2006). The historic image of the heroic Palestinian male fighter contrasts with
the reality of Palestinian men's lack of power and agency. In such a context,
breadwinning has come to symbolize daily resistance against the occupation
(Gokani, Bogossian, and Akesson 2015, 207).

Recent studies point out a similar dynamic among Palestinians living in
Israel because it is becoming more difficult for men to maintain their breadwinner roles. Roni Strier (2014, 401) interviewed unemployed men, who revealed
to her that "being a father means being responsible [and] carrying the burden
of the family's subsistence" and that "fatherhood means, first of all, providing for your wife and child." Both in Israel and in Palestine, the expression of

masculinity through resistance seems to be at stake, with provision emerging (or reemerging) as a masculine trait to be fulfilled.

Incarcerated men who have recovered their manhood and honor through militant mobilization and through tahrīb al nuṭaf can also recover their reproductive imperative and their role as breadwinner. A salary is in fact given to prisoners through their families by the Palestinian Ministry of Prisoners to help the wives meet everyday expenses. According to Nadia, "It has been very difficult to educate my children alone, but alḥamdulillah, they have grown up and the oldest are already married. I educated them by myself, and I paid everything thanks to my husband's salary. I also built the house thanks to that money. I built it over a year, gradually, and when it was built, I started to buy the furniture. This year I painted the wall; I did it gradually."

It is interesting to note that some husbands were either unemployed or precariously employed before being incarcerated. Some of them faced difficulty being breadwinners, and it is precisely the act of being incarcerated with a long sentence that allows them to fulfill their breadwinning role.

In the first intifada, "the practice of suspending everyday routine was an example of domestic (self-) nationalization that was concurrent with, and even complemented, a formally organized liberational and nation-state-building movement" (Jean-Klein 2001, 93), but from the second intifada onward, maintaining the everyday became truly political, a way to face the problems created by the occupation and the post-Oslo landscape.

CONCLUSION

The phenomenon of Palestinian men smuggling their sperm out of Israeli jails to impregnate their wives is relevant from many perspectives. Palestinian political prisoners are not biologically infertile, but life in captivity can put fatherhood at stake. Hegemonic masculinity (Connell 1985) in Palestine has been largely described in terms of fighting, resistance, and captivity. Rarely has the struggle been considered to have a twofold effect on manhood: on one side, it reaffirms a local concept of manhood, and on the other side, it can result in a lengthy detention that can limit procreation, putting fatherhood at stake.

In this chapter, I show how the availability of modern medical treatments allows the persistence and the coexistence of two "experiences of manhood": being incarcerated for political activism and being a father. Exactly as in Farha Ghannam's work (2013), wives actively work to help their male relatives materialize the notion of the real man and contribute in important ways to their standing both in private and public. Furthermore, as in Inhorn's (2012) work on "emergent masculinities," I consider this phenomenon in light of how Palestinian men engage creatively with new medical possibilities to overcome their enforced infertility in prison. Disrupting the dominant discourses on manhood in Palestine—which see Palestinians as dominated only by politics—I argue that the recent practice of taḥrīb al nuṭaf reflects another element that is supremely important for Palestinian men and women: to become parents and to have families.

NOTES

1. I thank Tamara Taher for the help in transcribing and translating my material.

2. The Arabic terms are transliterated following the *International Journal of Middle East Studies* system.

3. This is the only real name I have maintained because her case is well-known. All the other names have been anonymized.

4. I refer here only to the cases that have occurred in the West Bank, although other cases have been documented in the Gaza Strip. This also means that when I talk about Palestinians, I am referring only to the West Bank population. I am not taking into consideration those who live in the Gaza Strip or in the diaspora.

5. IVF treatment in West Bank costs around US$3,000.

6. For a detailed explanation of ICSI's origin and diffusion in the Middle East, see Inhorn (2012, 26–27).

7. For another example of how conflict can affect fertility, see Kilshaw (2008).

8. For another example, see Gürtin-Broadbent (2012).

BIBLIOGRAPHY

Allen, Lori. 2009. "Martyr Bodies in the Media: Human Rights, Aesthetics, and the Politics of Immediation in the Palestinian Intifada." *American Ethnologist* 36, no. 1: 161–180.

Asad, Talal. 2007. *On Suicide Bombing.* New York: Columbia University Press.

Baker, Abeer, and Anat Matar. 2011. *Threat: Palestinian Political Prisoners in Israel.* London: Pluto.

Berk, Elizabeth. 2014. "Political Infertility: Treatment as Resistance in Israel/Palestine." MA thesis, Washington University in St. Louis.

Buch Segal, Lotte. 2013. "Enduring Presents: Living a Prison Sentence as a Wife of a Detainee in Israel." In *The Times of Security: Ethnographies of Fear, Protest, and the Future,* edited by Morten Axel Pedersen and Martin Holbraad, 122–140. New York: Routledge.

———. 2014. "Disembodied Conjugality." In *Wording the World: Veena Das and Scenes of Inheritance,* edited by Roma Chatterji, 55–68. New York: Fordham University Press.

———. 2015. "The Burden of Being Exemplary: National Sentiments, Awkward Witnessing, and Womanhood in Occupied Palestine." *Journal of the Royal Anthropological Institute* 21:30–46.

Clarke, Morgan. 2009. *Islam and New Kinship: Reproductive Technology and the Shariah in Lebanon.* New York: Berghahn Books.

Connell, Raewyn W. 1995. *Masculinities.* Cambridge: Polity.

Demircioğlu Göknar, Merve. 2015. *Achieving Procreation: Childlessness and IVF in Turkey.* New York: Berghahn Books.

Fargues, Philippe. 2000. "Protracted National Conflict and Fertility Change: Palestinians and Israelis in the Twentieth Century." *Population and Development Review* 26:441–482.

Ferrero, Laura. 2016. *Zawjat Al-Abtal: Palestinian Women Building Families by Themselves.* Paper presented at the Doha International Family Institute conference, Doha, Qatar, October 17–18.

Ghannam, Farha. 2013. *Live and Die Like a Man: Gender Dynamics in Urban Egypt.* Stanford, CA: Stanford University Press.

Giacaman, Rita, and Penny Johnson. 2013. "'Our Life Is Prison': The Triple Captivity of Wives and Mothers of Palestinian Political Prisoners." *Journal of Middle East Women's Studies* 9, no. 3: 54–80.

Gokani, Ravi, Aline Bogossian, and Bree Akesson. 2015. "Occupying Masculinities: Fathering in the Palestinian Territories." *International Journal for Masculinity Studies* 10, no. 3–4: 203–218.

Gürtin-Broadbent, Zeynep. 2012. "Assisted Reproduction in Secular Turkey: Regulation, Rhetoric, and the Role of Religion." In *Islam and Assisted Reproductive Technologies: Sunni and Shia Perspectives,* edited by Marcia C. Inhorn and Soraya Tremayne, 285–311. New York: Berghahn Books.

Inhorn, Marcia C. 1996. *Infertility and Patriarchy: The Cultural Politics of Gender and Family Life in Egypt.* Philadelphia: University of Pennsylvania Press.

———. 2012. *The New Arab Man: Emergent Masculinities, Technologies, and Islam in the Middle East.* Princeton, NJ: Princeton University Press.

Inhorn, Marcia C., and Daphna Birenbaum-Carmeli. 2008. "Assisted Reproductive Technologies and Culture Change." *Annual Review of Anthropology* 37:177–196.

Inhorn, Marcia C., and Soraya Tremayne, eds. 2012. *Islam and Assisted Reproductive Technologies: Sunni and Shia Perspectives.* New York: Berghahn Books.

Jean-Klein, Iris. 2000. "Mothercraft, Statecraft, and Subjectivity in the Palestinian Intifada." *American Ethnologist* 27:100–127.

———. 2001. "Nationalism and Resistance. The Two Faces of Everyday Activism in Palestine during the Intifada." *Cultural Anthropology* 16:83–126.

Johnson, Penny, and Eileen Kuttab. 2001. "Where Have All the Women (and Men) Gone? Reflections on Gender and the Second Palestinian Intifada." *Feminist Review* 69:21–43.

Johnson, Penny, and Rema Hammami. 2013. *Change and Conservation Family Law Reform in Court Practice and Public Perceptions in the Occupied Palestinian Territory.* West Bank: Institute of Women's Studies at Birzeit University.

Joseph, Suad, ed. 1999. *Intimate Selving in Arab Families: Gender, Self, and Identity.* Syracuse, NY: Syracuse University Press.

Kanaaneh, Rhoda Ann. 2002. *Birthing the Nation: Strategies of Palestinian Women in Israel.* Berkeley: University of California Press.

Khalil, Naela. 2013. "Fatwas Allow Artificial Insemination for Wives of Palestinian Prisoners." *Al Monitor Palestine Pulse,* February 11.

Kilshaw, Susie. 2008. *Impotent Warriors. Perspectives on Gulf War Syndrome, Vulnerability, and Masculinity.* New York: Berghahn Books.

King, Diane E., and Linda Stone. 2010. "Lineal Masculinity." *American Ethnologist* 37, no. 2: 323–336.

Kleinman, Arthur. 1997. *Writing at the Margins: Discourses between Anthropology and Medicine.* Berkeley: University of California Press.

Kublitz, Anja. 2013. "Seizing Catastrophes: The Temporality of Nakba Among Palestinians in Denmark." In *The Times of Security: Ethnographies of Fear, Protest and the Future,* edited by Martin Holbraad and Morten Axel Pedersen, 103–121. London: Routledge.

Massad, Joseph. 1995. "Conceiving the Masculine: Gender and Palestinian Nationalism." *Middle East Journal* 49:467–483.

Muhanna, Aitemad. 2013. *Agency and Gender in Gaza: Masculinity, Femininity and Family during the Second Intifada.* Farnham: Ashgate.

Nashif, Esmail. 2008. *Palestinian Political Prisoners: Identity and Community.* London: Routledge.

Peteet, Julie. 1994. "Male Gender and Rituals of Resistance in the Palestinian 'Intifada': A Cultural Politics of Violence." *American Ethnologist* 21, no. 1: 31–49.

———. 1997. "Icons and Militants: Mothering in the Danger Zone." *Signs: Journal of Women in Culture and Society* 23, no. 1: 103–129.

———. 2000. "Refugees, Resistance, and Identity." In *Globalization and Social Movements,* edited by John A. Guidry, Michael D. Kennedy, and Mayer N. Zald, 182–209. Ann Arbor: University of Michigan Press.

Pitcher, Linda M. 1998. "'The Divine Impatience': Ritual, Narrative, and Symbolization in the Practice of Martyrdom in Palestine." *Medical Anthropology Quarterly* 12:8–30.

Rubenberg, Cheryl. 2001. *Palestinian Women: Patriarchy and Resistance in the West Bank*. London: Lynne Rienner.

Sa'ar, Amalia, and Taghreed Yahia-Younis. 2008. "Masculinity in Crisis: The Case of Palestinians in Israel." *British Journal of Middle Eastern Studies* 35, no. 3: 305–323.

Serour, Gamal. 2008. "Islamic Perspectives in Human Reproduction." *Reproductive BioMedicine Online* 17, no. 3: 34–38.

Strier, Roni. 2014. "Unemployment and Fatherhood: Gender, Culture and National Context." *Gender, Work and Organization* 21, no. 5: 395–410.

Taraki, Lisa. 2006. *Living Palestine: Family Survival, Resistance, and Mobility under Occupation*. Syracuse, NY: Syracuse University Press.

Vertommen, Sigrid. 2017. "Babies from Behind Bars: Stratified Assisted Reproduction in Palestine/Israel." In *Assisted Reproduction Across Borders: Feminist Perspectives on Normalizations, Disruptions and Transmissions*, edited by Merete Lie and Nina Lykke, 207–218. New York: Routledge.

Welchman, Lynn. 2000. *Beyond the Code: Muslim Family Law and the Shari'a Judiciary in the Palestinian West Bank*. The Hague: Kluwer Law International.

Yuval-Davis, Nira. 1987. "The Jewish Collectivity." In *Women in the Middle East*, edited by Magida Salman, 60–93. London: Zed.

LAURA FERRERO is Adjunct Professor of Anthropology at the University of Turin and Research Fellow at the Laboratory of Fundamental Rights in Turin, Italy. She is author of *Protagonists into the Background: Egyptian Femininities between Mobility and Immobility* (in Italian).

INDEX

NOTE: Page references noted with an *f* are figures.